MY FORMATIVE
YEARS

MY FORMATIVE YEARS

Translation of *Minha formação* by Christopher Peterson

Edited and with an Introduction by Leslie Bethell

Signal **Bem-Te-Vi**

First published in 2012 by
Signal Books Limited
36 Minster Road
Oxford
OX4 1LY
www.signalbooks.co.uk

Copublished in association with
Bem-Te-Vi Produções Literárias, Ltda.
Estrada da Gávea, 712, sala 502
São Conrado – Rio de Janeiro – CEP 22610-002
Brazil
www.editorabemtevi.com.br

English translation of *Minha formação* by Christopher Peterson
Introduction © Leslie Bethell

A catalogue record for this book is available from the British Library

ISBN 978-1-908493-66-8 Paper

Design: Baseline Arts
Cover Images: Bem-Te-Vi Produções Literárias/Joaquim Nabuco/ Studio Nabuco, Brazil
Illustrations: Bem-Te-Vi Produções Literárias/Joaquim Nabuco/ Studio Nabuco, Brazil
Printed in India

CONTENTS

INTRODUCTION

LESLIE BETHELL

OAQUIM NABUCO (1849–1910), lawyer, man of letters, diplomat, politician, journalist, historian and, finally, statesman, was a dominant figure in the literary, intellectual and political life of Brazil during the late Empire and early Republic.[1] He was what we would now call a public intellectual; indeed, since he spent almost half of his adult life in Europe (mainly in London, but also Paris and Rome) and the United States (New York and Washington), where he was also deeply engaged in current political, literary and intellectual debates, he was a trans-national public intellectual – in and from a country on the periphery of the 19th-century world system. He is best known, both inside and outside Brazil, for the central role he played in the abolition of slavery in Brazil in 1888 and, in Brazil, also for his "literary and political autobiography",[2] *Minha formação*, published in 1900.

— Early Years —

Joaquim Nabuco was born on 19 August 1849 in Recife, the capital of the province, later the state, of Pernambuco in the Northeast of Brazil, a region characterised by the large-scale production of sugar for the European market and by African slave labour. His mother Ana Benigna de Sá Barreto Nabuco de Araújo belonged to a wealthy family which had owned plantations in Pernambuco since the 16th century. His paternal grandfather and his great-uncle were born in Portugal, but both became ministers and senators of the

1 After more than 300 years of Portuguese colonial rule, Brazil declared itself an independent Empire in 1822. Brazil's first emperor D. Pedro I, the son of D. João VI, king of Portugal, Brazil and the Algarve, abdicated in 1831. After a nine-year Regency, his son D. Pedro II, aged fourteen, was declared emperor in 1840 and ruled until 1889 when Brazil became a Republic.

2 Nabuco's own description of *Minha formação* in the entry he submitted to *Who's Who* in 1906. It is reproduced (in Portuguese translation) as an appendix to the most recent edition of *Minha formação*, with an Introduction by Alfredo Bosi (Editora 34, 2012).

independent Brazilian empire. His father José Thomaz Nabuco de Araújo Filho, born in Bahia, was a prominent magistrate and politician who was about to become president of the province of São Paulo, Minister of Justice, senator and member of the Council of State.

Nabuco spent the first eight years of his childhood in Massangana, a sugar plantation (*engenho*) worked by slaves in Cabo de Santo Agostinho, fifty kilometres south of Recife, which was owned by his godmother (*madrinha*) Ana Rosa Falcão de Carvalho. He did not meet his father until 1857 when Dona Ana Rosa died and he joined his parents in Rio de Janeiro. He was educated at a school in Nova Friburgo in Rio de Janeiro province (1858–63), at the Colégio Pedro II, one of the city's best schools (1864–65) and, like many of his contemporaries who became leading figures in the literary, intellectual and political life of Brazil, at both of Brazil's foremost institutions of higher education, the Faculties of Law in São Paulo (1866–8) and Recife (1869–70), Brazil having no universities at this time.

In São Paulo Nabuco came into contact for the first time with anti-slavery (and republican) ideas circulating among the professors and students. As a final-year law student, he famously defended before the court of appeal in Recife a slave, Thomaz, accused of killing a man who was publicly flogging him and another who attempted to prevent his flight from custody. Effectively arguing against slavery (as itself a crime), flogging and legal execution, Nabuco secured a life sentence for Thomaz instead of the expected death penalty. At the same time, he wrote a lengthy student essay on "A Escravidão" (Slavery), or rather the first two parts of an essay: "O crime" (The crime) and "A história do crime" (The history of the crime). The projected third part, "A reparação do crime" (The remedying of the crime), was never completed.[3]

After the emancipation of over three million slaves in the United States during and immediately after the American Civil War (1861–65), Brazil was the last remaining slave state in the Americas.[4] The suppression of the

---

3 The 230 handwritten pages of "A escravidão" were donated to the Instituto Histórico e Geográfico Brasileiro by Nabuco's widow, Evelina, in September 1924: "yet further proof," she wrote, "of how slavery was his concern and abolition his ideal since almost childhood". The text was published for the first time in the *Revista do Instituto Histórico e Geográfico Brasileiro* in 1949. There is a modern edition edited by Leonardo Dantas Silva (Recife: Fundação Joaquim Nabuco/Editora Massangana, 1988).

4 Lincoln's Emancipation Proclamation (1 January 1863) declared free slaves in Confederate states in rebellion against the Union and was applied as and when these states came under the control of the Union. After the end of the War (and Lincoln's assassination) in April 1865, the Thirteenth Amendment to the Constitution (December 1865) abolished slavery throughout the United States.

Besides Brazil, slavery persisted in the Spanish colony of Cuba. It was abolished in January 1880, but continued under a system of *patronato* until October 1886.

transatlantic slave trade by the Brazilian government, under severe British pressure, in 1850–51 had dealt a decisive blow to the slave system in Brazil, since it was heavily dependent on the importation of tens of thousands of slaves from Africa each year.[5] Slavery in Brazil entered a long period of decline. Nevertheless, in 1866-67, when Agostinho Marques Perdigão Malheiro published his monumental *A Escravidão no Brasil* (Slavery in Brazil), which Nabuco had read in preparing his own essay on slavery, there were still 1.7 million slaves in Brazil.[6] Slaves, however, now constituted only 15–20 per cent of Brazil's total population (compared with 25–35 per cent in 1850). And there had been since 1850 a significant re-location of Brazil's slave population: from the North and North-East, where the sugar economy was in decline, to the Centre-South, where the production of coffee, now Brazil's leading export, was booming (the provinces of Rio de Janeiro, Minas Gerais and São Paulo now accounted for 70 per cent of the total slave population); and within the Centre-South, from the cities to the countryside (in Rio de Janeiro, where in mid-century 40-50 percent of the population were slaves, the slave population had largely disappeared), from subsistence and non-export agriculture to plantation agriculture, and from declining coffee areas in the province of Rio de Janeiro to expanding coffee areas in the interior of São Paulo.

There were few signs of a weakening of the Brazilian slave owners' commitment to slavery. Sugar and coffee planters were not turning to free labour from preference, nor yet from necessity, despite the rising cost of slave labour and the beginning of a problem of slave supply. And, although some individual voices (though precious few) could be heard denouncing slavery on the grounds of its injustice and its economic inefficiency, there was no widely-held abolitionist opinion in Brazil.

It was the Emperor D. Pedro II, in the late 1860s, who put the future of slavery on the political agenda for the first time. He had come to believe that slavery in Brazil could no longer be justified and that its decline since 1850 was irreversible and should be accelerated, though in a gradual, controlled fashion so as to ensure the minimum of economic and social dislocation.

5 On the abolition of the slave trade, see Leslie Bethell, *The abolition of the Brazilian slave trade. Britain, Brazil and the slave trade question 1807–1869* (Cambridge: Cambridge University Press, 1970). On the more recent, revisionist literature on the subject, see Jeffrey Needell, "The abolition of the Brazilian slave trade in 1850; historiography, slave agency and statesmanship", *Journal of Latin American Studies*, 32, 2001, pp. 681–711.

6 Brazil's first national census in 1872 indicated a slave population of 1.5 million.

In 1867 Nabuco's father, one of the leaders of the Liberal party, senator (for life), member of the Council of State (also for life) and an opponent of slavery – as (Conservative) Minister of Justice (1853–7) he had been responsible for the repression of the last, desperate attempts to import slaves into Brazil – agreed to chair a committee of the Council of State charged with drafting a bill whose main feature would be the liberation of children born of slave mothers. The young Nabuco followed the progress of this legislation closely and assisted his father – for example, translating documents published in the *Anti-Slavery Reporter*, the journal of the British and Foreign Anti-Slavery Society in London. In a letter written to his father in 1870, he confessed that his greatest wish was to see him president of the Council of Ministers for just two days so that he could abolish slavery by decree, thus becoming "Brazil's Lincoln" (*o Lincoln brasileiro*).[7]

The passage of the the Law of Free Birth by a Conservative government led by the *visconde do* Rio Branco on 28 September 1871, after a long and bitter struggle, cut off the internal supply of slaves in Brazil, twenty years after the suppression of the transatlantic slave trade had cut off the external supply. Thus, slavery was condemned to *eventual* extinction. No single slave, however, had been emancipated. As many planters had anticipated, the 1871 Law posed no *immediate* threat to existing slave property. Moreover, the children born of slave mothers (*ingênuos*), though nominally free, were to remain with their masters until they were eight years old (at which point they would be freed, with payment of compensation to their owners, or continue in semi-slavery until they reached the age of 21). And, as many who finally and reluctantly voted for it intended, the passage of the 1871 Law ended further debate in Parliament on the slavery issue for almost a decade.

After graduating from the Recife Law Faculty in November 1870, Nabuco had been uncertain about which road to take in life. He entered his father's law firm, but soon abandoned the legal profession. He dabbled with journalism, writing for *A Reforma*, the organ of the radical wing of Liberal party, where he defended a variety of liberal causes, notably the separation of Church and State. He wrote his first book *Camões e os Lusíadas* (1872)

---

7 Quoted in Carolina Nabuco, *The Life of Joaquim Nabuco*, translated and edited by Ronald Hilton (Stanford: Stanford University Press, 1950), p. 18. Carolina Nabuco was Joaquim Nabuco's daughter. Her life of her father was first published, in Portuguese, in 1928. The most recent biography is Angela Alonso, *Joaquim Nabuco* (São Paulo: Companhia das Letras, 2007).

in Portuguese, but he also wrote in French *Le droit du meurtre* (1872), an attempt to refute the famous pamphlet by Alexandre Dumas *fils*, *L'Homme-Femme*, on the right of a husband to kill a faithless wife, and *Amour et Dieu*, a book of poetry,[8] which he completed during his first visit to Europe.

Nabuco left Brazil for Europe, aged 24, in August 1873. He stayed there until September the following year, mostly in France and Italy, but with a month on Lake Geneva and a month in London. Intellectually, it was a transforming period in his life, and he fell in love with London, as we shall see. He returned to Brazil determined to be a writer, and began contributing articles on literature to the newspapers, engaged in public debates with other, more established writers, most famously with the novelist José de Alencar in the columns of *O Globo*, and, in late 1875, started work on a five-act play in French verse, *L'Option*, on the unlikely theme of the Franco-German dispute over Alsace-Lorraine.

In April 1876 Nabuco was appointed *attaché* to the Brazilian legation in Washington and entered on what proved to be a brief diplomatic career. In the event he spent only a year and three months in the United States, and more in New York than in Washington, and there is little evidence that he found it a particularly interesting country. His diary at the time consists mainly of reflections on God, love, women, marriage and French and English literature. On leaving the United States he confessed that he regretted not having made better use of his time there.[9] But he finished *L'Option*,[10] and wrote the first act of another play to be entitled *L'Amant de la Reine* or *L'Amant de la Princesse*.

In October 1877, to his great delight, Nabuco was transferred to the Brazilian legation in London, which was by far the most important of Brazil's legations abroad. (Britain was Brazil's principal trading partner and the principal source of capital throughout the 19th century.) He was in London, however, for only six months. In April 1878, following the death of his father, he returned to Brazil. And as his father had planned, and as his mother insisted, he somewhat reluctantly began a political career by contesting in Pernambuco on behalf of the Liberal party, and winning, an

---

8 Published in Paris in 1874.

9 Joaquim Nabuco, *Diários* 2 vols, I *1873–1888*, II *1889–1910* Rio de Janeiro: Editora Bem-Te-Vi/Recife: Editora Massangana, 2005, preface and notes by Evaldo Cabral de Mello, vol. I p. 220: 27 September 1877.

10 Published, posthumously, in Paris in 1910.

election to the Chamber of Deputies. He took his seat in Parliament in January 1879, aged 29. His first speech was on religious freedom, but he soon took up the cause of the emancipation of Brazil's remaining slaves, which was to be the main focus of his life for the next ten years.

— Abolition[11] —

During the 1870s the Brazilian slave population had continued its steady decline, albeit still relatively slowly: in 1879 there were still one and a quarter million slaves in Brazil. In Pernambuco and Bahia, where the sugar economy stagnated, there were still planters with hundreds, in some cases thousands, of slaves, and in the declining region of coffee production in Rio de Janeiro province landowners who had invested recently and heavily in slaves and had no obvious alternative labour force clung desperately to the slave system. On the new, expanding coffee frontier in the north and west of São Paulo province where slaves were increasingly difficult to obtain, increasingly expensive to buy and maintain, and a poor long-term investment, slavery continued to be the preferred system of labour for most planters – at least in the short-term until an alternative could be found. There was, however, in Brazil still relatively little serious public discussion of how in the long term to end slavery and provide plantation agriculture with a permanent supply of free labour.

The initiative that first brought Nabuco national renown as an opponent of slavery was a speech in Parliament on 30 September 1879 in which he denounced the British-owned St John d'El Rey Mining Company for continuing to use slave labour. The speech also brought him to the attention of the British and Foreign Anti-Slavery Society in London, which had been founded in 1839 after the emancipation of the slaves in the British Empire precisely in order to promote the abolition of slavery throughout the world. Nabuco was to develop an excellent working relationship with the Society, the most influential body of its kind in the world, and a close personal friendship with its Secretary Charles Allen which endured until

---

11 For a fuller account (in Portuguese) of Nabuco's role in the abolition of slavery in Brazil, see Leslie Bethell, "Joaquim Nabuco e a abolição da escravidão no Brasil", in *Conferências sobre Joaquim Nabuco* (2 vols, Rio de Janeiro: Editora Bem-Te-Vi, 2010), vol. I, *Joaquim Nabuco em Yale*, Kenneth David Jackson (org.), pp. 49–75.

Allen's death in December 1904.[12] "The frontier of the next decade," Nabuco assured Allen in April 1880, "shall not be crossed in Brazil... by any man calling himself a slave."[13]

The Liberals had been in power in Brazil since January 1878, after ten years of Conservative rule, and the newly elected Chamber was overwhelmingly Liberal. But the government led by the *visconde de* Sinimbú supported slavery unconditionally. In August 1880 Nabuco introduced an anti-slavery bill into Parliament. It was moderate inasmuch as it envisaged a ten-year period before the total emancipation of the slaves and offered compensation to the slave-owners, as Britain had done in its colonies half a century earlier. But it failed to make progress. Nabuco, however, continued to believe that the future of slavery was a matter for Parliament to determine. "Emancipation," he told Allen, "cannot be done through a revolution, which would destroy everything – it will only be carried by a parliamentary majority."[14]

In September 1880, Nabuco and a group of fellow abolitionists meeting in his home in Rio de Janeiro founded the *Sociedade Brasileira contra Escravidão* (Brazilian Society against Slavery). Nabuco himself was elected president and, as treasurer, his friend André Rebouças, a distinguished engineer of African descent (his father the son of a freed slave). From the beginning, Nabuco emphasised the need to mobilise public opinion, domestic but also international, in support of slave emancipation. And taking advantage of the parliamentary recess, he spent December through March in Europe, mostly in London, in order personally to raise international awareness of the continued existence of slavery in Brazil.

When the Chamber of Deputies was dissolved in June 1881 – with nothing achieved on abolition – Nabuco offered himself as a candidate for the first district of the *Corte* (the capital, Rio de Janeiro) in the elections to be held in October. Despite a strong campaign, he was defeated and forced to leave Parliament. In the newly elected legislature the abolitionists were an even smaller minority than before. Neither the Liberals nor the Conservatives were prepared to assume responsibility for a bill abolishing

12 On Nabuco's relations with Charles Allen and the other officers of British and Foreign Anti-Slavery Society, see Leslie Bethell and José Murilo de Carvalho (eds), *Joaquim Nabuco, British abolitionists and the end of slavery in Brazil: Correspondence 1880–1905* (London: Institute for the Study of the Americas, 2009). Original edition (in Portuguese), Rio de Janeiro: Academia Brasileira de Letras and Topbooks, 2008.

13 Nabuco to Allen, 8 April 1880, in Bethell & Carvalho (eds), op cit., p. 30.

14 Nabuco to Allen, 5 June 1881, in Bethell & Carvalho (eds), op. cit., p.46.

slavery, even for gradual abolition. In his frustration, and despite being accused by some of too readily abandoning the struggle, Nabuco left Brazil in December and returned to London, in what he called, in his farewell address to Brazilian abolitionists, "virtually forced exile".[15]

During his stay in London, this time for almost two and a half years, from December 1881 to April 1884, Nabuco earned his living as the foreign correspondent of Rio's leading newspaper, the *Jornal do Commercio*, and as a consultant to English firms with investments in Brazil, but devoted much of his time to promoting the cause of abolition in Brazil. In July 1882 he (unsuccessfully) petitioned the Brazilian Parliament for "the total abolition of slavery, either immediately or within a fixed period to be defined immediately" – though he still favoured indemnifying slave-owners for the loss of their slaves.[16] Above all, he worked closely with the British and Foreign Anti-Slavery Society, attending countless abolitionist meetings in London and a number of international meetings. With Charles Allen, he set up an efficient propaganda scheme, making use in particular of the *Times* newspaper, which was hugely influential in Britain and throughout the world ("the voice of civilization", Nabuco called it[17]) and which took a clear stance in favour of abolition. And in the British Museum and the late Richard Cobden's library in Brighton, Nabuco gathered material for one of his most important books, *O Abolicionismo* (Abolitionism).[18]

After almost two and a half years in London, Nabuco returned to Brazil in May 1884. He was tired and homesick. More important, the abolitionist movement outside Parliament had gained considerable momentum during his absence. In August 1883 thirteen abolitionist societies from five provinces had come together to form a *Confederação Abolicionista* (Abolitionist Confederation) committed to *immediate* abolition – and without indemnification. In March 1884, Ceará had become the first of Brazil's provinces to emancipate its slaves. The moment had arrived, Nabuco told Allen, for "some energetic kind of action" on his part.[19]

---

15 *O Abolicionista*, the journal of the Sociedade Brasileira contra Escravidão, 1 December 1881.

16 *Annaes do Parlamento Brasileiro* 1882 tomo II, p. 294; *Jornal do Commercio*, 15 July 1882.

17 Nabuco to Allen, 27 July 1883, in Bethell & Carvalho (eds), op. cit., p. 79.

18 *O Abolicionismo* was published in London in August 1883. There is an English translation: *Abolitionism. The Brazilian antislavery struggle*, translated and edited by Robert Conrad (Urbana, Il.: University of Illinois Press, 1977).

19 Nabuco to Allen, 31 March 1884, in Bethell & Carvalho (eds), op. cit., p. 84.

In June 1884 the Emperor, recognising the growing strength of abolitionism as a national political movement, invited Senator Manuel Pinto de Sousa Dantas to form a government, the sixth Liberal government in six years, prepared to introduce the first anti-slavery legislation since the Law of Free Birth in 1871, albeit legislation whose purpose was still *gradual* not immediate abolition. Dantas introduced a bill whose modest purpose was to free slaves over 60 years of age (not a large percentage of the slave population) – without compensation to their owners. It was radical only in the sense that it represented the first direct challenge to existing slave property in Brazil. But Dantas could not in the end unify the Liberal party behind his bill. At the end of July he was defeated on a motion of confidence and the bill had to be dropped.

D. Pedro, however, granted Dantas the dissolution of Parliament, and Nabuco immediately became a candidate for the first district of Pernambuco (the city of Recife). In the elections of December 1884 he campaigned for the first time on a platform of immediate abolition without compensation (and, equally radical, land reform). Nabuco drew crowds of thousands at meetings in the Teatro Santa Isabel in Recife. A great orator, he gave some of his most memorable speeches in favour of abolition in this campaign. Nevertheless, he was defeated, though only narrowly. And because of some irregularities, the result was declared invalid. In a second election in January 1885 the Conservative candidate chose to abstain and Nabuco therefore won unopposed, only for the Chamber when it met in May to overturn the result. However, in a by-election in another district of Pernambuco in June, Nabuco was re-elected to the Chamber.

Before Nabuco finally re-entered Parliament, after an absence of four years, Dantas had been defeated again and this time forced to resign. A much watered-down version of Dantas's original bill – slaves aged 60 and over would be freed but forced to work for three more years, at which point the slave-owners would receive compensation for their emancipation – was eventually passed by a Conservative government led by the *barão de* Cotegipe, on 28 September 1885, the 14th anniversary of the Law of Free Birth.

In new elections called for January 1886 Nabuco was again a candidate in Recife. And he was once again defeated in what proved to be a Conservative landslide. Disenchanted and disillusioned, Nabuco spent much of the following year writing for the Rio press and publishing pamphlets, including *O erro do Imperador* and *O eclipse do abolicionismo* in which he bitterly criticised the Emperor for having first encouraged the abolitionists with the choice of Dantas and then surrendered the government to the uncompromisingly pro-slavery Cotegipe. He eventually returned to London in April 1887 – this time as the correspondent of *O Paiz*. But he did not stay long on this occasion, returning to Recife in September to contest another by-election in which, again, the main issue was abolition. And this time he won, which he took to be an indication of how far abolitionist opinion had advanced in Brazil – at least in the North-East.

Following the passage of the Sexagenarian Law in September 1885 no further measures towards the liberation of Brazil's remaining slaves were expected from the Cotegipe government – and none was forthcoming. The political representatives of the slaveholding elite in Parliament continued for the most part to regard slavery as both indispensible and legitimate. Neither the Liberals nor the Conservatives favoured its outright abolition. Slavery was to be allowed to die naturally. And that, some abolitionists calculated, could take another thirty years.

The slave system's natural decline accelerated, however, in 1887 as a result of two new factors: first, mass desertions by slaves, encouraged and aided by the abolitionist movement outside Parliament which had grown in strength and become increasingly radical and militant;[20] secondly, an increase in the voluntary liberation of slaves by owners fearful of the total disintegration of plantation labour. Equally significant in the final demise of slavery in Brazil was the fact that the coffee *fazendeiros* of São Paulo, where the demand for slave labour was greatest, had finally been driven to find an alternative source of labour in the form of subsidised European, mainly Italian, immigration.

By the beginning of 1888, the majority of Liberals in Parliament were now – finally – in favour of abolition. The Conservatives remained divided, but in March Cotegipe was replaced by João Alfredo Correia de Oliveira, a leading figure on the reformist wing of the party, who had indicated to Princess Isabel (Regent in the absence of the Emperor abroad for medical

20 For an attempt to "re-contextualise abolitionism" by showing how the abolitionist movement interacted with the politics of abolition in Parliament, see Jeffrey D. Needell, "Brazilian abolitionism, its historiography and the uses of political history", *Journal of Latin American Studies*, 42/2, 2010, pp. 231–261.

treatment) his willingness to form a government committed to the emancipation of Brazil's remaining 250–500,000 slaves, now less than five per cent of Brazil's population.

Nabuco was in London at the time. He had travelled to Europe once again, his principal objective a meeting with Pope Leo XIII, whom in February he had finally persuaded to issue an encyclical condemning slavery in Brazil. He returned to Rio de Janeiro, via Recife, for the re-opening of Parliament – ready to lead the final battle for abolition. A bill for the immediate abolition of slavery without compensation was approved first by the Chamber of Deputies and then by the Senate. On 13 May, Nabuco, who for almost a decade had played a central role in the slow and uncertain progress of the abolitionist cause, had the satisfaction of addressing a large and enthusiastic crowd from a window of the Paço da Cidade (Paço Imperial) where the Princess Regent had signed the *Lei Áurea* (Golden Law) declaring slavery in Brazil extinct and liberating all of Brazil's remaining slaves.

— *Minha formação* —

The fall of the Empire and establishment of a Republic in November 1889, 18 months after the abolition of slavery (and the two events were not unconnected), brought an abrupt end to the political career of Joaquim Nabuco, a dedicated monarchist, when he was not yet 40 years old. Politically ostracised, believing (wrongly, as we shall see) that his public career was over, needing to make a living once again as a lawyer and a journalist (he had invested what money he had and, more important, his wife Evelina's money in Argentine bonds and lost 90 per cent in the Baring Crisis of 1890), and worried about his health which needed better treatment than was provided in Brazil, within a year Nabuco was back in London where he remained for nine months. He returned home at the beginning of July 1891, but immediately after the military coup that brought Floriano Peixoto to power in November he and his family left for Europe again (Lisbon, Paris and London).

Nabuco considered remaining permanently in Europe, but in September 1892 finally settled for "internal exile" in Rio de Janeiro, where he devoted the next six and a half years – the longest period he had lived in Brazil since his first visit to Europe in 1873 – to supporting the monarchist cause against the military dictatorship of Floriano (and military influence over Prudente de Morais, Brazil's first civilian president, elected in 1894) and writing for the press. His books *Balmaceda* (1895), on the Chilean civil war of 1891 ending with the suicide of president José Manuel Balmaceda, and *A intervenção estrangeira durante a revolta de 1893* (1895), on US support for Floriano when he faced a naval revolt with monarchist overtones in Rio de Janeiro, were both based on articles originally written for the *Jornal do Commercio*. In March 1896, finally accepting that the restoration of the monarchy was impossible, Nabuco decided to withdraw from politics.[21] He was one of the founders of the Academia Brasileira de Letras in 1897 and became its first Secretary General. And he completed the biography of his father which he had begun in 1894. *Um estadista do Império. Nabuco de Araújo, sua vida, suas opiniões, sua época* was published by Garnier, Rio's leading publishing house, in three volumes in 1897–98.

In 1896 Nabuco had agreed to write a series of articles for the pro-monarchy newspaper *O Commercio de São Paulo* in which he would reflect on his education, his intellectual formation (particularly his monarchist ideas), his early career as a man of letters, his discovery of the world outside Brazil, his life as a young diplomat and his political career dedicated to the abolition of slavery. Nineteen articles – in no particular chronological order – were published between April and July 1896 when the editor dispensed with his services on the grounds of cost. Three years later, at the end of May 1899, Garnier, the publishers of *Um estadista do Império*, contacted Nabuco, who was in Paris at the time, and he agreed to the publication of a book based on the autobiographical articles he had written in 1896, together with a few he had written for the *Revista Brasileira* soon after, and anything else he wished to add.[22]

On his childhood on the Massangana sugar plantation in Pernambuco, which he had not discussed in the articles written for *O Commercio de São Paulo*, Nabuco sent to Rio part of an unpublished MS on his religious beliefs written in French seven years earlier, after he had rediscovered during his recent visit to London, at the Jesuit church in Farm Street (under the "verbal lashings" of Father Peter Gallwey) and at the Brompton

---

21 *Diários* vol. II, pp. 111–112: 22 March 1896.

22 *Diários* vol. II, p. 161: 30 May 1899.

Oratory, the Catholic faith he had abandoned as a young man.[23] He also wrote three essays especially for the proposed volume: on his father, on Baron Tautphoeus, his old German tutor at the school in Nova Friburgo, and on his political and literary activities during the ten years since his public life ended (as he thought) with the fall of the Empire in 1889. The Preface was written in April 1900 – in San Sebastián, Spain. At the end of June, in Paris, Nabuco received his first copies of *Minha formação*. He was generally pleased with the book, he wrote in his diary, especially the chapters on his father, Baron Tautphoeus and Massangana, but at the same time he felt, like many authors on publication, "a sensation of emptiness, inadequateness, disappointment and displeasure".[24]

In the first three chapters of *Minha formação* Nabuco describes his intellectual formation in the Colégio Pedro II in Rio de Janeiro, in the Law Faculties in São Paulo and Recife and in the period immediately after his graduation, mainly writing for *A Reforma*, that is to say, between the ages of 15 and 24. It is evident that from early adolescence Nabuco read voraciously – in Portuguese, but also in English, in German and, above all, in French. He came under the historical and literary influence of Chateaubriand, Taine and Renan in France, Macaulay in England, Mommsen, Ranke and Curtius in Germany, Burckhardt in Switzerland. The French philosopher and historian Ernest Renan was, Nabuco writes, his "greatest literary influence in life, the most perfect intoxicant of the spirit, awed by a style with a quality unequalled in any writing, [his] intellectual *coup de foudre*".

Nabuco also read and was greatly influenced in his political thinking by Walter Bagehot's *The English Constitution* (1867). "I owe my unshakable monarchist bias to this little book, possibly no longer read by anyone in Brazil," Nabuco writes. "I extracted from it, transforming it in my own way, all the tools with which I worked in politics, except for my abolitionist work, which I based on a set of ideas derived from a different source." An entire chapter (Chapter II) of *Minha formação* is devoted to Bagehot who went a long way to persuading him that a parliamentary system, especially "English cabinet government", was superior to a presidential system and

---

23 *Foi Voulue: mysterium fidei* was published for the first time in 1971 by the Department of Portuguese Studies in the University of Aix-en-Provence; and in Portuguese as *Minha fé* (Recife: Fundação Joaquim Nabuco/Editora Massangana, 1985). A collection of Nabuco's moral and religious maxims *Pensées détachées et souvenirs* was published during his lifetime (Paris, 1906).

24 *Diários* vol. II, p. 191: 30 June 1900.

that "a secular monarchy like the English, with feudal origins, seeped in aristocratic traditions and forms, could be a more direct and immediately popular government than a republic". Republican inclinations from his student days associated with the liberal ideals of the French Revolution persisted, however. And Nabuco continued to read republican authors, for example, the French jurist, poet, abolitionist and close observer of US politics Eduard de Laboulaye, who was a great admirer of the US Constitution. Nabuco's "monarchist consecration" came, he writes, only with his first visit to Europe in 1873–74 which introduced him to the Third French Republic and its travails and gave him first, direct experience of the British monarchy and British politics.

Chapters IV-XVII of *Minha formação*, which comprise more than half the book, concern Nabuco's intellectual development between the ages of 24 and 29, beginning with the year he spent in Europe, and especially his five months in Paris, which represented "a personal metamorphosis, in my life the passage from chrysalis to butterfly".

In Paris Nabuco met, for a young man from Brazil, an astonishing range of leading political, intellectual and literary figures, notably Adolphe Thiers, who had recently been forced to resign as president of the Republic, Henri, comte de Chambord, heir to the French throne, George Sand, Edmond Schérer, Laboulaye and Renan, the *divin mâitre*, to whom, like Bagehot, Nabuco devotes an entire chapter of *Minha formação* (Chapter VII). His calling on Renan in his apartment in rue Vanneau was the highlight of the entire visit. "I have conversed with many spirited and distinguished men in my life," he writes, "but none has equaled the impression of this first conversation with Renan." It was pure enchantment, "as if I were the only spectator to an incomparable play... like Ludwig II of Bavaria in the darkness of the royal box, with the theatre empty, watching *Der Ring des Nibelungen* in a scene lit only for him alone."

Nevertheless, although Nabuco recognised that the "dominant cosmopolitan passion" for most Brazilians was Paris, "the strongest impression made on me," he writes, "was not Paris but London." It is evident from Chapter X of *Minha formação* that he was fascinated by London, the biggest city in the world, the centre of global economic and political power, the imperial metropolis – and by the "the majesty... the dignity... the confidence" it exuded. "The fact is I loved London above all other cities and places I visited," he writes. "Everything in London touched in me an intimate and reverberating chord." On seeing London for the first time he had felt a "desire to remain there forever". He returned to Brazil "touched by the beginnings of anglomania".

There can be no doubting Nabuco's love of Brazil, especially Rio de Janeiro (there is no place on earth, he writes, more pleasing *to the eye*), of his family and of his friends. But he was, he writes, "born cosmopolitan", attracted from his early years to the world outside Brazil, especially Europe, which to him represented civilisation, as it did to so many other intellectuals in the Americas in the 19th and early 20th centuries. He was therefore torn between *pátria* and Europe: "the sentiment in us is Brazilian," he writes, "the imagination European"; "on one side of the ocean we feel the absence of the world, on the other the absence of [our] country." In the end, he confesses, in a famous passage which brought him much criticism from his more provincial (or nationalist) fellow countrymen, then and since, that "[he] would not trade all of the landscapes of the New World, the Amazon forest, the Argentine pampas, for a stretch of the Via Appia, a curve in the road from Salerno to Amalfi, a part of the quay on the Seine in the shadow of the old Louvre."

Towards the end of his life, as ambassador in Washington, Nabuco was to become a huge admirer of the United States. But in the time he spent there as *attaché* in the Brazilian legation in 1876-77 his exposure to its "vulgar, violent republic", he writes, served merely to deepen his admiration for England. He has interesting things to say in Chapter XVI of *Minha formação* about politics in the United States, but he continued to believe not only that British institutions were superior, but that England was freer and more democratic than the United States, "the quintessentially free country". (There is no evidence that Nabuco had read Tocqueville's *Democracy in America* at this time although, intriguingly, at the end of Chapter XV he writes that he will in the following chapter describe his overall impression of the United States "which is today my idea of *democracy in America* [*democracia na América*]" – his italics.) He recognised the contribution being made to "material civilization", but "on the intellectual and moral level, including art, the United States has nothing to show". "If the United States [unlike France, Germany, England, Italy or Spain] suddenly disappeared," he writes, "one cannot specify what essential thing humankind would lose." And he showed little interest in the other America, Spanish America or, as it was increasingly called, Latin America.

On his return to London in 1877 as an *attaché* in the Brazilian legation, Nabuco stayed, as he had on his first visit in 1874 as a tourist, at 32 Grosvenor Gardens, the home of Francisco Inácio de Carvalho Moreira, who had been Brazilian minister in London since 1855, and who in 1864 had been given the title *barão de* Penedo. He received a warm welcome. Penedo had been a colleague of Nabuco's father at the Recife Law School and Nabuco himself had been a colleague of Penedo's second son, Artur, at the São Paulo Law School. 32 Grosvenor Gardens, which is the subject of separate chapter in *Minha formação* (Chapter XI), was a meeting point for London's high society. Nabuco met the Prince of Wales (the future King Edward VII), members of the British and European aristocracy – and the members of the Rothschild family, the semi-official bankers of the Brazilian government. The dinners, with food prepared by Penedo's famous cook Cortais, were especially memorable. "What prevented me from becoming a republican in my youth," Nabuco openly confesses, "was most likely the fact that I was sensitive to the aristocratic way of life."

Looking back on his life twenty years later, Nabuco recognised that the influence of England had been "the strongest and most lasting that I had received". This life-long admiration for England and things English is given full expression in the chapters in *Minha formação* on The English Influence (Chapter XII) and The English Spirit (Chapter XIII). Not only did the British constitutional monarchy and the British parliamentary system represent "the highest form of government", but England was the "only one *great* free country in the world, unshakable and permanent". (Switzerland was free, but small!) There was in England, he writes, "a feeling of equality of *rights* under the most extreme inequality of fortune and condition".

Nabuco's election to the Chamber of Deputies in 1878 brought about a "true formative change" in his life and in his thinking. It ended not only what he called his "literary period", in which among other things he had come to recognise his own limitations as a poet (*Amour et Dieu* was "virtually worthless", *L'Option*'s "only possible redeeming quality was that it was original"), but also his "intellectual dilettantism". He found a single political cause close to his heart, the emancipation of Brazil's slaves, and decided it was time for *action*. Apart from the chapter on Baron Tautphoeus (Chapter

XXV) and the concluding chapter on the years 1889–99 (Chapter XXVI), the final chapters of *Minha formação* are devoted to his struggle to abolish slavery in Brazil.

Various explanations are offered in *Minha formação* for when, how and why Nabuco became an abolitionist. First of all, there is the influence of his father: "No moral influence was as strong as my awareness of the relationship that bound me to him." Then there was the example of English and North American abolitionists, notably William Wilberforce and William Lloyd Garrison. Above all, he was, he writes, inspired by his own personal experience of slavery as a child in Pernambuco: "From childhood and adolescence I had the interest, the compassion and the feeling for the slaves, the seed that would produce the only flower in my career."

There is a well-known passage in the chapter on his childhood in Massangana (Chapter XX) in which Nabuco claims that his return there in 1869, as a student aged twenty, determined his decision to devote himself to the abolition of slavery in Brazil. He entered the small enclosure behind the little chapel of São Mateus that had been a cemetery for slaves. Standing among the crosses marking the graves, he reflected on the past and remembered the names of many of the slaves that he had known. "Thus it was," he writes, "that the moral problem of slavery was laid out for the first time before my eyes in all its clarity *and with its obligatory solution...* [my italics]. Then, right there, at twenty years of age, I resolved to devote my life... to the service of this most generous of races." The driving force behind his opposition to slavery was, he claimed, the "dear and blessed memory" of his childhood and of the suffering of the "black saints" he had witnessed. That is to say, it was a personal, emotional, indeed sentimental and essentially moral commitment to bring slavery to an end. It is no coincidence that he claimed to have read *Uncle Tom's Cabin* "a thousand times".

Minha formação was, however, written almost thirty years after this visit to Massangana. In his student text "A escravidão", written in 1870, and in his later writings, including *O abolicionismo* written in 1882–83, slavery was challenged with different arguments: it was a crime, an outrage against civilisation, responsible for the country's economic backwardness, an obstacle to political progress and to the construction of a nation. And, while there is no doubt that Nabuco was totally opposed to slavery throughout his life, there is no evidence, either in his extensive correspondence and his diaries, or in anything he did, in Brazil, in the United Sates or in Europe (for example, he had made no contact with the British and Foreign Anti-Slavery Society during his time in London in 1874 and 1877–78), that his decision to devote his life to its *abolition* was taken earlier than 1879, the year he entered Parliament for the first time.

Once embarked on his political career, however, Nabuco was fully committed to the cause, both inside and outside Parliament, in Brazil and in Europe, especially in London, until slavery was finally brought to an end in May 1888. In Chapters XXI–XXIV of *Minha formação* Nabuco gives us an invaluable first-hand account of not only of his own role in the abolition of slavery, including his eleventh-hour appeal to the Pope in the Vatican, but the abolitionist movement as a whole and its various leaders, politicians, intellectuals and journalists, both moderate and radical. The contribution of other abolitionists – André Rebouças, José do Patrocínio, Gusmão Lobo, Luís Gama, Antônio Bento, Joaquim Serra, João Clapp – is acknowledged, as is that of D. Pedro II and Princess Isabel, the landowners who for whatever motive voluntarily liberated their slaves, and not least the slaves themselves who at the end engaged in open revolt and abandoned the plantations.

Nabuco was painfully aware that the abolition of slavery in Brazil had not been accompanied by the "complementary social measures in favour of the freed slaves", such as land reform (what Rebouças called "rural democracy") and public education, that he had strongly advocated. The sad truth was that "the abolitionist movement stopped on the day abolition was decreed and retreated the day after". Nevertheless, it was his *hope* that "in time a more just society will be built on the ruins of slavery".

In Brazil, unlike, for example, in England, France or the United States, autobiographies by public men were extremely rare in the 19th century (and for that matter in the 20th century). *Minha formação* was regarded by some at the time as in bad taste, self-indulgent, narcissistic. But, as we have seen, Joaquim Nabuco did not set out to write an autobiography *per se*. He was invited, first by a newspaper and then by a publisher, to reflect on the influences that had shaped his literary, intellectual and political life. Apart from the chapter on Massangana, which was taken from an unpublished manuscript he had written earlier about his religious faith, there is nothing in *Minha formação* about his childhood or his deepest personal feelings, and there are no intimate details of his private life. Except for the chapters on Massangana and Tautphoeus, *Minha formação* was not, he wrote to a friend, "my intimate book" *(o meu livro íntimo)*. However, he added, he hoped to write that book one day.[25]

At the same time, Nabuco had no difficulty justifying the publication of *Minha formação*. In November 1901 he sent a copy (which he described as "a sort of autobiography") to Edgar Prestage, a young English scholar who was rapidly establishing himself as an authority on Portuguese literature and history.[26] "As one who committed the sin of autobiography...," Nabuco wrote in a covering letter, "I venture to say a few words to you in excuse of it, as against Mr. Asquith's strictures at Edinburgh." (Herbert Asquith, the deputy leader of the Liberal Party and future Prime Minister, had made "disagreeable remarks" against autobiographies in a lecture on Biography and Autobiography delivered to the Philosophical Institution in Edinburgh the previous day: "Self-consciousness was, as a rule, fatal to art, and yet self-consciousness was the essence of autobiography. No man ever sat down to write his own life... without becoming for a time an absorbed and concentrated egoist... the result was too often one of the most unappetising products of the literary kitchen."). For Nabuco autobiography was "the most interesting of 'lectures', and in fact a great many books only have interest for us for the parts of autobiography they contain... it is a great loss that so few men have told of their own experience and formation... after all, like confession in our Church, [autobiographies] are an attempt to truth." Great works like *Cicero's Letters* and Chateaubriand's *Mémoires d'outre-tombe* were autobiographical. But even when humble men like himself (sic) told their lives, "it is sometimes from an overwhelming sentiment of gratitude, and love, and memory".[27]

---

25 Joaquim Nabuco, *Cartas a amigos*, vol. I, *1864-98*, Vol. II. *1899-1909* (*Obras completas*, vols. XIII e XIV) Carolina Nabuco (org.) São Paulo: Instituto Progresso Editorial, 1949, vol. II, p. 93: Nabuco to Carlos Magalhães de Azeredo, 26 November 1900.

26 Edgar Prestage would become the first Lecturer in Portuguese at a British university, Manchester University, in 1908, and in 1923 the first holder of the Camões chair in Portuguese Language and Literature at King's College London.

27 Nabuco to Prestage, November 17 1901, Nabuco papers, Fundação Joaquim Nabuco, Recife, pasta 18, documento 342. The draft of a second, longer letter to Prestage was copied and inserted in his diary, along with a press clipping reporting Asquith's lecture; it is published, in Portuguese translation, in *Diários* vol. II, pp. 244-5. I am grateful to Evaldo Cabral de Mello, the editor of Nabuco's *Diários*, for drawing my attention to this correspondence with Prestage, and to Humberto França at the Fundação Joaquim Nabuco, José Thomas Nabuco Filho and Liana Pérola Schipper at Bem-Te-Vi Produções Literárias for locating copies of the two letters. L.B.

Minha formação has been compared, somewhat fancifully, to Montaigne's *Essays* and Rousseau's *Confessions*, even Proust *avant la lettre*, to John Stuart Mill's *Autobiography* (1873), John Henry Newman's *Apologia pro vita sua* (1864) and Ernest Renan's *Souvenirs d'enfance et de jeunesse* (1883), the latter certainly an inspiration, but most appropriately perhaps to *The Education of Henry Adams* (distributed privately in 1907 but only published posthumously in 1918).[28] It is now widely regarded as a classic in the Portuguese language. There are several modern editions of *Minha formação* in print and it continues to be read by successive generations of Brazilians.[29] It is published now for the first time in English in an excellent translation by Christopher Peterson as *My Formative Years.*

— Final Years —

Nabuco had been mistaken in thinking that his public life had come to an end in November 1889. In March 1899, on the eve of his 50th birthday, he accepted an invitation from President Campos Sales, who had been impressed by *Um estadista do Império*, despite its implicit defence of monarchical ideas and institutions, to become head of a special mission to London to prepare and present Brazil's case in its dispute with Britain over the boundaries of British Guiana, which was due to go to Italian arbitration. Ten years after the end of the Empire it was time, Nabuco thought, to put *pátria* above party, nation before regime, although he was much criticised for doing so by old guard monarchists. In May he was back in London – though in fact he was to spend most of the next twelve months in Paris, where, as we have seen, he was approached by Garnier about the publication of *Minha formação.*

Following the sudden death of his friend Arthur de Souza Corrêa in March 1900, Nabuco was appointed Brazilian minister in London, but he continued to regard the preparation of Brazil's case in the dispute with Britain over territory in Amazonia as his principal task. Indeed from

---

28 It was the Brazilian sociologist Gilberto Freyre who described *Minha formação* as "o *Education of Henry Adams* brasileiro". For an interesting comparison of the two works, and of autobiography in Brazil and the United States more generally, see Beatriz Jaguaribe, "Autobiografia e nação: Henry Adams and Joaquim Nabuco", in Guillermo Giucci and Maurício Dias David (orgs), *Brasil e EUA: antigas e novos perspectivas sobre sociedade e cultura* (Rio de Janeiro: Leviatã, 1994), pp. 109–141.

29 Joaquim Nabuco, *Minha formação* Brasília: Senado Federal, with an introduction by Gilberto Freyre, 1998; Rio de Janeiro: Topbooks, with an introduction by Evaldo Cabral de Mello, 1999; São Paulo: Editora 34, with an introduction by Alfredo Bosi, 2012.

January 1903 Nabuco based himself in Rome. And it was there on 14 June 1904 that he was summoned to the Quirinal, along with the British ambassador, to receive King Victor Emmanuel III's ruling broadly in favour of Britain. This was a devastating blow to Nabuco, but less than a week later he was informed by his friend the *barão do* Rio Branco, Foreign Minister since December 1902, of the decision to raise the legation in Washington to embassy status and invited to become Brazil's first ambassador to the United States.

After almost a year in which he moved between London, Paris and Rome, Nabuco left for the United States in May 1905. He spent the last four and half years of his life in Washington where, as he declared in a speech at a banquet given in his honour during the Third International Conference of American States held in Rio de Janeiro in July 1906, he dedicated himself to a cause (closer relations between Brazil and the United States) that had come to fill the void left in his soul by the successful achievement of another great cause (the abolition of slavery in Brazil).[30] Joaquim Nabuco died in Washington, aged sixty, on 17 January 1910.

*****

Leslie Bethell is Emeritus Professor of Latin American History in the University of London and Emeritus Fellow of St Antony's College, Oxford. He is the editor of the *Cambridge History of Latin America* (12 volumes, Cambridge University Press, 1984–2008), which is also being published in Portuguese, Spanish and Chinese. He is a member of the Academia Brasileira de Ciências and a *sócio correspondente* (one of twenty foreign members) of the Academia Brasileira de Letras.

---

30 *Gazeta de Notícias*, 24 July 1906, cited in João Frank da Costa, *Joaquim Nabuco e a política exterior do Brasil* Rio de Janeiro: Record, 1968, p. 93.

— Translator's Note —

The translation of *Minha formação* posed several technical issues, which I will outline here for the reader's clarification.

Joaquim Nabuco uses numerous phrases and expressions in Latin, French, Greek, Italian, and German without translating them into Portuguese for the original Brazilian readers of *Minha formação*, and I have maintained the same procedure in the English translation, with *simple italics* to identify these foreign terms and quotes (in addition to the expressions that Nabuco himself emphasizes with italics in the original Portuguese). Nabuco also adopts many terms in English, which I have marked in ***bold italics*** to prevent them from disappearing into the background English translation.

As Nabuco explains in his Preface, most of the chapters in *Minha formação* were originally published in a newspaper. Not surprisingly, therefore, when he quotes English-language authors he usually provides incomplete references and uses his own Portuguese translation. I made every attempt to locate the original English texts in order to avoid the inevitable differences produced by back-translation. The references are provided in my translator's notes. In a few cases, after an exhaustive search for the originals, it proved necessary to retranslate quotes into English, for which the reader's indulgence is requested.

This English translation is based on the 14th Edition of *Minha formação* (Rio de Janeiro: Topbooks, 2004), which I compared with the first edition (Rio de Janeiro: H. Garnier, 1900) and found to be entirely correct and consistent in both form and content.

Dr. Ricardo Salles, Associate Professor of History at the Universidade Estadual do Rio de Janeiro (UERJ) and author of *Joaquim Nabuco: um pensador do Império* (Joaquim Nabuco: a thinker of the Empire) (Rio de Janeiro: Topbooks, 2002), provided expert historical consultancy on key passages of *Minha formação*. In some cases Dr. Salles simply confirmed or corrected my interpretation of the text, while in others he offered more detailed explanations, especially in the chapters dealing specifically with 19th-century Brazilian history. However, I assume full responsibility for any historical inaccuracy that may remain in the English text.

For insightful comments during the translation, I am grateful to Sylvia Nabuco, José Thomaz Nabuco, Lélia Coelho Frota, K. David Jackson, Mário Hélio, João Almino, Liv Sovik, Iracilda Gonzalez, Priscilla Weaver, Jim Peterson and Lucas Peterson.

Christopher Peterson

— Editor's Note —

The translator's footnotes are identified with the initials T.N.; the notes prepared by Ricardo Salles (edited by Leslie Bethell) with the initials R.S.; and Leslie Bethell's additional notes with the initials L.B. There are also three notes by Nabuco himself (identified as Author's note).

There are so many names to be identified that rather than overburden the text with footnotes there is a Biographical Appendix with notes on Joaquim Nabuco's most important Brazilian, French and English (and also American, Portuguese, Spanish, German and Italian) contemporaries and a few lesser known figures from the previous generation. Well-known writers, philosophers, artists and composers from earlier periods referred to by Nabuco, with whom the reader will be familiar, have been excluded. Brazilian names are famously difficult to cite. The best-known last name appears in capital letters. In a few cases the first name by which a person was generally known (e.g. João Alfredo) is in capital letters. Those who had noble titles (baron, viscount, marquis) appear as they are most frequently cited, with cross references. The biographical notes were prepared by Alberto Taveira, revised by Liana Pérola Schipper and edited by Leslie Bethell.

Professor K. David Jackson of Yale University was tireless in his search for a publisher for this first English translation of Joaquim Nabuco's *Minha formação*. The project was enthusiastically supported throughout by Liana Pérola Schipper, Project Manager at Bem-Te-Vi Produções Literárias and, above all, by Vivi Nabuco, Joaquim Nabuco's granddaughter and publisher of Bem-Te-Vi Produções Literárias, who was also responsible for the publication of Nabuco's *Diários* in two volumes in 2005 and *Conferências sobre Joaquim Nabuco – Yale & Wisconsin* in two volumes in 2010.

For my children

PREFACE

MOST OF THE WRITINGS in *My Formative Years* first appeared in *O Commercio de São Paulo*, in 1895.* *Revista Brasileira* took up subsequent publication of the work, and never failed me with its support. The other chapters that I have added here come from an older manuscript. Only the conclusion is new. However, during the revision I inserted amendments and variations in some of the chapters. For reading purposes, the book thus dates from 1893 to 1899, and it contains ideas, views, and states of spirit from each of these years. Everything I say about the United States and England was written before the Cuba [Spanish-American] and Transvaal Wars, which marked a new era for the two countries. Some of the allusions to friends, like Taunay and Rebouças, now deceased, were made when they were still alive. For me it has been a simple distraction to compile these pages. However, it would have taken more than that to edit them and attempt to eliminate what no longer entirely reflects the changes I have undergone since first writing them.

Now that they are laid out before me in book form, and that I reread them, I ask myself what impression they will cause. They contain much of my life. Will they convey an impression of volubility, fluctuation, and dilettantism, followed by discouragement? Or rather, of consecration, by a perpetual vow, to a task capable of quenching the thirst for work, of youth's effort and dedication, and only after having fulfilled life's task – having quenched that thirst (and further, transformed by an earthquake during that time, with the creation of a new social milieu, requiring other kinds of action and other intellectual faculties for struggles of a different nature) –, resignation from politics after ten years of forced retreat, and in the face of a stronger intellectual enticement, that of a final perspective of a more beautiful and radiant world?... *Sed magis gratiarum actio...* (St. Paul).

---

* Nabuco's memory was at fault here. The articles were in fact published between April and July 1896. L.B.

As a whole, I fear, the impression will be mixed. Natural deficiencies will appear, disguised by the clemency of luck. Readers will see the ephemeral and the fundamental. In any case, I will not need to defend my own cause, because it will always be judged by the most generous of all races. If I observed something in studying our past, it is how futile our attempts are to subjugate, and how generosity always wins out. Pity he among us who has no other talent or taste than to debase his fellow man! Brazilians, by nature, are indulgent, sweet, enthusiastic, and kind, and each can count on the unlimited benevolence of all. In our history there will never be a Hell, not even a Purgatory.

However, I only authorize this book's publication with my *bon à tirer* because I am convinced that reading it will not weaken anyone's spirit for action and struggle or undermine their courage and resolution to fight for ideas they deem essential. Hopefully it will merely indicate some of the conditions for the triumph to be considered a national victory, or a human victory, and my life, without exactly being a work of art (a privilege granted to very few), will at least be seen with some parcel of beauty, and whenever it has failed to reflect brilliantly on the country, I may at least be consoled by having been affectionately harmless.

Politics, however, was not my dominant influence when I retraced these memories. I had already left politics by then.

"This morning, countless pairs of white, gold, and blue butterflies float against the backdrop of bamboo and ferns on the mountain. It is a pleasure for me to seem them fly, yet it would not be to catch them and pin them in a frame. I want nothing of them except the living impression, the flutter of nature's joy, as they cross the air, rustling the flowers. In a collection, of course, I would have them forever before my eyes, yet dead, like the dust conserved together by the lifeless colors. The only way for me to keep these butterflies forever the same would be to fix their instantaneous flight with my equivalent inner note. As with the butterflies, the same is true with all of life's other wonders. It serves us no purpose to gather up the remains. What matters is only the inner ray that strikes us, our contact with them, and this, they too carry away with them."

Years ago in Petrópolis I attempted, with this indecipherable stroke, to record an impression whose animate surroundings escaped me. Hopefully this fleeting trait of reality will explain the gaps in my book as a whole, and in many of its pages.

J. N.

San Sebastián (Guipúzcoa), 8 April 1900

CHAPTER I

SCHOOL AND LAW FACULTY

I REALLY NEED NOT HARK BACK TO MY SCHOOL DAYS, although that was probably where the layer was laid in my thinking that served as its foundation: the hereditary background for my liberalism. At the time (1864–1865), my father had finished his passage from the Conservative to the Liberal camp,[1] a march he had begun unawares since the *Conciliação* (Conciliation, 1853–1857),[2] but consciously and deliberately since the speech that came to be known as the *uti possidetis* (1862).[3] Brazil's political history had witnessed various migrations from the Liberals to the Conservatives. The men of the Regency[4], who entered public life or rose to power representing the idea of revolution, restricted their aspirations as they matured, taking advantage

1 For most of the Empire (1822–89) Brazil had two principal political parties – Liberal and Conservative, both monarchist, both dominated by landowning and slaveowning interests. The Liberal party had its origins in an alliance of politicians who were dissatisfied with the authoritarianism of Brazil's first emperor, D.Pedro I (1822–31), and who denied the legitimacy of the Constitution he had imposed in 1824. The Institutional Act of 1834 aimed at weakening the central authority in favour of greater autonomy for the provinces. The Conservatives opposed liberal political reforms and defended the centralization of political power, fearing the kind of fragmentation and instability that had occurred in Spanish America after independence. L.B.

2 Under the Brazilian parliamentary system during the reign of D.Pedro II (1840–89), the Emperor named the President of the Council of Ministers, or Prime Minister, who in turn chose the various cabinet members. The so-called "Ministry of Conciliation" named by Honório Carneiro Leão, the Marquis of Paraná, in 1853, included both Liberal and Conservative politicians in order to consolidate political unity and stability. Joaquim Nabuco's father, José Thomaz Nabuco de Araújo Filho, a Conservative at the time, became Minister of Justice. The period of broadly "conciliation" cabinets lasted until 1868 when the Emperor permitted the formation a wholly Conservative government led by Joaquim José Rodrigues Torres, Viscount of Itaboraí, following the resignation of the Progressive-Liberal Prime Minister Zacarias de Gois e Vasconcelos. L.B.

3 *Uti possidetis* refers to the diplomatic principle adopted by Brazil during the Empire and early Republic: in frontier disputes with neighboring Spanish American republics territory belonged to the country that actually occupied it. In his speech in 1862, Nabuco de Araújo argued that in practice the Conservatives occupied all the key positions of power (hence *uti possidetis*). A group of moderate dissident Conservatives led by Nabuco de Araújo (against the dominant *Saquarema* leadership – see note 5) began to align itself with the Liberals, giving rise to a new Liberal Party after 1868. R.S

4 The Regency (1831–40), from the abdication of Dom Pedro I in 1831 to the (premature) declaration of his son's majority in 1840, was a period of major turmoil, with Liberal tendencies prevailing, in the sense of weakening the central authority and facilitating a series of local rebellions: the *Cabanagem* in Pará, the *Balaiada* in Maranhão, the *Sabinada* in Bahia, and the *Farroupilha* in Rio Grande do Sul. L.B.

of experience, closing into the circle of petty ambitions and the desire simply for relative improvement that constitutes the conservative spirit. Yet Senator Nabuco was the one who launched, guided, and lured a great movement in the opposite direction, from the Conservative to the Liberal camp, from the old tradition to new experimentation, from the hieratic rules of government to the still-unshaped aspirations of democracy. He was the one who would embody the spirit of reform in Brazil's history – between the old "oligarchy" and the republic that would emerge from it the day slavery crumbled. He was our veritable political Luther, the founder of free will in the heart of the parties, the reformer of the old *Saquarema* church[5], which dominated everything in the country through the Torres, the Paulinos, and the Eusébios. Zacarias, Saraiva, and Sinimbu, with their great and small satellites, Olinda himself, with his independent orbit, did nothing else but take the route he designed with his intellectual initiative, a phenomenon of the same order as that of a prophet, and which for that very reason only allowed an almost impartial role for him in politics: that of oracle.[6]

In secondary school I still understood nothing of this, but I did know that my father's liberalism and what he said or thought at the time were dogma for me. I had not been invaded by the spirit of rebellion and independence, by the petulance of youth that later, in law school, would sometimes make me pit my way of thinking against his, rather than religiously assimilating his every word, as I would do today.

At fifteen or sixteen years of age, it was only natural that I follow my father's politics, among other reasons because this devotion was accompanied by a certain pleasure, a proud satisfaction. Among the childhood sensations engraved in my spirit, I recall one day when, after reading the daily news, our class inspector called me to his desk – he was an old actor from the São Pedro Theater who lived on the memories of his bit parts in plays and his veneration for João Caetano, to tell me with a great air of mystery that my father had been called to São Cristóvão[7] to organize the Cabinet. For me, to be son of the

---

5 The *Saquaremas* (so called because its triumvirate of leaders came from the Saquarema region in Rio de Janeiro) controlled the Conservative party from 1837. The leaders were Rodrigues Torres (Viscount of Itaboraí), Paulino José Soares de Sousa (Viscount of Uruguai and Rodrigues Torres' brother-in-law) and Eusébio de Queirós. R.S.

6 Biographical notes on all these Brazilian politicians – Joaquim José Rodrigues Torres, Paulino José Soares de Sousa, Eusébio de Quierós, Zacarias de Gois e Vasconcelos, José Antônio Saraiva, Viscount of Sinimbú and Marquis of Olinda – can be found in the Biographical Appendix.

7 The Emperor's residential palace in the São Cristóvão neighborhood of Rio de Janeiro. R.S.

Council President vibrated in my self-love more strongly, I imagine, than the prize for top marks our classmate Rodrigues Alves won every year. I felt my father's name glowing in me and rose in this ray of light: it was the beginning of a political ambition that crept into me. The air I breathed at home naturally fostered my first loyalties to the liberal cause. I recall that at the time I had a fascination for Pedro Luís, whose ode to Poland, *The Volunteers of Death*, I knew by heart. Later, in 1871, the slavery issue separated us, but still later we were reunited as members of the Chamber. At home I often saw Tavares Bastos, who took a liking for me, and the whole political group of the time. For me, as a young student, it was self-satisfying to walk up and down Ouvidor Street arm-in-arm with Teófilo Ottoni. It was a pleasure to go to *Diário do Rio* and speak with Saldanha Marinho and hear Quintino Bocaiúva, who to me was like the young Hercules of the press and whose attack on Montezuma concerning the capitulation at Uruguaiana[8] gave me my first example of a fearless polemicist.

Given my situation when I went to São Paulo to enroll in the first year of law school, I could not fail to be a liberal student. During my first year I founded a little newspaper to attack the Zacarias Cabinet. My father, who supported this Cabinet, wrote several letters urging me to concentrate on my studies and avoid newspapers and especially political positions, an attitude that showed – if not encouragement – at least a kind of tolerance on his part. I, on the other hand, highly prized my journalist's independence, my emancipation of the spirit. I wanted to feel free, and I considered myself committed to my class and to the law school, and thus skirted, without thinking of disobeying, my father's wish, who probably did not take my opposition to his sympathetic Cabinet very seriously. At the time I considered *Cartas de Erasmo*, which was sparking a conservative revival in the country, a masterpiece of political literature.[9]

Meanwhile, my own ideas were all mixture and confusion. My spirit had a bit of everything. Avid for new impressions, making my first contacts

8 In the first phase of the Paraguayan War (1864–1870), in which Brazil, Argentina and Uruguay joined forces in a Triple Alliance against Paraguay, Paraguayan troops had invaded Rio Grande do Sul. Initially successful, the invasion was eventually contained by the Allied forces. The Paraguayan commander Colonel Estigarribia surrendered to the Argentine president Bartolomé Mitre (commander of the Allied forces during the first two and half years of the war), Emperor D. Pedro II – on his only visit to the war zone – and President Venancio Flores of Uruguay at Uruguaiana on September 14 1865. The war would continue for four and a half years until the death of the Paraguayan dictator Francisco Solano López on March 1 1870. L.B.

9 *Cartas de Erasmo* (1864) were letters written to the Emperor under the pseudonym "Erasmus", by the novelist José de Alencar in which he criticized the Brazilian political system, especially the "Moderating Power", the personal power of the Emperor under the Constitution of 1824 to resolve conflicts between the legislative and executive branches of government. R.S.

with the great writers, with the prestigious books, with free ideas, I was enthralled and seduced by everything that was brilliant, original, and harmonious, awed by constant discoveries and the efflorescence of the spirit: all the branches were covered spontaneously with ephemeral roses.

Lamennais' *Les Paroles d'un Croyant*, Lamartine's *Histoire des Girondins*, Pelletan's *Le Monde Marche*, and Esquiros' *Histoire des Martyrs de la Liberté* were our generation's four Apostles, and Quinet's *Ashavérus* its Revelation. Victor Hugo and Henrique Heine must have been our favorite poets. However, I had not even (and I still have not) systematized or unified my reading. I read everything. For me, 1866 was the year of the French Revolution: Lamartine, Thiers, Mignet, Louis Blanc, Quinet, Mirabeau, Vergniaud, and the Girondists all swept successively through my spirit. The Convention was there in standing session. Even so, I also read Donoso Cortez and Joseph de Maistre, and I even wrote a little essay, with the infallibility of my seventeen years, on the Infallibility of the Pope.

Curiously, I can say that I did not possess a single idea, because I embraced them all. When I entered law school, I took my virgin Catholic faith with me. I will always remember my alarm, my outrage, my commotion, the first time I heard the Virgin Mary's name spoken in a libertine tone, yet I would soon have nothing left of that pristine image other than the gold dust of nostalgia. I would only return to Catholicism twenty some years later by a circuitous route that one day, if God grants me enough life, I will attempt to retrace. For the time being, suffice it to state that my greatest literary influence in life, the most perfect intoxication of the spirit, awed by a style with a quality unequalled in any writing, my intellectual *coup de foudre*, was that of Renan.

Politically speaking, the liberal foundation remained intact, without even a mixture of traditionalism. It would be difficult to find even a trace of conservative trends in all my thinking. I was liberal, lock, stock, and barrel. My weight and density were democratic to the fullest. At the time, José Bonifácio the Younger dominated the law school, with all his oratorical and charismatic appeal. The student leaders, Ferreira de Meneses, who had already graduated, but who was still a member of the movement and a literary youth leader, and Castro Alves, the republican poet and author of *Gonzaga*, drank up his words, absorbed in ecstasy. Rui Barbosa was part of this generation, but Rui Barbosa, now the most powerful intellectual machine in our country, whose countless rotations and forceful vibration remind one of the machinations that impel the great transatlantic steamers over the waves, took twenty years to mine the ore of his talent, to harden and temper the admirable steel that now characterizes his style.

However, my ideas floated in the midst of the various attractions of the time, between the monarchy and the republic, without a republican preference, perhaps only because of the hereditary background I mentioned and the easy political career that everything portended for me. A seductive and interesting manifesto – that is my impression of the time – *Le 19 janvier*, by Émile Ollivier, had left me in this state of hesitation and indifference between the two forms of government. I read Prévost-Paradol's *France Nouvelle* with true amazement, but despite all its appeal, it failed to sway me definitively towards the parliamentary monarchy. What decided the matter for me was *The English Constitution*, by Bagehot.[10] I owe my unshakable monarchist bias to this little book, possibly no longer read by anyone in Brazil. I extracted from it, transforming it in my own way, all the tools with which I worked in politics, except for my abolitionist work, which I based on a set of ideas derived from a different source.

---

10 *The English Constitution* (1867) by Walter Bagehot (1826–77), editor of the *Economist* (1860–77). L.B.

CHAPTER II

BAGEHOT

I DO NOT KNOW TO WHOM I OWE THE GOOD FORTUNE of learning about Bagehot's work, or if I found him by chance among the new releases at the Lailhacar bookstore in Recife. If I knew who put me in contact with that great English thinker, I would thank the person for helping me make his acquaintance, in 1869. That was the year I developed a close literary friendship with Jules Sandeau, to whom I was introduced, and I recall quite well, by the current counselor Lafayette, of the former *Atualidade* newspaper, where Farnese, Lafayette, and Pedro Luís, together with Tavares Bastos, were the leaders of the liberal youth movement. *Atualidade* may have been our first newspaper of a purely republican inspiration. They had sown the seed that sprouted later, during my time.

Before learning of Bagehot, I had already read a great deal about the English Constitution. I have before me a notebook from 1869 in which I copied the pages that most attracted my attention, a method of educating the spirit and acquiring one's literary style, which if I had the authority I would recommend to those who have decided to take up writing. I am convinced that no one writes except with the same phrases, the same wording – Renan would say the eurhythmics – that he used when he was twenty-one. What the writer does later, at a more mature age, is merely take the best of what he has written and discard the rest, cut out the weaker parts, the repetitions, everything that is out of tune or left over. Still, the cadence of the wording, the phraseology, will always remain the same. The phrasing of Lafayette or Ferreira Viana, of Quintino or Machado de Assis, even with the inevitable changes that come with age, is still the same with which they began. Of course I am not including in the writer's initial work the attempts that he makes to develop his own style. What I am saying is that the tempo is defined very early on, and for good, like one's physiognomy. In this notebook from my readings in 1869, during my fourth year in law school, I find in the table of contents a great deal on slavery, a great deal on Christianity, on English eloquence, on Fox and Pitt.

At that time I already considered the House of Commons the most prestigious assembly in the world, but the English royalty was still that of the four Georges, especially George III, the *bête noire* of Martinho de Campos, while the House of Lords, with all the old ceremonial trappings of the Tudors, for my liberalism, Americanized by Laboulaye, under the disguise of a historical carnival, was an odious aristocratic procession in the midst of the modern world. Of the two governments, the English and the American, the latter seemed freer, more popular. For Brazil, and for different reasons, as a form of government the constitutional monarchy, democratized by radical institutions, was still preferable to the republic, among other reasons because it already existed. But in theory, between the monarchy and the republic, if one was superior it was the latter. *France Nouvelle* – the last chapter of which was truly prophetic – with all its reasoned preference for the constitutional monarchy, as I have said, left me undecided, because in all its delicate apparatus the main part, or at least the part that perfected it, was the *king's right to dissolve Parliament*, the monarch's prerogative, and for our school this kind of dissolution was precisely the lever for personal government.

The English Constitution by Walter Bagehot is a book by a political thinker, not a historian or a jurist. Whoever reads the inextricable mass of facts contained in Stubbs' *The Constitutional History of England* or one of the brief overviews of an entire epoch, as Freeman suddenly unveils for us, will find nothing in Bagehot, historically speaking, that will not appear second-hand, so to speak. Yet what Freeman, Stubbs, Gneist, Erskine May, Green, and Macaulay failed to give us as perfectly as Bagehot (by the way, a layman in history and formal political science, a mere amateur) was the Constitution's secret, its hidden mechanism.

Freeman had shown in his little book *The Growth of the English Constitution* that this Constitution "was never made," that "in the great political struggles the voice of Englishmen has never called for... the enactment of new laws," but only "for the better observance of the laws which were already in force," that "the life and soul of English law has ever been precedent,"[11] and that measures to strengthen the power of the Crown have come in the end to widen the rights of the people. The entire book is full of suggestive ideas that shed light on a broad field of investigation for the spirit. Suddenly one finds a quasi-paradox of the kind that challenges all the moral ideas of historical experience. Saint Lewis, he would say, with his virtues and prestige, prepared the way for his successors' despotism. Will the reign of Pedro II not have the same effect? Says Freeman:

> But to win freedom as an heritage for ever there are times when we have more need of the vices of Kings than of their virtues. The tyranny of our Angevin masters woke up English freedom from its momentary grave. Had Richard and John and Henry been Kings like Alfred and Saint Lewis, the crosier of Stephen Langton, the sword of Robert Fitzwalter, would never have flashed at the head of the Barons and people of England.[12]

Bagehot lacked these retrospective intuitions, these local overviews. What he does have is the understanding, the divination of all the machinery he sees at work. Analyzing the English Constitution as if it were a cathedral clock, others would have better knowledge of the clock's history, the way it was built, the changes it has undergone, all the times it has stopped, or they would explain the symbolism of the figures it sets in motion when its powerful clapper announces the hours of the day. Bagehot, however, knows the actual mechanism better, which he simplifies, explaining it.

Bagehot, one can see, was a spirit with almost republican affinities, like Grotius, Stuart Mill, John Morley, and all the English Positivist Radicalism. Born into a banking family, he is another example of this singular attraction to speculative or political studies that one sometimes finds in English high finance, like Grote himself, Goschen, or Gladstone. His genius was of the kind that renews all the topics he discusses. I may be mistaken, but I believe that the English Constitution is a sphinx, and that he was the one who deciphered the riddle.

The ideas I owe to Bagehot are few in number, but they are all keys to political systems and concepts, veritable states of the modern spirit.

11 Edward Augustus Freeman, *The Growth of the English Constitution from the Earliest Times,* London, 1872, p. 55–56. T.N

12 Freeman. op. cit., p. 68. T.N

It was he, for example, who gave me the idea of what he called Cabinet government, as the soul of the modern English Constitution. "In Cabinet government," he says, "the legislative chooses the executive, a kind of commission, which it entrusts with the practical side of business, and the two powers thus function harmoniously, because the legislative can change its commission if it is not satisfied with it or prefers another. And yet – so delicate is the machinery – the executive is not absorbed to the point of servile obeisance, since it has the right to make the legislature appear before the electors, in order for them to compose a Commons more favorable to its ideas."[13]

This is the first idea, or set of ideas, that I owe to Bagehot: Cabinet government, the Cabinet commission in Commons, the Cabinet coming from Commons with the right to dissolve Commons, ministerial dissolution (not the Crown alone, nor the Crown with a Cabinet contrary to Commons): in short, everything that became common sense to me after that small book, but which it revealed and consolidated for the first time.

It was Bagehot who destroyed the two classical ways of explaining the English Constitution: the first, the notion that the English system consists in the separation of the three powers; and second, that it consists in the balance between them. His idea is that that the two powers, the executive and the legislative, are joined by a bond which is the Cabinet, and that in fact there is only one power, which is the House of Commons, of which the Cabinet is the principal commission. "The English system," he says, "is not an absorption of the executive power by the legislative power; it is a fusion of the two." This system's rival is what he called the Presidential system. These designations are now used by everyone, but they are all his. "The independence of the legislative and executive powers is the specific quality of Presidential government, just as their fusion and combination is the precise principle of Cabinet government."

Each of his words, comparing the two systems of government, deserves to be weighed. By summarizing these pages, I certainly contribute better to the education of young politicians, calling their attention to more delicate problems as compared to giving them my own ideas.

---

13 It was impossible to locate this first specific passage in either *The English Constitution* or Walter Bagehot's other writings, and thus it was retranslated into English from Nabuco's text. The subsequent excerpts from Bagehot were all located and quoted from the public domain file of the Gutenberg Library Project. T. N.

First, compare the two in quiet times. The essence of a civilised age is, that administration requires the continued aid of legislation. One principal and necessary kind of legislation is taxation. The expense of civilised government is continually varying. It must vary if the Government does its duty…If the persons who have to do the work are not the same as those who have to make the laws, there will be a controversy between the two sets of persons. The tax-imposers are sure to quarrel with the tax-requirers. The executive is crippled by not getting the laws it needs, and the legislature is spoiled by having to act without responsibility: the executive becomes unfit for its name, since it cannot execute what it decides on; the legislature is demoralised by liberty, by taking decisions of which others (and not itself) will suffer the effects.

In the financial disorder resulting from this lack of understanding between the executive and the legislative and this fabrication of budgets without the government, who is the principal party interested in perfecting the law of ways and means? Who is responsible? Who can be held accountable? Who can be removed from managing public affairs? "There is nobody save the legislature, a vast miscellaneous body difficult to punish, and the very persons to inflict the punishment." In England, the system is different. In a time of crisis, the Cabinet can turn to dissolution. In America, in order to resolve any clash of opinion between the executive and the legislative, it is necessary to wait patiently for one of their terms to expire. Until such time, they clash implacably, like two opposing parties.

Suppose there is no possible reason for conflict:

Cabinet government educates the nation; the Presidential does not educate it, and may corrupt it. It has been said that England invented the phrase, 'Her Majesty's Opposition'; that it was the first Government which made a criticism of administration as much a part of the polity as administration itself. This critical opposition is the consequence of Cabinet government. The great scene of debate, the great engine of popular instruction and political controversy, is the legislative assembly. A speech there by an eminent statesman, a party movement by a great political combination, are the best means yet known for arousing, enlivening, and teaching a people.… Travellers even in the Northern States of America, the greatest and best of Presidential countries, have noticed that the nation was not specially addicted to politics; that they have not a public opinion finished and chastened as that of the English has been finished and chastened.…

But under a Presidential government, a nation has, except at the electing moment, no influence… It is not incited to form an opinion like a nation under a Cabinet government; nor is it instructed like such a nation. There are doubtless debates in the legislature, but they are prologues without a play. There is nothing of a catastrophe about them; you can not turn out the Government. The prize of power is not in the gift of the legislature, and no one cares for the legislature. The executive, the great centre of power and place, sticks irremovable; you cannot change it in any event. The teaching apparatus which has educated our public mind, which prepares our resolutions, which shapes our opinions, does not exist. No Presidential country needs to form daily delicate opinions, or is helped in forming them.

The same holds true for the press, which is also prevented from removing the administration. In England, the *Times* has made numerous cabinets. Nothing of the like could happen in America. Nobody cares about the debates in Congress. They lead nowhere, and nobody reads the background articles, because they bear no influence on the outcomes.

Yet it is not only the legislative branch that is weakened by this division, it is also the executive.

In England a strong Cabinet can obtain the concurrence of the legislature in all acts which facilitate its administration; it is itself, so to say, the legislature. But a President may be hampered by the Parliament, and is likely to be hampered. The natural tendency of the members of every legislature is to make themselves conspicuous. They wish to gratify an ambition laudable or blamable; they wish to promote the measures they think best for the public welfare; they wish to make their will felt in great affairs.

In addition to this weakening caused by antagonism from the legislative, the Presidential system weakens the executive branch, *diminishing its intrinsic value.* "The statesmen from whom a nation chooses under a Presidential system are much inferior to those from whom it chooses under a Cabinet system, while the selecting apparatus is also far less discerning."

However, all these advantages are even more precious in troubled times than in calm ones:

A formed public opinion, a respectable, able, and disciplined legislature, a well-chosen executive, a Parliament and an administration not thwarting each other, but co-operating with each other, are of greater consequence when great affairs are in progress than when small affairs are in progress – when there is much to do than when there is little to do. But in addition to this, a Parliamentary or Cabinet Constitution possesses an additional and special advantage in very dangerous times. It has what we may call a reserve of power fit for and needed by extreme exigencies...

But under a Presidential government you can do nothing of the kind. The American Government calls itself a Government of the supreme people; but at a quick crisis, the time when a sovereign power is most needed, you cannot find the supreme people. You have got a Congress elected for one fixed period, going out perhaps by fixed instalments, which cannot be accelerated or retarded – you have a President chosen for a fixed period, and immovable during that period: all the arrangements are for stated times. There is no elastic element, everything is rigid, specified, dated. Come what may, you can quicken nothing, and can retard nothing. You have bespoken your Government in advance, and whether it suits you or not, whether it works well or works ill, whether it is what you want or not, by law you must keep it.

This system's flaws come into full view in times of war or complicated diplomatic relations. According to Bagehot, the system may be summed up as follows: *government by an unknown quantity.*

Hardly any one in America had any living idea what Mr. Lincoln was like, or any definite notion what he would do. The leading statesmen under the system of Cabinet government are not only household words, but household IDEAS. We have simply no notion what it would be to be left with the visible sovereignty in the hands of an unknown man.

I owe other ideas to Bagehot. Before reading him, I had the democratic bias against hereditariness, the dynastic principle, and the aristocratic influence. As this *democrat* taught me, what he referred to as the *dignified* parts of the English Constitution, "those that excite and preserve the reverence of the population", are as important as the *efficient* ones, "those by which it, in fact, works and rules." Phrases like the following are engraved in my thinking: "A second and very rare condition of an elective government is a *calm* national mind – a tone of mind sufficiently staple to bear the necessary excitement of conspicuous revolutions. No barbarous, no semi-civilised nation has ever possessed this. The mass of uneducated

•

men could not now in England be told '*go to, choose your rulers*'; they would go wild; their imaginations would fancy unreal dangers, and the attempt at election would issue in some forcible usurpation. *The incalculable advantage of august institutions in a free state is, that they prevent this collapse. The excitement of choosing our rulers is prevented by the apparent existence of an unchosen ruler.*[14] The poorer and more ignorant classes – those who would most feel excitement, who would most be misled by excitement – really believe that the Queen governs. You could not explain to them the recondite difference between 'reigning' and 'governing'; the words necessary to express it do not exist in their dialect; the ideas necessary to comprehend it do not exist in their minds. The separation of principal power from principal station is a refinement which they could not even conceive. They fancy they are governed by an hereditary Queen, a Queen by the grace of God, when they are really governed by a Cabinet and a Parliament – men like themselves, chosen by themselves."

All the pomp, majesty, and apparatus of the royalty thus became part of what I considered the necessary means to govern and to satisfy the imagination of the masses, whatever the society's culture. The royalty thus belonged naturally to what Herbert Spencer called ceremonial institutions, like trophies, presents, visits, obeisances, titles, etc. Says Bagehot, "No feeling could seem more childish than the enthusiasm of the English at the marriage of the Prince of Wales. But no feeling could be more like common human nature. The women – one half the human race at least – care fifty times more for a marriage than a ministry." And he adds, "So long as the human heart is strong and the human reason weak, royalty will be strong because it appeals to diffused feeling, and Republics weak because they appeal to the understanding."

The main idea I received from Bagehot was that of the practical superiority of the English Cabinet government over the American Presidential system. In addition, a secular monarchy like the English, with feudal origins, seeped in aristocratic traditions and forms, could be a more direct and immediately popular government than the republic. "When the American nation has chosen its President, its virtue goes out of it, and out of the Transmissive College through which it chooses." The

---

14 Nabuco's italics.

House of Commons, however, elects and dismisses the Cabinet, so that the government is always in the hands of the national representation. If a disagreement arises between them in which the Cabinet believes it has public opinion on its side, it dissolves Commons, and within days the nation has spoken. Comparing the two governments in terms of public opinion, the American system appeared to me like a clock that keeps time in hours, while the English keeps time down to the second.

CHAPTER III

1871–1873 *A REFORMA*[15]

I GRADUATED FROM LAW SCHOOL HAVING OVERCOME THE BIAS that makes certain spirits reluctant to accept the monarchist form of government, namely the prejudice against the non-electiveness of the head of state. I clearly saw this non-electiveness as the secret to the superiority of the monarchist over the republican mechanism, condemned to periodic interruptions, synonymous with revolutions for some countries. To insist on the clockwork metaphor, for me the republic was a clock whose spring soon had to be replaced, while the monarchy was a kind of perpetual timepiece. It was no small debt I owed to Bagehot, without whom – without understanding and accepting parliamentary monarchy as an apparatus more sensitive to public opinion, quicker and keener to grasp its fleeting nuances, meanwhile preserving government tradition and the constant pursuit of the nation's destiny – I would have been dragged irresistibly into the nascent republican movement. Even so, I did not control my fascination for the movement immediately, or all at once.

In 1871 the Rio Branco Cabinet was in power. During those three years, 1871, 1872, and 1873, I wrote a number of political articles for *A Reforma*. However, other matters occupied my mind more than politics. Life, society, the world, literature, art, even philosophy enticed me more than politics. From a very early age my spirit was preoccupied by something that both attracted me to politics and in a certain sense acted as an amulet against it: slavery. From 1868 onward I viewed everything in our country through this prism. During law school, I acted as defense attorney in three jury trials, and all three defendants received life sentences of forced labor. My friend

15 The newspaper *A Reforma* was the organ of the radical wing of the new Liberal party, an alliance of Liberals and dissident Conservatives who joined forces after 1868 when D. Pedro II invited the Conservatives (who were the minority in the Chamber of Deputies) to form a new cabinet following the resignation of Zacarias de Gois. See notes 2 & 3 above. L.B.

Alberto de Carvalho would no doubt laugh at these rulings, since all three crimes were committed by slaves, or rather imputed to them (I have to be consistent with what I probably said to the jury). During my fifth year of law school in Recife I drafted a book that I still have, a sort of unpublished Perdigão Malheiro[16] on slavery in Brazil. I translated documents from the *Anti-Slavery Reporter* for my father, who was the most prominent influence from 1868 to 1871 in consolidating the idea of emancipation, drafted as a bill of law in 1866 by São Vicente (Pimenta Bueno). I am convinced that the initiative, the desire to submit the issue to Parliament, came from the Emperor, who did not rest until he succeeded (the first time by Zacarias, the second by Rio Branco). I have already stated publicly that I have a copy, signed by the Emperor, of his letter in response to the French abolitionists, the letter that was the point of departure for everything.[17] I was fascinated by my father's stance on the issue. I wanted him to receive at least the glory as Brazil's Sumner. I remember how happy I was in 1869 when he told me that he had agreed with Sales Torres Homem to push the idea in the Senate, and that Sales was writing a Plato-like dialogue on slavery.

As I said, it had not been easy for me to resist the attraction of radical democracy. In 1871 the Emperor was organizing his first visit to Europe. An article I wrote in *A Reforma* entitled "The Emperor's Journey" clearly reveals my narrow monarchist inclinations. It is still a young man's writing. There is nothing but youthfulness in it, but each writer's individual style is already fixed. It no longer changes. Not only is it immutable, but twenty years later, when I consider resuming a literary style of writing, I am forced to return to the phrase-forming I used when I was twenty-one. The article is *quasi*-republican. My new British ideas had still not taken full charge. They lacked the force to overpower the partially fantastic projections that Laboulaye and his magic lantern had recently cast of the American world.

---

16 Agostinho Marques Perdigão Malheiro (1824–81) published his classic study of slavery in Brazil, *A Escravidão no Brasil*, in 1866–67. L.B.

17 In 1866, the French Abolition Society had sent a letter to D. Pedro II demanding that he take measures for the gradual emancipation of the slaves in Brazil. Under instructions from the Emperor, the Minister of Foreign Affairs Martim Francisco Ribeiro de Andrade replied that "the emancipation of the slaves...is only a matter of form and opportunity", and that as soon as circumstances allowed (he was referring to the end of the war with Paraguay) the government would take steps on the matter. The emancipation of children born to slave mothers was already viewed as a possible solution to the problem of slavery. In April 1867, the Council of State (a standing advisory body to the Emperor and the government) discussed a bill for this purpose drafted by José Antônio Pimenta Bueno, Viscount São Vicente. Nabuco's father, Nabuco de Araújo, was one of its principal defenders. On September 28 1871 a Law of Free Birth was enacted by a Conservative cabinet led by the Viscount of Rio Branco. R.S.

I thus recommended to the Emperor that rather than going to old Europe, he should visit young America:

"Above all, he would understand one thing. When he saw the United States leading the world's industrial and moral progress, he would understand that kings might very well be a mere hypothesis, a luxury, a superfetation. Upon seeing a fully liberal and free society, governing itself without a king, he would understand that in certain epochs, the people are able to dispense with any kind of tutorship. Seeing the family institution honored and respected" – here I was referring to the purity of the home and Americans' respect for women – "and transformed into a religion in its own right, seeing religion turned into the moral bond of souls, with a fragmentation of denominations to the point where there are nearly as many churches as there are individuals, all of which leads to none other than greater tolerance and brotherhood, and watching civilization grow," – on virgin soil – "like a tree with enormous roots and a great shadow; witnessing the vanguard of progress occupied by a republic" – did I not deserve the first Laboulaye prize? – "the Emperor would abandon the monarchist temple wherein kings worship. Meanwhile, witnessing the power that passes from a soldier to a lumberjack, to a tailor, always the same, whole and perfect, he – preserving his love for family, which would even grow, because his family would no longer be synonymous with the dynasty – would forego his veneration for hereditary succession."

That was my language at twenty-one, with a minimum of monarchism and a maximum of republicanism, produced by this preference for a monarch with no hereditary succession, with no ceremonial usages, with no veneration, all on the same level, like the White House with its government of the people. Only gradually did the influence of the monarchist system grow and prevail over this spontaneous radicalism, this inflexible egalitarianism. At twenty-one years of age I certainly would never have appreciated my father's political maxim in the Senate: "The relative utility of laws is preferable to their absolute utility." For me, nothing was relative.

During those years, the Liberal Party led the Rio Branco Cabinet wherever it wanted. Liberal opinion certainly wielded much more power over that Cabinet than the Sinimbu Cabinet or any other from its own party – except for the Dantas Cabinet, because in the latter the President of the Council was sensitive to the slightest censure by liberalism. In fact, the Rio Branco Cabinet was a reformist one, the like of which had not existed before the Paraná Cabinet, or since. The government itched for reforms, perhaps not by its own inclination, but to disarm the Liberal opposition. It was only Conservative in the traditional sense on two points: in its prejudice against direct elections, which was probably the Emperor's position as well, and in relation to the balance of power in the River Plate. In its foreign policy it maintained a firm Conservative tradition, or rather the traditional policy pursued before the Triple Alliance, and it is most likely that if the Alliance's Liberal policy had continued after the war in the peace treaties, it would have created a very different situation in the River Plate than the stability and peace that resulted from this change in attitude by the Conservatives. In all the rest it was an innovative Cabinet, the likes of which the Liberal Party would never have produced. The liberals provided all the fabric for the reforms. The clothing's pattern was entirely liberal, but the conservative tailor cut the fabric so deftly with his shears that he left the entire liberal haberdashery across the street in tears. Particularly on the issue of religion, the Rio Branco position could only have been called conservative because it was Pombaline, ultra-royalist. The Liberal Party, rather than rejoicing, claimed it had been robbed, and demanded its patents, its copyrights.[18]

At the time, and for many years, radicalism dragged me with it. For example, I was among the most active voices in the Masonic campaign of 1873 against the bishops and the Church. I even defended the ideas of Feijó for a national Church, independent of Roman discipline. I gave lectures, wrote articles, published pamphlets. Today, I would not take back a word of what I said then, advocating for the most perfect freedom of religion. More than ever, I understand now that after the splendid experience with the pontificate of Leo XIII, the Church has everything to gain with freedom, and the world's future may belong to the alliance, already achieved under

---

18 Under the Constitution of 1824, in the Portuguese regalist tradition, Catholicism was the religion of the state in Brazil and the Church came under state control. In Brazil, in contrast to most Spanish American republics, Church and state coexisted in relative harmony in the period after independence. When, however, Pope Pius IX (1846–78) began his attempt to reform the Church and establishing the supreme authority of the Papacy, reform-minded, ultramontane bishops and priests in Brazil began to resent, and resist, their subordination to the state. This led finally to the crisis between the state and the Church of 1872–75 in which the bishops of Olinda and Para were arrested, tried and sentenced to jail and hard labor, mainly over their refusal to allow freemasons in the *irmandades*. There was intense and bitter hostility to the Pope and the "Romanizing" of the Brazilian Church among politicians and intellectuals. But the government eventually backed down, and granted the bishops amnesty. Although tensions remained, relations between state and Church improved in the final years of the Empire. And under the republican Constitution of 1891 Church and state were finally separated. L.B.

the current Pope, between the Catholic Church and democracy. Under Leo XIII, liberalism would never be subject to suspicion, and this pontificate is probably not a *fortunate accident*, but a definitive point of departure, marking a new era in the history of Catholicism. What I do need to renounce, in favor of the moths that ate it, is everything I wrote in those pamphlets with any spirit of antagonism against religion, with an utterly arrogant misunderstanding of religion's role and of the need, above all else, to argue for its influence, its formative, reparative, and consoling effect, in our public life and in our national customs, as the foundation for future generations. Still, at that time, how could I have appreciated a statement like the following, truer now than ever, but whose depth and scope I only realize now – by Senator Nabuco in 1860, on the Senate floor: "In my opinion there are two pressing needs in our country's moral situation: the first is to spread the religious principle in the interest of family and society..."? I can say, using the new scientific jargon, that back then nothing was static for me, everything was dynamic.

A Conservative Cabinet that sets out to conduct liberal reforms necessarily produces great confusion in the Liberal camp. For a youth like myself who was just beginning to pursue an independent political life in the press and in the party's club, the Cabinet's politics hardly mattered. My target remained the same. Nevertheless, instinctively, listening to my lifeblood, rather than discussing with the conservative government that was conducting the liberal reforms, I preferred a dialogue with the faction that had broken away from our party to form the Republican Party. Even then, for me the form of government begin to prevail over all other matters, except for the issue of the slaves. But the September 28 law[19] had already been enacted, followed by a kind of truce with slavery. Therefore, taking the monarchist view, I launched a battle in *A Reforma* against the newspaper *A República*. While in 1871 I could aspire to the American Laboulaye prize, in 1873, the year of my monarchist consecration, I entered the contest for the English Bagehot prize, again with the articles from *A Reforma*. The following passage suffices to demonstrate, as compared to "The Emperor's Journey", the change I had undergone in two years:

19 The Law of Free Birth (1871)

"One really needs to be fooled – whether by words or by symbols – to call the king in the parliamentary system a tyrant. Nor can one even compare a Lincoln to a Victoria. The American President governs, administers, has thousands of civil service jobs at his disposal, heads his party, and has full responsibility over the government and powerful initiative. He can be a Washington or a Johnson[20], if you will. The English sovereign has no power whatsoever. Parliament names the minister that he appoints, and he can appoint no other. This imposed minister becomes the head of state, submits the bills, which the sovereign cannot refuse to sign, and dissolves Commons if it gives him a vote of no confidence. And while the minister *governs*, the king only *reigns*. Does this English tyrant not have much less power than the American *chief executive*?"

I no longer strayed from these ideas, as we shall see. They are nothing like the ideas I espoused in 1871, when I was swept away by enthusiasm and passion. These are the forms of the spirit that allow intelligence to take another shape. They have transparency, the clarity of evidence, as if they were, and indeed they really are, the first theorems of political geometry.

---

20 A reference to Andrew Johnson (1808–75), the 17th President of the United States (1865–69), following the assassination of Abraham Lincoln, and the first US president to be impeached (in 1868). L.B.

CHAPTER IV

THE ATTRACTION
OF THE WORLD

DURING THE YOUTHFUL YEARS THAT I HAVE JUST BEEN
RETRACING, politics certainly excited me greatly. In any scene
in the world, the political game interested me, gripped me, and
shook me. For that very reason I was not, nor was I ever, what they call a
true politician, a spirit capable of living politics with a small p and giving it
my best. During my life I have lived Politics with a capital P, I mean politics
that is history, and I still live it today, but of course much less than before.
But as for politics per se, which is local, national, partisan politics, I have
this double inability: not only a whole world of things appears superior to it,
but also my curiosity or my interest always focuses on the most complicated
or intense part of the action in the contemporary universal drama.

I am more a spectator of my century than of my country. For me, the
play is civilization, and it is staged in all the great theaters of humankind,
now connected by the telegraph. When the scene takes place in Brazil,
a greater fondness, a closer interest, a more intimate connection give
it a special importance for me, but this is not to be mistaken for pure
intellectual emotion. It is a domestic pleasure or pain that touches my
heart, not a great play that grips or overwhelms my intelligence. Abolition
in Brazil held my interest more than all the other facts of my time. The
ousting of the Emperor shook me more deeply than all the other falls from
thrones or national catastrophes that I witnessed from afar. And finally, I
have never experienced another sensation so full, so prolonged, so alive, for
months on end, as in the last revolt, when the cannons of civil war could
be heard at sea and the silence of terror on land was worse still. Yet there is
hardly any politics in any of this. In all three cases, politics stood still. What

existed was the universal drama I mentioned, transported to our land. The same could not be said of the party struggles or of what the professionals consider exclusively *political*. The latter is a kind of assimilation, like any habit, which limits curiosity to a narrow visual field, like closing one's eyelids. I never experienced the politician's special enjoyment in the partisan struggle. I pursued the moral side of politics, imagining it as a kind of modern chivalry, the errant knighthood of principles and reforms. I experienced in it the emotions of the rostrum, sometime even popularity, but I never passed beyond that point, that threshold. Official politics never tempted me. Its delight was never revealed to me. I never renounced imagination, curiosity, or dilettantism to take even the first vows of obedience. I only glimpsed from afar the hyacinth blue and purple veil of the *Sanctum sanctorum* (in fact, from so far away that to me it looked like an old green and yellow portiere), behind which the President of the Council contemplated alone, face to face, the majesty of the Moderating Power.[21]

This means that my political ambition was all purely intellectual, like that of the orator, the poet, the writer, or the reformer. Of course there is no greater ambition than that of the statesman, and I would not dream of reducing the eminent men in Brazilian politics who deserve that name to the status of professional politicians. Still, to be a man of government, it is indispensable to fix, limit, and focus one's imagination on the country's affairs and be capable of sharing, if not the parties' passions, certainly their premises, to enjoy a perfect communion of life with them, *individuae vitae consuetudinem*. Thus, even if I had possessed the necessary qualities, which I did not, the incompressibility of my human interest excluded me from politics. Politically speaking, I fear I was born cosmopolitan. I could never have restricted my faculties to the service of a local religion or have renounced their tendency to burst out spontaneously.

Thus, for example, during the years of my life that I have been describing, in 1870 my interest was not in Brazilian politics, but in Sedan. In early 1871 it was not in the formation of the Rio Branco Cabinet, it was in Paris burning.[22] In 1871, for months, it was in the struggle for emancipation, but

---

21 See note 9 above.

22 Sedan (September 1870) was the decisive battle in the Franco-Pressian War of 1870–71. The defeat of France led to a popular uprising and the formation of the Paris Commune (March-May 1871). L.B.

was this not the year when God's finger was pointed at Brazil? In 1872, my spirit was occupied by the [third] centennial of *The Lusiads*. I was publishing a book on Camoens, and for someone who is working on a book, although it may lack any literary value, as demonstrated by Teófilo Braga, there is little time or interest left to focus on events around him. As I said, 1873 was the year of my monarchist consecration, but also – which proves that reason matures by parts – the year in which I criticized the Church with all the iconoclastic furor of youth, believing that I was saying new things that it had never heard before in nineteen centuries of struggle, convinced that it would tremble under the blows of the terrible hyperboles I hurled against it in pamphlets and articles published in *A Reforma*: theocracy, ultramontane invasion, Jesuit conquest! Despite all this, in my mind 1873 was the year of my first journey to Europe, a personal metamorphosis, in my life the passage from chrysalis to butterfly.

I can no longer – fortunately or unfortunately is a question that would take me a long time to unravel – feel what I felt at 24 years of age, when for the first time I took a steamship (and today I would prefer to sail) to Europe. Since I have already seen Leo XIII in the *sedia gestatoria* and had the good fortune to speak at length and alone with the Pope, I believe I would no longer travel to meet any great personage, except perhaps the Emperor of China. Since I did not meet any Moorish king in Granada, I can do quite well without having met Abdul-Hamid in the Bosphorus. I might even be content to know the Emperor of China through the description given to me (if I saw them again) by two *rising men* in the upper echelons of European diplomacy, friends of mine, who had the occasion to penetrate the inviolable sanctuary and ponder the boyish figure of the Unknowable under the duress of the Japanese war. What interests me about him, what I can imagine quite well, is not his throne of silk cushions, his spokesman, his pipes, his incense burners, or his necklaces. It is the originality that surrounds him, as marvelous as the supernatural itself. It is the accumulated psychology of centuries.

In 1873, however, my ambition to meet all sorts of famous men was boundless. I would have sought them out at the ends of the earth. The same was true for places. I wanted to see all the world's vistas, everything that has elicited a cry of admiration from an intelligent traveler. In this capacity as a camera, I only regretted not having the gift of omnipresence. My wanderlust also passed. I run no risk whatsoever by reading any new geography book, an Elisée Reclus from cover to cover. I only get restless now when I read a good page from Pausanias or Strabo, with their ancient names. The most precious tomes on my personal bookshelf are my Baedekers, where various places are still earmarked. If I could, I would visit them again by taking the pilgrim's ticket (no one says staff anymore), but only the places that evoke one of my life's impressions, as I would have said years ago, or one of humanity's great impressions, one of its revelations in art or religion.

In terms of travel or landscapes, what would tempt me today? Perhaps the pure restitution of a far-off atavism? My maternal [great, great, great...] grandfather, João Pais Barreto, who moved to Pernambuco in 1530 and founded the Cabo estate,[23] was from Viana[24] – perhaps it would be Lima, if I could be certain that I would see it with the same impression as that of the Roman soldiers who called its banks Champs Elysées and gave it the beautiful name of Letes. The truth is that with each passing day I feel the call of the cradle stronger. I am increasingly bound to Brazil by this singular law of the heart that binds man to his fatherland, and all the stronger, the more unfortunate that land and the greater the trials and tribulations it endures.

At the time, however, in my era before Christ, immersed in the polytheism of youth, the entire world attracted me equally. Each new source of fascination from art, nature, literature, and even politics was stronger than the last. I wanted to meet the celebrities from all the parties. Next to the Pope, the noblest figure in Europe for me was the Comte de Chambord, who had just turned down the French crown so as not to renounce the white flag, a Henry V, hardly similar to Henry IV, and yet I had the good fortune of spending an evening in the home of monsieur Thiers.[25]

---

23 The year 1530 is allegorical here and refers to the decade in which the colonization of Brazil began. São Vicente was founded in what is now the state of São Paulo in 1532. The website of the Joaquim Nabuco Foundation quotes Cabo as having been founded officially on October 28, 1580. R. S.

24 Viana do Castelo in the north of Portugal. L.B.

25 About this visit my diary from 1874 contains the following entry: "January 10. In the evening I went with Itajubá (our arbitrator in Geneva) to the home of Monsieur Thiers, Hotel Bragation, Faubourg Saint-Honoré. Introduced to Monsieur Thiers, Madame Thiers, Mlle Dosne. Introduced to Jules Simon. This visit allowed me to see Pierrefonds, Coucy, Reims, Tarascon, Arles, and the great Chartreuse. Spoke with Monsieur Thiers about Brazil. *His opinion about the inequality of the Negro race, from which derives the right not to enslave it, but to force it into labor, as the Netherlands do with the Javanese.*" Author's note. Author's italics.

Itajubá refers to Marcos Antônio de Araújo, Baron of Itajubá (1805–84), named by the Emperor to the five-member international board to arbitrate between the United States and England in the case of the *Alabama* after the Civil War. T.N.

For me, a trip to Europe under such circumstances could hardly have failed to be, and indeed was, that eternal nudge to the pendulum of my imagination. Based on my sentiment, my attitude, my use of life, I believe that in my modest way I have been one of the most consistent figures in Brazilian politics. I even believe I will go down in history as a single-minded man, *persona unius dramatis*, to the extent that my monarchist fidelity can be considered, like that of André Rebouças, as the ultimate commitment, an expression of gratitude, an episode in the liberation of the slaves. But as for the spontaneous affinities, the natural sympathies, the inner movement of the spirit, it would be difficult to find a pendulum with a broader arc than that of my imagination and my curiosity. Who is this political man, the dilettante and traveler, attracted equally to everything, who admires the great social constructions, whatever the system of architecture, convinced that the same spirit inhabits them all, because the *creative* spirit is all one and the same?

We Brazilians, and the same can be said of the other American peoples, belong to America because of its new, floating sediment, that of our spirit, and to Europe because of its stratified layers. The latter tend to prevail over the former, as long as one has the slightest culture. Our imagination cannot fail to be European, that is, to be *human*. It does not stop at the First Mass celebrated in Brazil, to continue thereafter recomposing the traditions of the savages that guarded our beaches on the day of discovery. It continues in all the civilizations of humanity, like that of the Europeans, with whom with have the same common background of language, religion, art, law, and poetry, the same centuries of accumulated civilization, and thus (as long as there is a ray of culture) the same historical imagination.

We are thus condemned to the most terrible of instabilities, which explains why so many South Americans prefer to live in Europe. It is not the pleasures of social climbing[26], as the lavish lives of South American millionaires are labeled in Paris. The explanation is deeper and more complex. It is the attraction to the affinities that have been lost, but not erased, that are in all of us, from our common European origins. The instability to which I refer derives from the fact that the American

---

26 The original Portuguese term is *rastaquerismo*, from the French *rastaquouère* (c. 1880), or "individual of South American or Mediterranean origin with a dubious means of subsistence and an ostentatious, over-luxurious lifestyle, in poor taste". *Dicionário Houaiss da Língua Portuguesa*, Editora Objetiva, Rio de Janeiro, 2001, p. 2387. T.N.

landscape – the life, the horizon, the architecture, and everything around us – lacks the historical background and the human perspective, while Europe lacks the fatherland, that is, the way each of us was shaped at birth. On one side of the ocean we miss the world, on the other, the country. The sentiment in us is Brazilian, the imagination European. I would not trade all the landscapes of the New World, the Amazon forest, the Argentine pampas, for a stretch of the Via Appia, a curve in the road from Salermo to Amalfi, a bit of the quay on the Seine in the shadow of the old Louvre. In the midst of the luxury of the theaters, the fashion, the politics, we are eternal *squatters*, as if we were still cutting down the virgin forest.

I know quite well, just to give Rio de Janeiro as an example, that there is nothing more pleasing *to the eye* than perhaps – and the choice would be impossible – the parks of São Clemente, the pathway along the Paineiras aqueduct towards Tijuca, the São João bridge, with Sugarloaf, viewed from Flamengo at sunset. But all of this is still a stretch of the planet of which humanity has not taken possession. It is like an earthly paradise before man's first tears, a kind of kindergarten. I am not implying that there are two humanities, a higher and a lower, and that we belong to the latter. Perhaps some day humankind will renew itself through its American branches, but in the present century the *human spirit* – of which there is only one and which is terribly centralist – is located on the other side of the Atlantic. The New World, for all purposes of aesthetic or historical imagination, is a veritable solitude, in which that spirit feels as far from its reminiscences, from its associations of ideas, as if the entire past of the human race had been erased from memory and he must babble all over again, learn to spell again, like a child, everything he learned under the sky of Attica.

In a superb Spanish book, a tribute to the Society of Jesus, *Pequeñeces*, a novel by the Jesuit priest and great author L. Coloma, there is a character who is constantly asking, *"Usted me entiende?"* We all know someone who punctuates his sentences with that annoying *"...understand?"* that irked the Marquis of Paraná to no end. The speaker's "understand?", which attempts to force the listener not to miss anything he says, is very different from the habitual formula with which the idiotic Marquis of Villamelon expressed what he lacked the strength to think. There are also points, ideas, and feelings that the writer would like to express by another *Usted me entiende*, merely raising the tip of the veil on his thinking, alluding to it vaguely, without specifying anything, in fact, without saying anything. Each man is just an aesthetic ray that exists inside his thinking, and as long as we ignore the nature of that ray, we have no idea of who the man really is. In this confession of my political background, in order not to reveal just the mask, the persona, I should provide a kind of photograph of the symbols that were imprinted and reproduced most indelibly in my brain. Thus the reader will recognize that politics was nothing more than a refraction of that sliver of light that we all have in our spirit.

The instability to which I refer has been greatly modified. The duality disappeared in part, although not as perfectly as in my friend Taunay. He, despite his crusader's blood, despite having written his masterpiece in French, and despite his brilliant propaganda against nativism, is the most genuine *nativist* I know, because he does not even conceive of life in another land, with other natural surroundings. A Brazilian from head to toe is one who cannot live except in Brazil. In my youth I was a wanderer, as was the Emperor himself in his old age. However, torn between the fatherland, which is feeling, and the world, which is thinking, I realized that the imagination could break the mold in which my rough little sculptures were baking under the tropical sun, *Ustedes me entienden*, and I let go of Europe – history, art – only holding on to what is universal in religion and literature.

CHAPTER V

FIRST JOURNEY TO EUROPE

I N VARIOUS WAYS MY FIRST JOURNEY TO EUROPE helped attenuate the republican tendencies I might have had, while reinforcing my monarchist side. First of all, French republicanism, the kind practiced in Brazil, has a ferment of hate, an egalitarian predisposition that leads logically to demagogy – its greatest figure is Danton, the man of the September Massacres –, while even radical liberalism is both compatible with the monarchy and even appears to ally itself with the aristocratic temperament. If I had to personify liberalism, I would call it Lafayettism, since Lafayette was the principal representative of the *gentilhommes libéraux* of 1789. Narrow republicanism – which in times of crisis goes hand in hand with demagogy, and when exasperated by danger or excited by sudden, unpredicted accession to power, leads to the bloodthirsty outbreak of Terror – is a feat of mental reclusion. It only occurs when the spirit closes itself off in some philosophical system or religious fanaticism, in some sort of doctrine or social prevision, and isolates itself entirely from the outside world. Intolerance is, or was, the characteristic of French aggressive republicanism, and intolerance is fear of freedom and of the world. It is a phenomenon of intellectual retraction, producing a naïve hypertrophy of the personality.

The republican embryo probably existed in me as well. I have no doubt that, had I been born in another condition, if my father had not belonged to the highest sphere of politics, if I had not discovered – like so many others that rebelled – a way of overcoming the terrible *multi sunt vocati, pauci vero electi* of the old oligarchy, I too would have followed the republican movement of 1870, which included some of the spirits that fascinated me. If that had happened, however, I am certain that later on the abolitionist movement would have set me apart from such republicanism, and that on

May 13 I would have cast my lot with the liberating monarchy. If, despite everything, I had remained republican until November 15 – and had been born in any condition whatsoever, as long as I were the same person I am, and had received the same basic foundations of the soul ever since the cradle –, I have not the slightest doubt that the shock of the Emperor's exile would have shattered my republican fantasy and restored me to the sincerity and clarity of my political senses.[27] One way or another, my European journey in 1873 destroyed the seed of any and all republican inclination, any trace of fanaticism that I might have harbored in my innermost being.

My sojourn did not last long, only a year. The inner spirit it created had antecedents in my relations in the small circle of the diplomatic corps in Petrópolis and the Court, in contact with foreign attachés and secretaries, some of the latter now foreign ministers themselves and even ambassadors. A *cosmopolitan* or *worldly* spirit is characterized by an understanding of opposing solutions to the same social problems, through tolerance for all opinions, by equal familiarity with coreligionists and adversaries, by the idea, first and foremost, that *good society* takes precedence over any party. This political way of being is not necessarily eclectic, much less skeptical. It is only incompatible with fanaticism, that is, with intolerance in whatever form. The trip to Europe was the great shift that consolidated an anti-systematic tendency that I already had, buffering my predominantly political inclination until 1879, when I entered Parliament for the first time. Yet even in Parliament, after my first year, when the excitement of the rostrum made me confront and take interest in the party struggle, from 1880 to 1889, when that career ended for me once and for all, I can say that the effect of my shift away from party politics in 1873 continued, because throughout my time in the House I served under a broader banner and took my stance on politically neutral ground, namely the emancipation of the slaves.

The journey that made a definitive imprint on my political evolution lasted only a short time, as I have already said. I left in August 1873 and returned to Rio de Janeiro in September 1874. On this first trip to Europe I spent less than a year. Of these eleven months, I spent approximately five in Paris, three in Italy, one on Lake Geneva, one in London, and one

---

27 Slavery was abolished on 13 May 1888. The Empire was overthrown and a Republic proclaimed on 15 November 1889. L.B.

in Fontainebleau. The reason for this month in Ouchy and the month in Fontainebleau is that when I travel, whenever a place speaks to me, I let myself be gripped by it and forget to leave. That is what happened later when I planned to spend the customary hour in Niagara to see the falls, and I allowed myself to stay twenty-some days without succeeding in tearing myself away from that spectacle until I had entirely absorbed it.

The month in Ouchy meant that, not counting Lausanne, the first walks along the banks of the lake, on one side towards Coppet, on the other towards Clarens, the visits to Geneva with the obligatory pilgrimage to Ferney, placed me in perhaps the most interesting literary theater in modern Europe, next to Weimar, because Clarens was the scene for *The New Heloise*,[28] and it was full of the eloquence of Rousseau, Ferney, and the last years of Voltaire. Coppet, that of the royalty of Corinna with her court coming from Paris, from Germany, from Italy, not to mention Lord Byron. Most of all, in this stretch of land intellectually linking the 18th to the 19th century, what would have bound me to Ouchy forever (if I had several eternities in this life) was the lake, its landscape, its frame.

I spent the month in Fontainebleau for a different reason. It was not the castle or the forest themselves that held me. It was that I was returning from England, having spoken English with everyone for the first time, fascinated by London, touched by a bit of Anglomania, which was the disease of society in France, and thus even this belies the French construction of my spirit, while Fontainebleau, with the repose of its symmetrical gardens, its fresh waters and shadows, its tranquil silence, was the most admirable retreat I could desire in this month of my life, which I may call my Thackeray month. This was the ideal cloister during which, secluded with *Vanity Fair*, *Pendennis*, *The Newcomes*, and I don't know what else, with no dictionaries, guessing at what I was unable to translate, understanding everything, I exhausted myself to tears in my impression of the great English novelist – which I later did with George Eliot and Trollope, but never, I regret to say, with Dickens, nor with Sir Walter Scott.

Of course, a spectacle that one may never forget can open and close before one's eyes in just minutes. In a matter of months I visited Italy, but only the great ancient capitals, I also regret to say. I did not even make

---

28 *Julie* or *The New Heloise*, Jean-Jacques Rousseau's great epistolary novel published in 1761. L.B.

the artistic pilgrimage through Umbria. I spent two hours before the four monuments of old Pisa, which inspired Taine to his most eloquent page. Yet how can one forget this undying revelation? Did Keats not say it all with his verse:

A thing of beauty is a joy for ever?

Not only is this "joy" of which he speaks truly beautiful "for ever", an inner ray incorporated into life, never again to be extinguished, whatever the trials and tribulations; but also, a single ***thing of beauty***, a single fragment of true beauty, suffices to illuminate all of human existence. No man will have fully understood two great works of art, the Greek column and the Gothic arch, a Michelangelo and a Piero della Francesca, or two different views of nature, the ocean and the mountain lakes, the snow-covered landscapes and the Oriental skies. In no case, however, can one feel a work of art *in passing*, that is, without it producing a vibration in us, corresponding to the artist's effort and feeling when he composed it.

If the artist took years for his creative thinking to reach fruition and was still moved by it when he died, how could his impression penetrate us in minutes? For example, I *saw* the Cathedral of Reims with Rodolfo Dantas on a day we *stole* in Paris, to use the parlance of the *boulevard*. I stopped by to see the Cathedral of Amiens. I *stole* another day in Paris to wander around the Cathedral of Rouen. I visited Strasbourg to see the great Münster by Erwin von Steibach. With Artur de Carvalho Moreira, one of the finest spirits from our academic generation, I did a tour of the historical castles of Loire: Chenonceux, Amboise, Blois, Chambord. Just hours for all of this! For Francis I, Diane de Poitiers, the French Renaissance! Later, since I wanted to linger more, I chose not to go with my same traveling companion (who devoted years of his intellectual life exclusively to the *Goethekenners*) when I visited Goethe's cities: Frankfort, Leipzig – I saw Strasbourg, but without thinking of Frederica -, Wetzlar, and Weimar. Everywhere I went, as I did in 1892 in Coimbra, Alcobaça, Mafra, and Batalha, I passed too quickly to let the impressions take hold of my spirit. An hour in the Cathedral of Reims! It would have been an outrage, an insult to that divine façade, except that I was there in a truly humble spirit, without glancing critically at the cathedral's sublime portal or all its incomparable legend, as a gamin would throw pebbles at it. An hour in Amiens! In this *Parthenon of Gothic architecture*, as Viollet-le-Duc called it, and holding the *Bible of Amiens* by John Ruskin, who envied the lowly cathedral guard whose daily job was to dust its unparalleled wooden sculptures!

One can see many things in passing, but then nothing is revealed. The first condition for the spirit to receive the impression of any great creation, whether that of God or the times (nothing is purely individual), is repose, the occasion, passivity, erasing one's own thought; giving the divine form the time it needs to reflect in us, to allow us to understand and admire it, revealing to us the original thinking from which it was born.

Of all these places in Switzerland, Italy, Fontainebleau, Paris, or London, I have nothing more than literary impressions. This journey's greatest effect was thus to erase politics for an entire year, to suspend my political faculty, which – having been suspended, interrupted – was broken and never again became the mainspring of my spirit. Yet I could not have stayed in France at such a period of transformation, like 1873–74, and at times in contact with political men, nor have penetrated English society, without the grand European politics having exerted a positive influence on my spirit, in addition to the negative change, as I mentioned, due to the fact that I was so removed from the local Brazilian scenario and impressed by art. Despite it all, I had indelible political affinities that might, at most, be relegated to a secondary plane, subordinate to purely intellectual attractions. I will speak of this *positive* change now.

CHAPTER VI

FRANCE IN 1873–1874

T HE FIRST TIME I STAYED IN PARIS was during such a historically
interesting period that a spirit like mine, subject to strong
political temptations, could not fail to focus on the spectacle of
the events, despite my artistic and literary fascination. Even so, one can
easily understand how the attraction pulling against politics, because of
the splendor of constant revelations, was even more powerful that the
contemporary drama. In Rio de Janeiro or São Paulo, when the sensation
of a great event grasps someone who feeds on politics, he finds nothing
around him to counteract the pull or serve as a counterweight. Fortunately,
such rare events are *great*. However, for a young Brazilian arriving in Paris
for the first time, it is almost impossible to imagine an event that could
make him indifferent to the marvels that greet him with each step, or a
political sensation not soon dampened or overpowered by the sensation
of art.

The struggle between the Duc de Broglie and Monsieur Thiers, the
theater of the Palace of Versailles converted into the National Assembly,
the Trianon ceding its rooms for Bazaine's war council, did indeed attract
me, and I was one of the anxious spectators who witnessed this time of
debates in that assembly and that shared in the emotion of that grand
military process, hardly generous in spite of it all.

I will never forget the cold November mornings in which my dear friend
José Caetano de Andrade Pinto, later state counselor, and I crossed the
promenades of Versailles in an open carriage to take our places on Marshall
Bazaine's own platform, behind him, practically the only ones (perhaps
because we were strangers and foreigners) who had the courage to occupy
that place to watch the prosecution, the defense, the cross-examination.

At the last moment, when they ordered the Marshall's private platform closed, we moved to the *prétoire*. What emotion we felt when the Duc d'Aumale, standing, like all the Council, which formed a semicircle around him, the red sash of the Legion of Honor draped across his grand uniform, the plumed hat on his head as if on a battlefield, holding a large sheet of paper on which was projected the reflector of a lamp held behind him by an imposing *huissier*, with the solemn air of one who after twenty-five years of exile spoke once again before France, read the three *Oui, à l'humanité*, which whistled through the entire hall like a platoon's bullets!

I will always remember, too, the session of the National Assembly that voted on Mac-Mahon's Septennate as a provisional, dilatory truce between the Restoration, temporarily impeded because of the white flag, and the Republic, which they did not want to proclaim. If during those seven years, the Comte de Chambord had died with the Duc de Magenta still in power, who knows whether the Comte de Paris might not have mustered the votes of the *Chevaux-légers* and the high finances of the *Centre Gauche*! I wager to whomsoever reads me that after a speech by the Duc de Broglie, with his nasal accent, his academic perfection, his manner (and manners) from the *ancien régime*, seeing the old Dufaure take the rostrum and improvise, without cadenced phrases, without clauses embedded one inside the other like a literary mosaic, taking the speech by Mme. de Staël's grandson in his hands and crumpling it, giving it whatever shape he wished until no one could recognize it any more, witnessing such a duel, between elegance and eloquence, is a joy one never forgets.

And I did not hear Berryer! There, in Versailles, I still found the remains of the great parliamentary generation that began in the Restoration and that brought it traditions, its oratorical school, to the Chambers of Louis Philippe. I don't need to say that all this interested me in my innermost being, intellectually speaking, but a mere glance at any page of my diary from that time suffices to show how my interest was divided and my spirit was tugged in opposite directions by nearly equally valuable sensations.

Thus, for example (the italics are to highlight the sudden oppositions): "November 19. The Septennate session (which voted to extend the Marshal's powers). November 21. I began attending Bazaine's trial. November 22. *Visit to Ernest Renan.* January 2 (1874) Chateauroux. January 3. Morning. Route de la Châtre. Poplar trees pummeled by the wind. In Nohant at 11 o'clock. They had been waiting for me since the eve, had a room for me. Maurice Sand and his wife, Calamatta's daughter. They invite me to have lunch. George Sand arrives at noon. We chat until 3. Asked me to stay for a while at Nohant. We spoke of Renan, the *Giaconda*, the theater, Bressant, and the Emperor, whom she had not seen. January 4. Orleans, Cathedral. The homes of Jeane d'Arc, Agnès Sorel, Diane de Poitiers. *News of the fall of Castelar*. January 3. We went to the *Château* de Chambord. Stone staircase *à double rampe*. The FF and Salamanders of Francis I. The *Bourgeois Gentilhomme*, 1670. *Souvent femme varie*. *Château* de Blois. The room of Henri II. Spiral outer staircase. French Renaissance. January 10: Visit to *Monsieur Thiers*."

For many, perhaps the first day they saw the *Venus de Milo* or *La Gioconda* was indifferent in comparison to their minor political preoccupations. However, I could never have even remembered that I had once been a politician, when standing before the marble of marbles or Leonardo's fleeting color or evanescent brushstroke. In politics itself, I found myself divided by the most absolute possible duality. In feeling, in temperament, in reason, I was as exalted a partisan of Thiers as any French Republican, but in historical and aesthetic imagination, I was a Legitimist. In other words, given the imperfect and incomplete artist inside me, the figure of the Comte de Chambord reduced Thiers to morally insignificant proportions. For one and the same man who harbors a lyricist and a politician, legend casts a shadow twice that of history.

During this period to which I refer, the Republic was still at stake in France. Thiers had been forced to resign and was replaced, to his surprise, by his Chief of Staff, Marshal Mac-Mahon, who had absolute control over the Army. The reconciliation between the Comte de Paris and the Chief of Staff of France had taken place at Frohsdorf on August 5. The horses for the king's solemn entry into Paris were being negotiated when the ministry retreated, feeling powerless to impose the white flag on the troops. One could say that the Restoration had been aborted, but from one minute to the next, Henri V could take inspiration from the precedent of Henri IV and accept the flag of the Revolution. Recently, General du Barail, who was minister of war under the Duc de Broglie, confessed that if the Comte de Chambord had wished, the monarchy rather than the Septennate would have been proclaimed.

"The Marshal," he wrote, "was convinced that the Prince would give in to a patriotic argument, namely the fear of attracting the animosity and even the guns of Germany on his country." Recent testimony by the Duc de Broglie and the Ambassador in Berlin, Comte de Gontaut-Biron, indicate precisely the same, that is, that the Comte de Chambord realized that the Restoration would mean war with Germany and wished to spare France a second and worse mutilation. Who knows as well, given these diplomatic revelations, if this was not the same secret ulterior motive for Thiers to desert the monarchy?

Whoever saw the old statesman devote himself to consolidating the Republic, with all his prestige and power of persuasion, ever since he raised France from the battlefields where she lay wounded and rescued her from the power of the Paris Commune still in flames, might think that one does not dedicate oneself so fully to a cause that one does not hold dearly. The truth is that if Thiers had invested half the effort and work in restoring the monarchy that he did to consolidate the Republic, the royalty probably would have been proclaimed, perhaps still in Bordéus. For a long time it was he who tipped the scale between the parties. One cannot fail to be moved when reading his speeches from 1871, when he found himself caught between the two sides of the Assembly and invented fine points to keep them from treating each other as enemies in the face of the foreign invader, all of which were subtle distinctions, as between *constituting* and *reorganizing*, between *renouncing* and *reserving* constituent power.

I was like a blatantly Thierist politician, that is, a de facto republican in France. Yet this did not mean that I felt republican in principle, on the contrary. The Third Republic in France was founded by monarchists. It was a transaction by monarchist statesmen, like Thiers, Dufaure, Rémusat, Léon Say, Casimir Périer, Waddington, and the entire *Centre Gauche*.

"It may sound paradoxical," wrote one of the skilled editors of the *Quarterly Review*[29] with admirable clarity in 1890, "but the main obstacle to a monarchist restoration in France is the growing conservatism that has always been inherent to the French character in the midst of excitement and turmoil. The people know that a change in the form of government can only be achieved by means of a revolution or as the result of war, and shrink

29 *Quarterly Review*, the literary and political review published in London from 1809 until 1967. I was unable to locate the specific issue, and I therefore retranslated the quotes into English based on Nabuco's text in Portuguese. T.N.

from the prospect of one or the other eventuality, preferring to accept the status quo, even though it causes no enthusiasm."

This French conservative spirit, enemy of sudden changes, even for the better, is well illustrated by the following anecdote, as told several years ago by a *Times* correspondent. During the June barricades, when the cannons were heard in the streets of Paris, a platoon was sent to guard the Foreign Ministry. The commanding officer, with his sword drawn, stormed into the Secretariat, but he stopped at the door to one of the office rooms, noticing that the civil servants continued to work calmly at their desks, as if nothing was happening. Seeing him, the director stood up, holding a stack of papers ready for the Minister to sign, walked up to the officer, bowed, and asked quite naturally and with the greatest deference: "Do I have the honor of addressing the new government?"

This conservatism, principally by the agency of Thiers, thus founded the Third Republic. The same conservatism prevented the liberal bourgeois spirit, which can be called *Centre Gauche*, from divorcing itself from the Third Republic. No analyst can deny that the quintessence of this conservatism was monarchist, more sincerely monarchist than the *fronde* spirit of the restoration *coteries*.

This first great foreign school in which I learned could not make me a republican in sentiment, just as it did not make any of its founders republicans in sentiment. Likewise, it did not make (nor does it make) republicans out of the English liberals or conservatives or the crowned heads of Europe, which – with no ill will towards France – prefer the Republic to the Royalty or the Empire. Nor does it make a republican of the Pope, who powerfully protects the current French system. For me, the greatest effect of that attitude by Thiers and the members of Parliament in the July monarchy was that it gave me grand experimental proof that the form of government is not a theoretical, but rather a practical and relative question of time and situation, which in relation to Brazil provided powerful nourishment for my monarchist predilection. The main effect was thus to destroy the latent republican seed, the seed of intolerance and fanaticism. And this was Thiers' greatest service to modern France, that of eliminating the old Jacobin monopoly over the republican idea.

The same writer in the *Quarterly Review* concluded, "Although on the one hand the genuine royalist sentiment is almost extinct, on the other the republican sentiment has also cooled down. The new generation is republican in the sense of not believing in the possibility of a monarchist restoration. Meanwhile, the ardent republicanism of the old doctrinaires is nearly as dead as advocating the divine right of kings." This change, which is now complete, began in 1871, and was the result of adherence by, not conversion of, the *Centre Gauche* to the republican situation created for France in Europe by the defeat at Sedan. This dual and equal attenuation of monarchism and republicanism formed the natural atmosphere for contemporary liberalism and modern political culture, and just as it favored the Republic in France, it should have favored the monarchy in Brazil. This was the great political influence that my stay in France in 1873–74 had on me. My task now is to describe the rival influence I experienced, which I will call my literary influence, thanks to which I returned from Europe considerably less political than when I left.

CHAPTER VII

ERNEST RENAN

AFTER I FINISHED LAW SCHOOL, LITERATURE AND POLITICS alternated in occupying and defining my ambitions. During my first years after graduation, the prevailing force was politics, but it shifted to literature during my trip to Europe in 1873, when my literary period began, lasting until 1879, when I entered the Chamber of Deputies.

I always read a great deal of everything during the period in which I considered myself more a politician than a man of letters. In philosophy, I had absorbed a little of Spinosa, Plotino, Kant, and Hegel. The most sonorous and sustained note in each of them vibrates the same in my spirit even to this day, when I appreciate the grandeur of Catholic philosophy and place St. Thomas Aquinas alongside Aristotle and Plato. In religion, I was under the influence of Strauss, Renan, and Havet, and I took fragments from each of them to shape my own personal story of Jesus Christ. Spiritually, for many long years I inhabited the lonely and silent banks of Lake Genezareth, albeit from Flamengo Beach in Rio de Janeiro. In literary critique I was completely imbued with Sainte-Beuve, Taine, and Scherer, although not as much with the latter as after I met him personally, which I will discuss later. In poetry, I had moved from Lamartine to Victor Hugo (almost exclusively *Hernani*), and from Victor Hugo to Musset, as later I would move from Musset to Shelley, and from Shelley to Goethe, at which stage I stopped, but where I do not expect to die, because I have Dante before me, which does not mean that I do not hear the echoes of the grand new rhymes by Banville, or that I do not admire the strong relief sculpting of José-Maria Heredia. In prose, Chateaubriand and Renan shared the empire of my interests with Cicero, whose letters are perhaps the worldly book that I would take along if I had to live on a desert island. The phrase, the eloquence, the portrait, and the historical staging of Macaulay also exerted a permanent influence on my spirit. Today, I would have to add Mommsen, Curtius, Ranke, Taine, and Burkhardt. As for the novel, which is imagination encompassing and shaping life, I would remain under the impression of Jules Sandeau. I lived in the shadow of his ancient castles, rebuilt by the modern bourgeoisie between two societies, the old and the new, which he wished to merge by love. Still, even stronger than Sandeau's poetry of the soul, which was magnificent and to which France will one day return, was the indescribable impression, at once aristocratic and feminine, left on me by the last charming studies by Cousin on 17th-century society.

All of this formed my spiritual background, the humus of my intelligence, when my literary phase began, when I felt an irresistible inner drive to enter literature. The previous period was one of receptiveness, of planting seeds, of assimilations. My impression is that reading had been my greatest pleasure. Now came the need to produce, to create, and a singular fact occurred as the result of all these years of reading in French: I read very little in Portuguese, I still had not started reading in English, and I had forgotten the German of *Maria Stuart* and *Wallenstein*, to the true disappointment of Goldschmidt, my old tutor. As a result, I felt urged, indeed coerced by the very spontaneity of thought, to write in French.

A brilliant reader of the *Revista Brasileira* whose various qualities include perhaps the most precious of all, a generous dose of kindness, marveled at my affinity for French. In fact I am not revealing any secret when I say that my wording is definitely a free translation, and that nothing would be easier for me than to translate it back into the original French. I am surprised that the same does not happen with everyone who has read as much French as I, or even more, and whose intellectual life has been principally French, that is, in all its work of acquisition. Perhaps they assimilate more readily than I, or have I developed a greater ability to imitate? I don't know the answer, but this susceptibility to the French influence appears natural in those who receive nearly everything in French and who dread translation. Meanwhile, until it becomes literary second nature, Portuguese purism requires constant surveillance, precise rectification of all one's work in intellectual acquisition.

To put it bluntly, the truth is that while I admire the strength, the finished touch, at times the grandeur of the [Portuguese] vernacular style with its sieve of imperceptible holes to block any foreign imperfection, and with which our language modernizes while appearing to preserve its ancient tone, my cerebral phonography nevertheless adapted itself to reading in foreign languages. To reproduce the sonority of the grand Portuguese prose, I lack the inner echo that reverberates and extends within me – in curiously more intimate and profound gradations as they fade out – from the indefinable whisper of a page from Renan, for example. There it is, Professor Graça Aranha[30] has the confession of my deficiency in our language, whose strong, resistant, primitively rough fiber I regret not possessing. Perhaps for this very reason I limit myself to writing, as he has observed, with the threads and hues of Portuguese that fit my French loom.[31]

The moment in which this fever for French verse overwhelmed me – to top it all, it was in verse that I felt compelled to compose – was whimsically poorly chosen, since it coincided with my first visit to Europe. Nor is there any doubt that I caught the fever as a result of my journey. From the artistic impression, the historical impression, the literary impression of the Old World, there welled up within me the unknown source of the Muses, which in others has sprung from love and youth. I gathered verses on everything I saw, like others gather pebbles or ivy leaves from the Coliseum, from the Forum, from Posilipo, from Sorrento, from Pompeii, from Lake Geneva, from Versailles. I collected these verses in a book, *Amour et Dieu*. God in the title was everything that was left from a long poem on Eternity that I had conceived in Ouchy, a sort of theist rebuttal to the *De Rerum Natura*. When I began to write these verses, I ignored the fundamental rules of French prosody, like alternating rhymes, but I soon became familiar with the secrets of hiatuses and hemistiches. My verses in *Amour et Dieu* sounded to me – and the author's self-delusion is one of Creation's finest stratagems – not exactly equal, but similar to the best from the decadence in which France had already entered. In fact, these verses were virtually worthless. Not that they were all bad, but because their possible value, as

30 The "brilliant reader of the *Revista Brasileira* " to whom Nabuco replies in these two paragraphs is José Pereira da Graça Aranha (1868–1931), writer, jurist, diplomat, and together with Joaquim Nabuco, a founding member of the Brazilian Academy of Letters. T.N.

31 Brazil was engaged at this time in a major debate on its national identity, in which the issue of language played a key role, including the relationship between the Portuguese of Brazil and that of Portugal. Nabuco wrote in French as easily as in Portuguese. This chapter of *Minha formação* led Mário de Andrade (1893–1945) to caution the young poet Carlos Drummond de Andrade (1902–1987) against what he called "Nabuco's disease" (in an ironic parallel with the recently-discovered Chagas' disease), as an infirmity affecting Brazilian intellectuals in their craving to copy French models. R.S.

if I had been opening a new pathway to the imagination, was in fact a road well traveled, a sort of *via sacra* of the ancient processions, in which spirits far superior to my own had already raised votive columns all along the way. Besides, what might have sounded pleasant in them was really just poetic declamation, not poetry. It belonged to rhetoric, or to eloquence, but not to art, which is solely creation.

Since I have touched on the matter of the author's self-delusion, I will digress here with a reminiscence that may caution younger poets against one of the most frequent traps in the path from youth to old age, that of the praise we curry, or even merely desire.

In 1872, when Alexandre Dumas *fils* wrote the pamphlet *L'Homme-Femme*, finishing with the famous *Tue-la!*, I published in Rio de Janeiro a letter in French to Ernest Renan with the title *Le Droit au Meurtre*. A friend delivered a copy of the letter, with my compliments, to Renan, whom I almost considered a *divin mâitre*. Today, I am aware – literarily speaking – of the weak points in the Renanian *manner*, but at that time I was the most completely mesmerized of Renan's many admirers in Brazil. My emissary was Artur de Carvalho Moreira, of whom I have already spoken, and Chamfort could have written the letter Artur later sent me, telling of his mission. According to Renan, *L'Homme-Femme* was nothing but a *méchant paradoxe*, not worth refuting, *une plaisanterie*, not to be taken seriously. When I visited Paris the following year, one of my first visits was to Renan. He remembered my name and promptly granted my request to spend a few moments with him as a courtesy visit. I still have his brief note: "*C'est moi qui serai enchanté de causer avec vous. Tous les jours vers 10 heures, vous êtes sûr de me trouver. Votre très affectueux et dévoué – E. Renan. Rue Vanneau, 29.*" Three days later I was climbing the four flights of stairs at Rue Vanneau 29 and entering the very same modest "apartment" that Carvalho Moreira had depicted for me in his letter. Within minutes Renan appeared before me. I have conversed with many spirited and distinguished men in my life, but none has equaled the impression of this first conversation with Renan. The impression was one of enchantment, as if I were the only spectator to an incomparable play. In that small library, with the wonderments of that unrivaled spirit pouring out before my eyes, I felt literally like Ludwig II of Bavaria in the darkness of the royal box, with the theater empty, watching *Der Ring des Nibelungen* in a scene lit for him alone.

I left this interview not only fascinated, but also appreciated, acknowledged. Renan gave me letters of introduction to the men of letters I wanted to meet: Taine, Scherer, Littré, Laboulaye, Charles Edmond, who later introduced me to George Sand, and Barthélemy Saint-Hilaire, through whom I met Monsieur Thiers. We established a friendly relationship from the first day, and of course when I printed my *Amour et Dieu*, I sent him one of the first copies. Here is his reply:

> Sèvres, 15 août 1874. Cher Monsieur, J'ai tardé plus que je n'aurais dû à vous dire tout ce que je pense de vos excellents vers. Je voulais les relire et, puis, j'espérais quelque vendredi vous voir à Paris. Oui, vous êtes vraiment poète. Vous avez l'harmonie, le sentiment profond, la facilité pleine de grâce. Si vous voulez venir après demain, lundi, vers trois ou quatre heures, rue Vanneau, vous serez de me trouver; nous causerons. Je suis prêt à faire tout ce que vous voudrez pour la Revue et les Débats. Malheureusement ces recueils sont depuis longtemps brouilles avec la poésie. Ce sont des vers comme les vôtres qui pourraient les réconcilier. Croyez à mês sentiments les plus affectueux et les plus dévoués. – E. Renan.

Is it not true that for a young Brazilian writing in French for the first time, such a letter must have produced the feeling of making history in life? Now read this revealing page from *Souvenirs d'Enfance et de Jeunesse*, by which I was certainly not the only one to be inspired. I will commit the crime of translating Renan:

> To my knowledge, since 1851 I have not uttered a single lie, except of course the pleasant lies of repartee, the accommodating lies of polite jesting, which all men of conscience allow, and also the minor literary subterfuges, as needed, in favor of a higher truth, in the search for a well-balanced phrase or to avoid a greater evil, like stabbing another writer. Let us suppose that a poet shows us his verses. One is obliged to claim that they are admirable, because otherwise it would mean saying that they are worthless, thereby mortally wounding a man whose only intent was to pay us a kindness.

As for me, if a vague recollection of my verses occurred to Renan so many years later when he wrote this graceful irony, the great writer was mistaken on one point: he would not have stabbed me by saying that my verses were worthless, rather than telling me they were admirable. George

Sand also wrote to me about my book: *"Il est d'une rare distinction et les nobles pensées y parlent une noble langue"*, and curiously, Madame Caro also referred to *"l'oeuvre qui exprime dans une noble style la plus noble sympathie pour notre malheureuse patrie."* All these compliments, all this *nobility*, I received and guarded preciously as proof of the French people's characteristically generous kindness and courtesy. But as for the value of my verses, my lasting impression, that erased all the others, was that of the cold, impenetrable, yet polite, thoughtful, and kind silence of Edmond Scherer. I retold this episode to caution any budding talent against the powerful seduction of literary eutrapelia. Among us Brazilians, I know one master in this spirited art, Machado de Assis, but I expect no confessions from him. According to San Filippo de Neri, "He who cannot conform to the loss of his own honor will never make progress in spiritual life." The young writer who cannot resign himself to sacrificing his literary "honor" will never make progress in literature.

CHAPTER VIII

MY POETIC CRISIS

Now, THE REASON WHY I WOULD INEVITABLY FAIL IN POETRY: if what I wrote in *Amour et Dieu* were new, I could certainly be proud of my thinking, although even so I would not be a poet. But it was not new. Consider these quatrains:

La terre est une triste et bien sombre demeure:
Pour que l'homme s'attache à ce terrible lieu,
Il faut que le poète avec lui souffre et pleure,
Et lui fasse espérer l'adoption de Dieu.

Car Dieu toujours est loin, et notre humble prière
Ne le fait point descendre à ce séjour du mal;
En vain nous l'appelons et crions: Notre Père!
Il n'est encore pour nous qu'un soupir, l'idéal.

If no one had said the same before, this *humankind awaiting God's adoption*, which is still a *sigh of the heart*, would be the seed of an enticing philosophy. However, this passage is merely a translation – in weak and poorly crafted verse – of what Renan had taken from the Germans and had expressed perfectly in the most elegant of his prose. What fooled me in my verses, seeming sonorous and lofty, pertained not to poetry but to eloquence. Here is an ode to France; it is Alsace-Lorene that speaks to Germany:

Tu penses arrêter le sang de notre vie,
En t'emparant des rails de nos chemins de fer;
Nous avons cinquante ans pour changer de patrie,
Pour nous enrôler, tous, contents, dans la landwehr?

Ah! la force t'inspire autant de confiance
Que nous en puiserons dans le droit éternel?
Nous sommes les deux bras mutilés de la France,
Qu'elle tend toujours vers le ciel!

Madame Caro wrote to me in her note of thanks: "The two maimed arms raised skyward, I trust, will finally vanquish fate." The two maimed arms might have been the two knees doubled in prayer, or the shackled feet, or the liver of Prometheus of the Vosges devoured by the black eagle of Prussia, eternally reborn. All of this pertains to the realm of rhetoric and political pamphlet: it is a libel in hemistiches, like Barthélemy's *Némésis*. Nothing is more contrary to poetry than emphasis, platitude, and pathetic oratory. Where the lawyer or soapbox begins, the poet ends.

The fact is that I lack the form of verse, where the idea takes shape by itself and emerges with the timbre of true rhyme, which no artifice or effort can imitate. This explains minor poetry, free poetry, what one can call the music of poetry. As for grand poetry, the poetry of imagination and creation, romance, even ballad, I would be incapable of it, due not only to my absence of talent, but to a lack of courage to inhabit the solitary realm of creative spirits, those who live naturally among figures extracted from themselves, without a life of their own, automats of their intelligence and their will, as if daydreaming. At this stage, where everything is fictitious, everything unreal, everything fantastic, poetry is as terrifying to me as Pythias' *adytum*. Even when the figures are pleasant, tender, and human, the creation always involves something mysterious and terrible. The intrinsically complete abstraction from the outside reality, from the world of the senses, would make me dizzy.

In addition to the poetry of feeling and creation, there is another poetry. Verse is the noblest form of thought, the purest crystallization, and it has thus been said that what cannot be expressed in verse is not worth preserving. Yet this poetry, which mounts these gems of ideas in the most lasting and perfect settings, virtually belongs to the class of proverbs, in which human wisdom is condensed and perpetuated. In Homer it merges with history, in Dante with Catholicism, in Goethe with art and science. Its domain is that of the highest geniuses.

The poetry within my reach could only be a modest individual note. But as I said, I did not find within myself the key to verse, whose inner resonance is not to be confused with that of any artificial timbre. Even if I had received the gift of verse, I would have floundered, because I was not born an artist. As a writer, and everything should be seen in a relative light, I believe I received a bit of feeling, a bit of thought, a bit of poetry, which added all together can produce a certain measure of rhythmic prose, even in someone who lacked verse. As for art, I received nothing but the aspiration to it, the sensation of an incomplete, unformed organ, the grieving that nature had left me out of the chorus, the vacuum of the missing inspiration. *Ustedes me entienden.* According to Novalis, "Only an artist can interpret the meaning of life." I was entirely deprived of this faculty of *interpreting*, of creating the slightest representation of things, and all the more so for a reality higher than reality itself, as Goethe put it. Not everyone who has the gift of verse is an artist by nature, and not every artist has the gift of verse. Prose possesses them like poetry. As for me, I received a share of neither verse nor art.

It is quite unique how the title of artist is bestowed among us Brazilians. I have often read and heard of Rui Barbosa as an artist, based on his prose. In the same sense, one could call Krupp[32] an artist. Smelting is an art in some way, a cyclopean art, like that of Rui Barbosa – it would be no exaggeration to say – based on the blocks of ideas he raises and the lightning bolts he forges, making him a veritable intellectual Cyclops. But an artist? Is there a layer of art in him? If there is, naturally, it still lies unbeknownst to the writer himself, under the overlapping erudition and reading. I myself once suggested that no one knows what diamond Rui Barbosa would reveal to us if he had the courage to cut away mercilessly at the *mountain of light*, whose grandeur has overshadowed [sic] the Republic, and polish it down to a small gem. Take another, José do Patrocínio, who is not an artist either, although in his prose one finds the gold vein of poetry, the lode, fleeting of course, and which is lost at every turn in the political bedrock. One could extract pure poetry from it; from the palettes of his phrase, at least paint a portrait, that of the *blonde mother of the slaves*[33], as from the breath of his

32 Alfred Krupp (1812–1887), the German steel-maker, who was a friend of D. Pedro II. T. N.

33 A reference to Princess Isabel, the daughter of D. Pedro II, who as Regent at the time signed Brazil's Abolition Act on 13 May 1888. T.N

eloquence in the struggle one could construct a bas-relief for a triumphal arch: the *Chant du Depart* of abolition. Neither does he possess the faculty of verse, in which he would fail as he did in the novel, because his intellectual reflection has the vibration and speed of a lightning bolt, while verse is by nature diamantine. For this very reason, although his prose sometimes displays a touch of poetry and almost the heat of the creative sentiment, it still does not pertain to art, unlike that of Chateaubriand and Renan, because it is not a style. It has no government, only measure. It reflects the confused action, the constant upheaval of an unbalanced time, without an instant of calm or eternity in his work, which is brilliant as a whole. Now consider a quite different example. Would anyone fail to feel the intrinsic music in Constâncio Alves? He belongs to the order of the songbirds. His prose warbles, rises, and trills. Yet if he wished to reduce his melodious inner irony to a work of art, what would be left of it?

I said I lacked the gift of verse. Poetic timbre can be recognized in any quatrain. Take Olavo Bilac, for example. I cannot speak of Luís Murat, who takes a greater flight of the imagination, because so far I have instinctively respected his art's chaos. I sense that his talent has the elements of poetry, except for the order, the main element, but which fortunately for him can be acquired, while the others are inherited. His confused and intricate forms suggest a molting, and I wait for the time in which his youth has expended it violence and he enters the forest of the Muses, taking silence and tranquility into his soul. Said Goethe of Oeser: "It was he who taught me that the ideal of beauty is to be found in simplicity and repose, and thence it follows that no youth can be a master." I will wait to speak of Murat until he finds his Oeser. Take Bilac, however. Suffice it to read *Profession of Faith* in *Panóplias* to see that he was born with verse, that it is not an effort or a chore, but the free, open, natural expression of thought:

Invejo o ourives quando escrevo;	I envy the goldsmith when I write;
Imito o amor	I imitate the love
Com que ele em ouro o alto-relevo	With which he crafts a flower
Faz de uma flor.	In gold relief.

It is not my purpose to ask whether this craftsman always adheres to the rules of the craft in his work, which he sculpted so perfectly. Yet his hand holds the chisel, and no one can be mistaken about the kind of metal he is worthy of fashioning.

What I wish to emphasize is that it was not until the year I spent in France in 1873–74 that I aspired to become a writer, through contact with great spirits of the time, who received me as warmly as I might have wished, especially Renan, Scherer, and George Sand.

Renan counseled me, and I hereby pass this advice on to the new generation of writers, to devote myself to historical studies. Nothing is more ungrateful or futile than literary production that an individual extracts entirely from within himself, and that is what happens when the talent lacks a serious literary profession. There are studies like the humanities that prepare the spirit for a career in literature. Those with such a background can claim that they possess the tools of their trade, but in addition to the tools, they need to choose the raw material. The material for our writers includes customs and society in the case of novelists or playwrights, readings for critics, and life itself, or impressions, for poets.

Meanwhile, the raw material on which young writers draw tends to be inconsistent, ephemeral, partly coarse, party useless or insufficient, and thus the output is nearly all facile, improvised, with no prior work, no investigation, no time, no element that reveals continuity, ambition. Lacking the discipline and the emulation of a specialty, what happens? One's intelligence acquires the habit of waste, of indolence, of parasitism. The talent slackens and loses all its specific weight. We thus have an idle literature. Our literary field consists of *flâneurs*. In fact our epoch has witnessed a considerable increase in what Matthew Arnold has called the inaccessibility of ideas, in which this new Philistinism will reduce the art of our literary banquets to one single genre of delicacies, the **nature** genre. The reader public, the modern benefactor of the letters, whose generosity has been so widely extolled, is nothing more than a half-cultured Maecenas, even in France and England. To counsel young Brazilians to devote themselves to disinterested historical studies is to counsel them into misery. But the laws of intelligence are inflexible, and the output of a spirit that feeds only on its own imagination can only become increasingly frivolous and worthless.

I did not take advantage of Renan's advice until too late in life, when I began to prepare my father's biography, which is a perspective on the entire epoch of Dom Pedro II. But the advice is there for those who wish to develop and perfect whatever literary talent they possess, rather than frittering and wasting it. Still, his advice had an impact on my spirit – if not to discipline myself, at least to make me appreciate the value of work and research and understand the uselessness and vacuity of the purely personal and spontaneous (unless it is something uniquely characteristic of that writer).

From my conversations with Scherer, what impressed me was his admiration for the English novel, which appeared to be the house literature – Adam Bede, Jane Eyre, etc. My Anglo-Saxon foray began with Thackeray, whom I read at the time, as I said, during my retreat in Fontainebleau. Concerning my poetry, the great critic maintained the kind of disheartening silence of the physician who is incapable of deceiving the naïve patient who has just been examined and who attempts to surprise and probe the doctor with insidious questions about the reality of his condition.

The poetic fever that had gripped me with my first draft of *Amour et Dieu* was not about to recede easily. I wanted to rescue this draft, which I found inferior and imperfect, to replace it, and the seed of an idea contained in one of its poems split away from it and filled my spirit with the extravagant proportions of a grand drama in verse. I will speak of this play later. Evidently, very little was left of the militant politician after this first trip to Europe. In Paris and Italy, I had exchanged political for literary and critical ambition, that is, with a thick European layer in my imagination, a layer impermeable to local politics, to party ideas, platforms, and passions, isolating myself from everything in politics that did not pertain to aesthetics, and thus also from republicanism, because my political aesthetics had started to become exclusively monarchist.

CHAPTER IX

LEGATION ATTACHÉ

DURING THE NEXT FIVE YEARS (1873–78), for me politics was secondary, almost indifferent, but in relation to the monarchy this same state of spirit led to a process of consolidation, because thanks to all the fascination of the arts and poetry, my political aesthetics, according to the expression that served my purpose, was closed off, isolated, crystallizing in its monarchist form. The reader may be certain that my claim does not contain even a trace of the self-admiration that Jules Lemaître referred to as *moral narcissism*. Among the springs in my machinery, none had the elasticity or the strength of what I call the aesthetic spring. My aesthetic judgment always was, and still is, imperfect, instinctive, oscillating, like a gyrating compass needle. In order to embark in one direction, I lacked the necessary resolution, strength of character, courage, and spirit of sacrifice. Meanwhile, throughout life I have aspired to the Absolute, always failing, because in intellectual life – unlike spiritual life, where in the words of one of its great guides, there is nothing that looks like a mooring place – there is a mooring place, but it is religion, and until very recently I considered religion the haven of women and children. Some moral magnet always moved me throughout my career. My mistakes were deviations from idealization. I would never have been able to profess an idea, a belief, or a principle that was not an aesthetic magnet for me. Therefore, if my aesthetics had been republican, that is, Athenian, Roman, Florentine, the monarchy would never have made me unfurl its flag in the field of imagination, like an errant knight. Whenever I hoisted it, to feel my dignity, my pride, my spirit expand, it was necessary for the monarchist sign to act in me, as a partnership of art that is mixed with history and in some way makes it divine.

This process of idealization by which the monarchist form penetrated my aesthetic conscience and combined with my idea of art was my principal political influence from 1873 until 1879, when I took a seat in the Chamber of Deputies. During this time I had returned to Europe and lived a year in the United States. This period included the influences of England and English society, of North America and the diplomatic career, and the further development of my literary influence, under which I returned from Paris in 1874.

The latter was so strong that during the two years I spent again in Rio de Janeiro, I took no part in politics. At the Emperor's request, I gave several lectures at the Glória School on what I had seen of Michelangelo, Raphael, and the great Venetian painters. I was a literary collaborator of *O Globo* and waged a controversy with José de Alencar, during which I fear having treated the great writer with youthful presumptuousness and prejudice (I say I *fear*, because I never read those pamphlets again and I do not recall how far my critique went, or if I offended Alencar in his most profoundly *national* side: his Brazilianness). I also wrote in a magazine, *A Epocha*, which appeared and soon died out, along the lines of *Vie Parisienne*. Starting in late 1875 I immersed myself in composing a play in French verse, the writing of which absorbed me for more than two years.

My play's plot was based on the Alsace-Lorraine problem. This illustrates very well the political background of my imagination. Fortunately for the intelligence that was born with this diathesis, politics has as-yet poorly defined sides that border on art, religion, and philosophy, that is, to use Hegelian language, with the three spheres in which the world spirit is manifested. Since my play had a French source and a sentimental motif, as a literary composition it attempted to rise above the spirit of nationality, aiming at the unity of justice, of right, of the ideal among nations. I based its plot on the affinities and sympathies linking modern intellectual France to the Germany of Klopstock, Wieland, Lessing, Schiller, Goethe, Heine, de Herder, Winckelmann, Jean Paul Richter, Johannes Muller, Novalis, the Schlegels, Kant, Fichte, Hegel, Schelling, Bach, Gluck, Haydn, Mozart, Schubert, Schumann, and Beethoven, in a word, to the 19th-century *alma parens*.

By an apparent anomaly, although I was politically Thierist or republican in France, my play came out all legitimist and Catholic. The characters were taken for me, not by me (intellectual output is involuntary), from the old *bedrock* with the layers of the grand French traditions. This means that the unconscious – the only talent in any of us, our only creative power – was distinctly monarchist for me, whatever the cause, whether instinct or culture.

For my spirit, such a literary composition could not fail to be a strong political model. So as not to speak of this play again, since its only possible redeeming quality was that it was original, I have to tell that after writing and rewriting, copying and recopying, I finished it in 1877, in New York. My diary from that year contains the date on which, after a dinner, with an author's inflexibly inflated ego, I inflicted a reading of these five acts on a small gathering of friends that included the Baron Blanc, then the Italian Ambassador in Washington and more recently Minister of Foreign Affairs. He will have forgiven me for this sacrifice, to which he submitted voluntarily. The European riddle of Alsace-Lorraine, which is the basis for the Triple Alliance, will have imposed more vexing and tiring evenings on him in the Consultation than that reading in the Buckingham Hotel.

My political indifference at the time and the literary predisposition that I have just described led me to enter diplomacy in 1876. I had wasted five years since graduation, during which time it would never have occurred to me to accept a position from a conservative minister, since I was a liberal. Prejudice, the partisan extreme, prevented me from such an apostasy. But during those five years my intransigence finally wore out, and the idea now sounded plausible, although it had never occurred to me before that public positions are not the monopoly of the party in power, but should be entrusted to those best equipped to occupy them. Neither had it occurred to me that the post of legation attaché was in keeping with my capacity and social situation. On the contrary, it was several rungs below my previous pretensions. When I graduated from law school I believed that only a position as consul or ambassador would have satisfied me. My ambition progressively shrank as I experienced life. I do not mean to say that it shifted from the personal to the real, from the ephemeral to the lasting, that is, that it gradually increased. Thank God, however, among the contests that shape the struggle for life, my ambition never clashed with that of anyone else.

Perhaps I felt a tinge of the disdainful voluptuousness in the proverb: "Glory delayed is glory cold." Since my ambition was all in my imagination and surfaced when I was just eighteen or twenty, by definition whatever eventually befell me in life already arrived late. I now realize that luck has always smiled on me at the proper time, when I was prepared to assimilate it, and that whenever fate has passed me by, that particular favor no longer served my purpose, and I would have failed to benefit from it. At the time, however, my youthful impatience blinded me to the generosity of Fortune's veto when it excluded me from something I was not inwardly prepared to enjoy. I had not the slightest idea that a great public life needs to be illuminated like the architecture of Ruskin, by the lamps of sacrifice, truth, beauty, and obedience. Talent, form, eloquence, and outer shine meant more to me than the inner spirit of faith, continuity, and submission, which alone inspires and shapes the true human standards.

At any rate, I have the fondest and most grateful memories of that position as legation attaché, the only diplomatic post I have ever occupied. I could never have accepted another. Indeed, soon afterward I entered the Chamber of Deputies, where my position as a militant abolitionist became incompatible with the political system behind slavery. And once slavery was abolished, another forced abstention soon emerged for me: the defense of the monarchy against the political parties. The Baron of Cotegipe signed my nomination, which was certainly no cause for scandal. I could have easily earned my position as attaché through a public examination, in any Ministry of Foreign Affairs without patronage. And I lack the kind of gratitude by which others measure in millimeters a favor or service they receive. I ignore the art of analyzing or dissecting (by secret intentions and fortuitous circumstances) a kindness, distinction, or benefit bestowed in such a way that the beneficiary is sometimes the one who generously binds and obliges the benefactor. If the Baron of Cotegipe had named me Plenipotentiary Ambassador, his credit with me would have been no greater than for this nomination to the lowest rank in the diplomatic career.

CHAPTER X

LONDON

PERHAPS I COULD SUM UP MY PROCESS of political consolidation
merely by saying that the monarchy is an integral part of England's
moral atmosphere, and that the English influence was my strongest
and most lasting.

When I first landed in Folkestone, entering England, I had spent months
in Paris, had crossed Italy from Genoa to Naples, had stopped for a long stay
on the banks of Lake Geneva, and could not forget the gentle view of the
banks of the Tagus, from Oeiras to Belém, with such a sweet, smiling tone
as no horizon has ever appeared to me since. I had passed everywhere as a
traveler, sometimes lingering as long as necessary to receive the impression
of the places and monuments, the intimate shape of the landscapes and
works of art, but detached from it all, in the continuous inconstancy of
my imagination. Yet as I looked through the *wagon* window on a summer
afternoon and saw for the first time the lawn that covers the clean ground
and rolling hills of Kent, and the next day, leaving the little *apartment* they
had reserved for me near Grosvenor Gardens, I unveiled, one by one, the
rows of palaces on West End, crossing the great parks, finding St. James'
Street, Pall Mall, Piccadilly, with the high tide of the *season*, this aristocratic
multitude on foot, on horseback, or in open carriages, going twice a day to
the Hyde Park *rendez-vous*, and day after day I penetrated countless other
areas of the city, getting to know the populace, all the English demeanor,
race, character, customs, manners. I felt my imagination overwhelmed,
vanquished. My wanderlust was satisfied, exchanged for the desire to
remain there forever.

Sometimes I entertain myself by imagining which people I would save
if humankind had to be reduced to only one. I would hesitate between

France and England. Rather, I know quite well that whoever eliminated early 19th-century Germany from the wave of ideas, poetry, and art would eliminate its best. However, between France and England I am always left undecided. My duty, perhaps, would be to rescue France. Madame de Staël once asked her friend Talleyrand, "If Madame Récamier and I fell into the river, which of us two would you save first?" He replied, "*Oh! madame, vous savez nager.*" England, too, can swim.

The French genius has all the rays of the human spirit, especially the aesthetic rays. The English genius does not have them all, and has a unique opacity in spiritual points, which deserve the name French, and in nearly all of those that deserve the name Athenian. England – and this comparison has often been made – is the China of Europe, in the sense that it has an unyielding individuality, incapable of sharing a common countenance with other countries. Latins, Germans, and Slavs would form one single family, due to their countless common traits, before the English would fail to be a *sui generis* type, set apart from the collective European type. Thus, France alone would represent humankind better than England. It has more universal attributes, more creative faculties, more central qualities, a greater sum of human heritage, of evolutionary possibilities, than the English particularity and exclusiveness. On the other hand, the English race appears to be healthier, more resilient; even to have more vigorous genius and creativity, a greater supply of life and strength, although strength without imagination and culture (which in English has been foreign, at least to a major extent) can degenerate into brutality and egotism. These are the reasons for my hesitation when I imagine a new Great Flood and ask myself which country, in the highest interests of human intelligence, would merit the privilege of building the Ark.

Whatever the explanation, I never experienced the unbridled pleasure of living in Paris that was (and still is) the dominant cosmopolitan passion around us. London, not Paris, made the strongest impression on me. For me, London was what Rome would have been had I lived between the 2nd and 4th centuries A.D., and one day, transported from my transalpine village or from the depths of Roman Africa to the peak of Mount Palatine, had seen unfold at my feet the sea of gold and bronze on the rooftops of the basilicas, circuses, theaters, hot bathes, and palaces. For me, a 19th-century provincial youth, London was like Rome for the provincials in the time of Adrian or Severus: *the City*. This *universal* impression of the City that flaunts itself above all others, queen of the world for the *milliarum aureum*, could only be maritime in the 19th century. I felt this *sovereign* impression as distinctly as if humankind were still all centralized. The effect of this impression of domination was a feeling of *finality* that only London gave me: not of intellectual finality, like the Athens of Pericles, the Florence of the Medicis, or the Rome of Leo X for the man of art, 17th-century Versailles for the man of the court, Rome of the Catacombs for the man of faith, ancient Rome for the man of the past, Niebuhr, Chateaubriand, Ampère, and little late 18th-century Weimar for the man of letters, or this century's Paris up to Renan and Taine for the man of culture. It was a material finality, if I may use that expression, of an overwhelming grandeur and unlimited empire.

What is the source of London's universal impression, followed by this feeling of finality, which may be entirely subjective? (But which I think is not.)

I believe what gives the *metropolis* this *imperial* ascension is its gigantic mass, its undefined perspectives, the eternal Egyptian solidity of its buildings, the immense squares, and the parks that suddenly open up at the mouths of the streets, like meadows where huge vast herds could graze under the shade of old trees, on the banks of lakes that deserve to belong to Earth's natural relief. The latter, for me, is London's dominant trait: a foreigner would suppose he has entered the countryside, the suburbs, when he is actually in the heart of the city. It is the same impression, yet incalculably greater, caused by the *Domus Aurea*: "...the jewels and gold, long familiar objects, quite vulgarized by our extravagance, were not so marvelous as the fields and lakes, with woods on one side to resemble a wilderness, and, on the other, open spaces and extensive views."[34]

And my amazement did not stop there. It continued with the broad strip of the Thames, with the colossal bridges crossing it and the monuments sitting on its banks from Chelsea to London Bridge, especially the mass of buildings in Westminster, the low line of Parliament houses, the most grandiose shadow that architecture has ever cast on earth. And the City

---

34 A reference to Nero's "Golden House", as described by Tacitus in *The Annals*, Book XV, AD 62–65. Nabuco was probably quoting from the Portuguese translation by José Liberato Freire de Carvalho, *Annaes de Cornelio Tacito*, Paris, 1830. The English excerpt here is from *Complete Works of Tacitus*, New York, 1942, p. 379. T.N.

around the Bank of England, with the Royal Exchange next door and Lombard Street in front, the money market, the world's true *comptoir*. Here, on the streets covered with planks to muffle any noise, a unique impression is made by the throng that wastes not a minute, indifferent even to itself, from which nothing could distract a gaze or extract a syllable, transporting under its arms, in its briefcases, masses of capital that entire *wagons* would be needed to carry if it were in cash, the checks going to the Clearing House, the billions sterling crossing from bank to bank, imported, re-exported by telegraph to the ends of the earth whence they came. The passerby stops in the midst of the ebb and tide of gold, realizing he does not hear the pounds clinking. He only perceives the continuous, subterranean fluctuations of the counter-currents of metal through their tangible effect: the discount rate.

What also gives London its tone of majesty and dominion is the dignity, the silence that envelopes it, the calm, the tranquility, the repose, the confidence it exudes. It is the concentrated, reserved, at times severe air of its countenance, and at the same time the urbanity of its manners. It is the seclusion in which one lives in its very midst, in the center of its most densely populated streets, the isolation one experiences in its cathedrals and in the British Museum, in its parks, in its theaters and clubs. In my view this seriousness and reserve characterize an imperial, energetic, and responsible race, conscious of its virile and magnanimous strength. And there is yet another noteworthy, characteristic feature, the utmost expression of force and sovereignty: this world metropolis is not a cosmopolitan city, but an English city.

Compared to London, Paris is a work of art, immortally beautiful, next to a Pelasgian wall. It is an Erechtheion before the Memnonium of Thebes. Of course, nowhere else in the world is there an architectural perspective like that stretching from the Arc de Triomphe across the Champs Élysées to the Louvre, along the quay of the Seine to Notre-Dame. London lacks this impression of art that covers all of old Paris like a Greek frieze. For the artist who needs outer inspiration in architectural forms, living in the midst of beauty achieved by human genius, London is to Paris as Khorsabad is to Athens. The joyous and festive French genius is entirely different from the great English apathy, and in Paris one comes face-to-face with the masterpieces of French art. On that point there is no comparison. For the intellectual who needs a daily artistic tour to revitalize, and for the man of spirit and high society, Paris is the first home, because it combines art with the joy of living in their most delicate and elegant forms. London has nothing that matches the French aspiration, now decadent and evanescent, to turn all of life into an art, an aspiration whose masterpiece was 17th-century politeness and 18th-century spirit. Leaving aside the grand art that has committed such infidelities with the French genius as to produce Goethe, Beethoven, and Mozart outside of France, the lesser arts – and I do not use the term lesser art for the work of the great woodcarvers, inlayers, and furniture-makers, of Riesener, Boulle, Beneman, and Gouthière – are still exclusively French, as they were Greek in Cicero's Rome. The joy of living in London is not art, but comfort. It is not rules, measures, or the tone of manners, but freedom and individuality. It is not decoration, but space and solidity. Paris is a theater in which everyone, of whatever trade, age, or country, lives by acting for the crowd of passersby. London is a convent in the form of a club, in which those who find themselves in the silence of the grand library or the dining halls do not notice each other, and each feels indifferent to all. In Paris, life is a limitation; in London, an expansion. In Paris it is bondage, bondage to art, to the spirit, to etiquette, to society, a pleasant bondage, but always bondage nevertheless, demanding constant self-vigilance by the actor before the audience, who observe everything, notice everything. London is independence, naturalness, and insouciance. *Ceci tuera cela.*

Perhaps it was this side of English life that seduced me. The artistic impression is by nature tiring, exclusive, and beyond a certain pitch, uncomfortable, like any excessively strong vibration. I would not wish to be condemned to spend an hour a day contemplating the *Gioconda* or even the Venus de Milo. In order to renew my short faculty of admiring and enjoying a work of art, I need long intervals of rest (of lethargy, to tell the truth). London was this penumbra that admirably frames my weak aesthetic gaze. There, *excusez du peu*, I had the marbles of Phidias at my disposal. There was no artistic or literary period, if I wished to spend half an hour – more than which I would could not have withstood – that I would not have found represented in the British Museum, the National Gallery, South Kensington, and the other national collections. For me this proximity sufficed. As for all of life's other pleasures, as I said, I preferred the naturalness, the calm, the repose, the grand perspectives, the isolation, the oblivion of London to the constant vibration of Paris, a cosmopolitan vibration of spirit, pleasure, and art, through an atmosphere of luxury, struggle, and theater.

I know quite well that another life exists there, with indifferent, solitary recluses in the great capital, in little cloisters of silence and meditation, where the outside noises do not reach the thinker or the artist. Without it, Paris could never produce its great thinking. To live isolated from the bustle of Paris, better to be separated from it by the English Channel than by the Seine, like my friend Rio Branco[35], who closed himself off on the Rive Gauche with his Brazilian library, his exams to correct, and his closest friends from the Institute.

The fact is that I loved London above all the other cities and places I visited. Everything in London struck in me an intimate and reverberating chord: its broad meadows and woods, and the blackened brick of its buildings; the dizzying hustle-bustle of Regent Circus or Ludgate Hill, and the nooks in Kensington Park, in the shadow of centuries-old trees; its hot summer days, when the asphalt softens underfoot, the foliage covers with dust, and the air exudes the dry heat of a sauna; and its delicious days in May and June, when the highest windows become hanging gardens and the great baskets in the parks fill with tulips and hyacinths; its moonlit nights, making Park Lane appear to me as if in fog, with its street of palaces, a stretch of Venice, and from Piccadilly, looking out over the fog in Green Park towards the lighting around Buckingham Palace, the eternal illusion of the opposite side of the bay in Rio de Janeiro, viewed from the esplanade in Glória, as well as the city's dark, gloomy, foggy days, which I would not have traded for the blue of the Mediterranean or the purity of Attica; its traits as the world's largest city, the splendid beauty of its race, the slightest details of its proper countenance; the luxurious shop windows of Piccadilly and New Bond Street and the *hansoms* that stopped in front; the *Times*, the *Pall Mall Gazette*, the *Spectator*, and the books with their vellum paper, large, clear font, and supple gold-embossed leather covers; the tranquility of the clubs, the seclusion of the churches, the Sunday silence, and the hustle, the bustle, the trampling of Charing Cross and Victoria Station, the

---

35 José Maria da Silva Paranhos Júnior, Baron of Rio Branco (1845–1912), politician, lawyer, historian, diplomat and Foreign Minister 1902–1912. Son of José Maria da Silva Paranhos, Viscount of Rio Branco (1819–1880). T.N.

huge wave of all classes and all cities scattering from London on Saturday afternoon to the seacoast resorts, the summer homes, the banks of the Thames.

All of this, I realize quite well, was none other than my own youth, with perhaps the difference that it was my youth that colored the other places, animated and absorbed them, while in London such color overflowed naturally from all the city's springs.

I paid dearly for this feeling later on, because in London I felt the mortal withering of the human tree that each of us harbors and on which our spirit merely alights, like a bird on the highest branches. My tree's physical and moral roots needed the earth in which they were formed. Its leaves needed our [Brazilian] sun. Even so, years later I thanked London for restoring me, meanwhile more than compensating for that initial feeling of exhaustion. It was in London, thanks to forced concentration, which would have been impossible without the fog, that my mind first focused on the riddle of human fate and the solutions proposed throughout history, and that gradually, in the secluded Jesuit church on Farm Street, where Father Gallwey's verbal lashings taught me that my religious anesthesia was not absolute, and later, in the Brompton Oratory, breathing that pure and diaphanous spiritual atmosphere impregnated with the breath of Faber and Newman, my heart was able to gather together the broken pieces of the cross and thereby recompose my forgotten childhood emotions.

CHAPTER XI

32, GROSVENOR GARDENS

I SPOKE OF LONDON AS IF IT WERE THE ONLY CITY FOR ME, because London combined in one single impression all the different sensations I had felt, or later felt, in Paris, Rome, Pisa, Venice, New York, Boston, and Washington. For each of these cities, one needs to transpose race, climate, art, and the past to get the equivalent English impression, while in London I had the following sensations: the supreme life one feels in Paris, the enchantment of Rome or Florence, the radiant death of Pisa, the maritime power and solidity of Venice, the opulence, youth, and human beauty of New York, the silence and intellectual distinction of Boston, and the indestructible and gigantic civil institutions of Washington with its Capitol. All of this transposed, as I said, reducing the impression of the Forum to that of London Tower, or that of Catholicism to Protestantism, as if to say from the Pope to the Archbishop of Canterbury or from the Vatican to Lambeth Palace.

I am not one of the solitary, the strong, who survive by themselves and live on art, history, landscape, and thought alone. London with its grandeur, empire, vast interior horizons, statues, Parthenon frieze, winged bulls of Assyria, and Raphael Cartoons would have suffocated me in solitude if I had not found within it a close circle in which to rest my imagination from the acuity and plenitude of all those impressions. Without a pliant mediator I would not have stayed there, despite all my affinities. If I had to define happiness, I would say that it is admiration, the realization of shared beauty with those with whom we feel at home. The link for me was 32 Grosvenor Gardens.

I lack the space in these few pages to paint the portraits of the lord and lady of the house. I will only say of the former, in his Oxford doctoral clothing, that his diplomatic figure is as irreparably lost to Brazil as the 16th and 17th-century Venetian ambassadors are to Venice.[36] Of the Baroness of Penedo, the following trait will suffice: having lived for more than thirty years with the English court and society, she never neglected even her most humble friends, and always practiced the hospitality of her London mansion in the finest Brazilian style, with the very same affability to all, which goes to show what a proud and noble family the Andradas are.

My closest friends at Grosvenor Gardens included: Rancés, the Marquis of Casa de la Iglesia, the handsomest man of his time, who for all I know, to atone for his fine profile, later founded some Trappist Monastery in Andaluzia; the Marquis Fortunato, who represented the defunct Neapolitan royalty as faithfully as if Francesco II still inhabited Capodimonte; the elderly John Samuel, who told us stories of the old Brazil, having lived and pioneered fashion in Rio de Janeiro at the time of Pedro I; another elder, Saraiva, London's very own Portuguese dictionary, summer and winter in a full-length coat, with a long, unkempt beard, his skin engraved like a Spanish altarpiece, with a pile of books under each arm and in every pocket, first and last friend of Dom Miguel in England, and who since 1834 had consoled himself from the exile, poverty, and cold in London with his tomes and his listeners.

I also met Mr. Clark, famed correspondent for *Jornal do Commércio*, whom I later succeeded, the *bête noire* of Zacarias, one of these **old gentlemen** that England can send abroad as a certified national specimen, because he represented everything essentially English: profile, character, tradition, manner, prejudice, wit, insular pride; and Pellegrini, the *Vanity Fair* cartoonist, one of the Neapolitan artists that took cold, stuffy English society by storm with his joyous loquacity, contagious smile, and irresistible mime.

I should also mention Mr. Youle. For fifty years he has served as the London dispatcher for his friends from Brazil and Portugal. He welcomes them all, shelters them, showers them with favors, going to the bother of traveling to Germany for some lad whose father wants him placed in a house in Hamburg; taking the Calais train, no sooner than he has arrived

---

36 No. 32 Grosvenor Gardens was the home of Francisco Inácio de Carvalho Moreira, Baron of Penedo (1815–1906), Brazilian minister in London (1855–89). In 1864 he received an honorary doctorate from the University of Oxford – apparently the first Latin American to do so. L.B.

from Scotland or Manchester, to leave a girl at the Sacré Coeur in Paris who no longer wants to stay in Rohampton; going to Lisbon and if necessary to Madeira to accompany a patient fleeing the English winter; always ready, tireless in his role as purveyor to Brazilians and Portuguese in England, for half a century, and besides, an oracle in the City, in the large banks, on matters of the two countries' commercial interests.

These were some of my close friends from 1874–76, the period I am referring to, not to mention the countless Brazilians who found a home-away-from-home there. In previous times I know the long list had included, among others, Musurus Pachá and Don Juan, father of Don Carlos of Spain, Dr. Gueneau de Mussy, faithful doctor to the exiled Orleans family, and the republican Dupont, banned from the Empire, companion of Ledru-Rollin and Louis Blanc, the old Baron Leonel de Rothschild, the Marquis de Lavradio, a model of the Portuguese distinction and urbanity that appears to outshine all the other aristocracies.

At that time, the Brazilian Legation was at its apogee: it belonged to the handful of houses with the privilege of receiving the royalty, that is, the Prince and Princess of Wales. I heard many arguments in favor of the monarchy during my youth, but none had the persuasive force, the evidence, of these two, one on the Pincian, the other in Hyde Park: Princess Margarita de Saboya and the Princess of Wales. For the republicans of good aesthetic faith (let us leave both the barbarians and the anchorites aside), I would dispense with any other arguments. The modern monarchy would do well to sustain itself by enacting the Salic Law in reverse, that is, further neutralizing the neutral power by establishing a royalty exclusively of women. This would be real experimental politics, not only drawing inspiration from Queen Victoria's splendid and peaceful jubilee and Spain's relative calm, despite cruel times, during the reign of Dona Maria Cristina, but rather based on the masses' profound interest in theater when the leading player is a woman. The triumphant entry of Napoleon's remains into Paris will never compare to Tacitus' account of the field of Mars on the "awesome day" when Agrippina brought Germanicus' ashes to be deposited at Augustus' grave. If the prestige of the woman's position is combined with radiant youth and beauty, her scepter becomes a fairy's magic wand. When the queen's beauty is perfect, she has a glow of her own, a combination of goodness and sovereignty, of personal charm and national grandeur, of reliance on

Fate or even fear of it, of protection and succor for those who take shelter under her cloak, forming the dual projection, upward and downward, of the people towards the throne and the throne towards the people, which on the spiritual order made the Queen of Angels compare herself to the rainbow. In addition to the English royal family and the surrounding high society from Belgrave and Mayfair, the Legation was visited by foreign princes, both reigning and dethroned, like a young imperial prince, pierced with an asseguai in Kafirland, and whose death, so inglorious it seemed predestined, always reminds me of Saldanha's death at Campo Osório.[37]

It was for this society that the famed Cortais – inspired by the glories of the great chefs – formed the cortege of his architectural dishes, veritable masterpieces with which he later attempted to drive the Italian crown bankrupt, or so they told me. I also heard that at one of these later banquets on the Quirinal, and again following the tradition of culinary masters, he expressed his gratitude by serving one of his compositions with the following inscription on the royal card: *à la Penedo*. On that day the Brazilian diplomat must have said, as Chateaubriand did when they named a *beefsteak* after him, "Now I can really never die."

A creation by Monsieur Cortais for the crowned heads, with all the attendant pomp and circumstance, including a group of *professional beauties* from English high society, could not have failed to entirely erase from the mind of a young Brazilian legation attaché the prestige, if there still was any, of the royal decapitations by the Convention or at Whitehall.[38]

The reader will please not take me for a sybarite simply because I bowed before a great chef as if before an artist. *"Il en faudrait au moins un à l'Institut,"* Talleyrand used to say. If one compares the Dinner of Trimalchio to a *menu* created by a French master chef, or a belly dance to the minuet, civilization has certainly placed a huge distance between sensuality and elegance.

---

37 Admiral Luís Filipe de Saldanha da Gama (1846–1895), a monarchist, was one of the principal leaders of the Naval Revolt in Rio de Janeiro aimed at forcing the resignation of Floriano Peixoto, who as Vice President had taken over the presidency when General Deodoro da Fonseca, the first president of the Republic, resigned in November 1891. When the revolt failed, in part because of the support given to Floriano by a US naval squadron in Guanabara Bay, Saldanha da Gama went South and joined the Federalist Revolution which had begun in in Rio Grande do Sul and spread to Santa Catarina. Saldanha was killed in June 1895 at Campo Osório in one of the last battles of the Revolution. In 1896, Nabuco published a book on the episode, *A intervenção estrangeira durante a revolta (Foreign intervention during the revolt)*. R.S.

38 Nabuco expresses his monarchist sympathies with this ironic reference to the beheading of Louis XVI and Marie-Antoinette by the French National Convention in Paris in 1793 and of Charles I on a scaffold outside the Banqueting House at Whitehall in London in 1649. T.N.

Of all the senses, taste is truly the least prone to intellectualization, which allows a lesser degree of asceticism. Even the cup of bouillon served to Madam de Maintenon in Saint-Cyr or the cup of afternoon tea that comforts Queen Victoria on the terrace at Osborne is always a material enjoyment. It cannot undergo its transformation until the scent of roses and violets becomes pure nostalgia. Artistic cuisine is prone to idealism, because its main target is not taste: it aspires to leave the taste buds with a vague, light, immaterial sensation, nothing but a perfume, like a wine's bouquet, while giving the sense of sight the durable impression of an oil painting, a still life by a master. Yet what painstaking color, that of its sauces, sherbets, gelatins, and *primeurs*!

Still, there is real, true poetry in the healthy, natural food of the fatherland. There is sentiment, tradition, family worship, religion, in home cooking, in the country's own fruit or wine. For us, from the North of Brazil, raised on sugar plantations, the aroma steaming up from the great molasses caldrons inebriates us throughout life with the air of childhood. And just as there is poetry in each country's cooking, there is a *quid* of art in ornamental cuisine, the culinary art of refinement, which seeks to rise up through its design and form to the very reason for the banquet – and to make history, to make politics...

I beg the reader's pardon for my confession, but I could not fail to mention the foreign worldly influence in my formative years, the aristocratic, artistic, sumptuous influence I described. Just as I witnessed it in a royal banquet in Grosvenor Gardens, I might have observed it in a ball hosted by the Astors in New York. It is the same impression as an afternoon outing in Villa Borghese, a *drawing room* morning in London, a great day at the races in Ascot; the same as the Queen's jubilee in Westminster and the jubilee of Leo XIII at the Vatican. I cannot deny that I experienced the magnetism of the royalty, aristocracy, fortune, and beauty, just as I felt the pull of intelligence and glory. Fortunately, however, I never felt such influences without the corresponding reaction. I never really felt them to the point of losing my awareness of the more important issue, human suffering, and thanks to this I did no more than pass through a society that fascinated me, before trading the diplomatic life for the cause of the slaves.

Yet if I were only capable of receiving a political and social impression, and after my father's death, then slavery, the partisan oligarchies, and any false understanding on my part of the Emperor's role and the monarchist function might have led me to burn my Bagehot and enlist under the American flag. On the other hand, when my career depended on it, if I had received the exclusive impression of art, I might just as easily have leaned politically towards the republic. That is how I explain, in Portugal, the republicanism of Ramalho Ortigão, Bordalo Pinheiro, and Oliveira Martins in their political debuts: as a revolt against the unsightly character of the institution, that is, of the reign in which they began their careers. It is also my explanation, among us Brazilians, for the republicanism of Castro Alves, Ferreira de Meneses, my friend Pedro de Meirelles, Salvador de Mendonça, Quintino Bocaiúva, Lafayette Rodrigues Pereira, Pedro Luís, and others. What prevented me from becoming a republican in my youth was quite probably the fact that I was sensitive to life's aristocratic influence.

CHAPTER XII

THE ENGLISH INFLUENCE

T HE WORLDLY, ARISTOCRATIC IMPRESSION was purely a buffer
against politics for me, as the artistic impression of Italy and the
literary impression of Paris had been. The effect of society, like
that of the arts and letters, was none other than to prevent the development
of the revolutionary seed that the French readings had sown in my spirit
during my twenties. Without those influences, left to my own impulses,
just as my innate liberalism degenerated into radicalism – which in me
was purely a phenomenon of stagnation in a closed political space – my
radicalism would have degenerated into republicanism.

A distinguished writer whom I often find in the *Revista Brasileira*,
Prof. Pedro Tavares, of the type I refer to as *premature* republicans, has
expressed surprise more than once at what he calls a deviation in my
political evolution. He contends that liberalism naturally emerges, develops,
and ends in republicanism. But can he be certain that if Mirabeau had
lived, he would have joined the Convention? It is the same, for example, as
criticizing Lafayette for not having embraced the republic in France after
having helped found it in America. The fact is that republicanism (and
I am speaking of sincere, true republicanism) harbors an ideal, but also
resentment towards the position of others, just as socialism, communism,
and anarchism include an ideal, but also envy, almost always the point of
departure for the revolutionary impetus.

Without the *opposing* influences of the imagination, I might have
leaned towards the republic, like so many others who later regretted it.
Those influences only contained me because they shifted or distracted me
from politics. Still, I had a political temperament by nature. Sooner or later
politics was bound to seduce me again, and only a positive influence that

created a second nature in me and modified the absolute, radical tendencies in my temperament could have made me a monarchist in mind and feeling, as I became. This influence was the contagion of the English spirit, or what I was able to grasp of it.

My time in England left me the conviction, later confirmed in the United States, that there is only one *great*, free country in the world, unshakable and permanent. Switzerland is a free country, but it is a small country. The United States is a great country, but without even mentioning its justice system, the Lynch law (which is in the country's blood), the mass abstentions of its best people, and the discredit in which its politics is mired, the country has 7 million inhabitants – the entire colored race – for whom civil equality, due process, and constitutional rights are permanent and hazardous mirages. France is a great and free country, but without a deeply rooted spirit of freedom, always subject to the turmoil of revolutions and glory.

What leaves such a deep impression from England is first and foremost the government of the House of Commons: the sensitivity of that machinery to the slightest oscillations in public opinion, its swift movements and concentrated strength in repose and reserve. Even greater than the authority of the House of Commons is that of the judges. One can say that only England has judges. In the United States, the law may wield more weight than power does. That is what gives the Supreme Court in Washington its prestige as the world's foremost court. Yet there is only one country in the world where a judge is stronger than the powers-that-be, and that is England. The judge overrides the royal family, aristocracy, money, and even more importantly, the parties, the press, and public opinion. He does not occupy first place in the state, but he does in society. The stable boy and the *groom* know they are meant to serve, but they do not fear abuse or violence on the part of their employers. Despite their centuries of nobility, their historical residences, their wealth and social position, the Marquis of Salisbury and the Duke of Westminster are certain that before a judge they are equal to the humblest of their servants. This, in my view, is the greatest impression of freedom that England has made on me. Anglo-Saxon dignity is based on a feeling of equality of rights under the most extreme inequality of fortune and condition.

Except for this idea of justice that grew and took shape in me as I read the courts section in the *Times*, an unparalleled practical course in liberty, all I did in England was to confirm first-hand the precision, perspicacity, and acute spirit of Bagehot. Based on what I saw, heard, and knew, his little book explained itself, made itself clear, sensitive, and palpitating in what had previously been obscure and impersonal. It helped me understand the mechanism by which he formulated his theory: for me, it became a veritable gospel of constitutional law. One thing was to have assimilated those ideas right after graduating from law school, and another was to watch the system itself at work, to receive the living impression of what I had merely learned theoretically or memorized.

This dual influence of the English government and English freedom was by nature monarchist. I could not have failed to lean inwardly towards the monarch, knowing that the freest government in the world was a monarchist government. Even so, an intelligent foreigner would not be unshakably monarchist in his own country simply because in England the government reached a higher degree of perfection than in the United States, which adopted a republican system. Since we in Brazil lacked the historical elements that English freedom presupposes, and since I did not want to make the greatest possible mistake in politics – that of copying institutions that had *developed* in different societies – I could not repel the Republic in Brazil simply on grounds of preferring the English monarch over the American Constitution. I needed something more in relation to the form of government to avoid letting myself get dragged easily in one or the other direction.

The transformation, rather the modification of the political ideal that I experienced in England, was still preliminary, a preparation for the impenetrability that I later showed to republican proposals. Thus far I had found the republican system superior to the monarchist on the matter of human dignity. It was in England that I felt that nowhere else had our race ever reached the same level of moral pride as in a monarchy. With the dynastic privilege, which my radicalism had also rejected, I now realized quite well, all that was done in the 19th century was to take advantage of the oldest and most glorious national tradition to neutralize the state's first position. The monarchist concept was the following: that of a government in which the highest position in the hierarchy is excluded from the contest. The concept was as simple as that of a scale, or an axle. No right was transformed as much in the Western 19th century as the royal right, which changed from divine to passive. If the King of England wants to influence politics with his own ideas and initiative, he has to abdicate and – if the hypothesis is admissible – get himself elected to the House of Commons or head for the House of Lords. The difference in authority is infinitely greater between the Czar and Queen Victoria than between Queen Victoria and the President of the United States. Personal government is possible in the White House; it is impossible in Windsor Castle.

The so-called royal privilege is thus an honorary position, a national tradition, and a public convenience, almost an algebraic formula for the equilibrium of forces, conservation of energy, and perpetual motion. It is as absurd for someone to feel resentful in the dignified existence of this fixed point in the political system as to resent the existence of the Earth's axis or the North Star. In viewing the throne's occupant, for many it is impossible to ignore the man or woman, the accident, the person, in order to see the function, the traditional existence, and the law of political motion. Such individuals may lack symbolic imagination; but if symbolism were to disappear, we can be certain that the ideal would also disappear from religion, poetry, art, society, and the state.

The constitutional monarchy thus became the highest form of government for me. To my mind, the absence of unity, permanence, and continuity in government that many consider the superiority of the republican system became a sign of inferiority. In my opinion, this republican ideal of a state in which everyone can compete for first place, starting in primary school, became an unappealing utopia, a paradise of the ambitious, and a kind of asylum specializing in megalomanias. This was certainly not the purpose of the human evolution we all pray for every day when we repeat the *adveniat regnum tuum*. To forego the monarchist idea is not as easy as it seems. *Even the planetary system is monarchist*, says Schopenhauer. The universe is the monarchy par excellence. Rather than *Cosmos*, Humboldt could have entitled his book *On Monarchy*. The central idea of the Infinite, that is, God, cannot fail to be the true ideal in the entire sphere of human intelligence and activity. To this day, force, transformed into law and tradition, has produced the monarchist ideal; one day it will come from science, intelligence, virtue, and sanctity. The human ideal, all of it, the entire religious, social, and artistic aesthetic, we can be certain, is contained in the line: "God created man in his own image."

I found republicanism in England in spirits of the first order. There was more or less conscious republicanism in Spencer, Mill, Bagehot, Bright, Morley, George Eliot, and G. Henry Lewes, but it was a kind of republicanism *sine die*, preserved in the monarchist sentiment to prevent it from becoming corrupted. England would not be the free nation it is if its character did not contain a fiber that prevents worship of the royalty from degenerating into superstition, or *loyalty* from becoming servility. In the English heart, loyalty to the House of Commons precedes loyalty to the monarchy, with no exception even among the royalty, who themselves feel like the nation. This background of republicanism – latent, even forgotten, but which at the slightest provocation would resuscitate, as under the Stuarts – far from being incompatible with monarchism, is what has preserved it, restricting and reducing the royal power to the function it is today, purely moderating, and only rarely and provisionally arbitral. For those who profess it, this republicanism is no impediment – on the contrary – to bowing before the queen and defending the integrity of her evanescent prerogative.

As I said, however, not even this profound change in my political ideals would have sufficed to prevent me from joining the republican movement in Brazil, given certain contingencies. I could have been ideologically monarchist and at a given moment considered the republic the best government in practice, just as one can be ideologically republican – and many are in England itself – and make the monarchy one's *noli me tangere*. In addition, I could have allowed myself to be dragged along by a wave of enthusiasm, partisan solidarity, political friendships, or even some interest that managed to disguise itself and bore into my spirit – in the form of a sacrifice to the public cause. For spirits who can see the opposite sides of issues, the good and the bad, ideas are poor, weak, defensive. To sustain political faith, one needs more than the clarity of intelligence. If there is no sentiment that touches the heart, or a kind of point of honor imposing itself on one's character, a uniform spirit of conduct is indispensable, a certain rule of direction. In my particular case, what saved me from the republican illusion was just a touch of the English spirit.

CHAPTER XIII

THE ENGLISH SPIRIT

WITHOUT THIS TOUCH OF THE ENGLISH SPIRIT, my conviction that England's political system is superior would not have sufficed. The aristocratic sensation of life that I have described would not have withstood the first clash in the party struggle. What I mean by the English spirit is the tacit rule of conduct that all of England appears to obey, the center of moral inspiration that rules all its movements. I saw very little of England, I regret to say, but I did see places so wonderful that they nearly prevented me from wanting to see the rest, except for Oxford, for which I have reserved a place in my inner gallery, waiting to hang up a little oil portrait of it. For example, I saw Canterbury, and cherish the memory of the calm silence and grandeur of that imposing mass withdrawn into itself. During a week in Cowes, Southampton, and the Isle of Wight, I saw a colorful, moving, and joyous little trace of England-on-the-sea. I traveled by carriage – could there be a more completely fantastic day? – from Stratford-on-Avon, passing through Warwick, to Kenilworth. I spent days on the banks of the Thames, between Windsor and Henley, and had clear visions of heaven on Earth. It is truly the most perfect illustration for Genesis 2:10: "A river flowed out of Eden to water the garden."

Wherever I went, England left me with the same impression: ivy-covered ruins, old engravings exhibited in Pall Mall, wheat stacks in the harvested fields, carved castles in the midst of wooded parks, old roadside inns, boats moored at Cliveden Grove, grand transatlantic ships at the Southampton docks, always with the same English stamp embossed on everything. The feeling was the same for England viewed from within, with all the security of its resources, and from without, unassailable on its high white *cliffs*, at the foot of which the sea opens up like a great moat.

However, I will now speak of the English spirit from an exclusively political perspective, and in the even narrower sense, whereby it manifests itself in the reformist movements and its influence on innovative spirits. Politically, the English spirit can be broken down into a spirit of tradition, a spirit of reality, a spirit of strength and generosity, of progress and improvement, and the spirit of an ideal: Anglo-Saxon and Christian world supremacy.

In England, veneration lends an almost sacred authority to precedent, while eliminating the individual approach with which other peoples focus on all historical or national matters. Queen Victoria is more than the august monarch whose portrait every English family worships in its inner *lararium*; she is the Norman, Plantagenet, and Tudor royalty. What is true for the Queen is true for the Constitution. The latter is nothing more than a letter of proxy issued by the English nation in its own best interests to the House of Commons, and even so, a mandate for which the instrument has never been seen. No great jurist drafted it, no statesman conceived it: the Constitution took shape spontaneously, unconsciously, like the English language, the perpendicular architecture, and the *nursery rhymes*. Tradition, as the basis for the national temperament, produces in the English the faculty of admiring an institution's historical mass, like the architect admires a Gothic cathedral's grandeur and detail. For the English, if freedom is man's greatest attribute, if he feels it as the development of personality, then order is the true social architecture. Order encompasses and permeates the entire English system, which perpetuates itself more than that of revolutions, unlike the Latin system, which lives blithely on turbulent political ground, subject to constant tremors. Hence the English love of the law, and the sympathy, interest, and even fondness for the authority in charge of enforcing it. Hence, too, the judge's prestige and the popularity of court rulings that strike terror in the criminal's mind, unlike the ease he finds in countries where the self-preservation instinct is decaying.

When such an organization exists, with a virtual superstition for custom, and is accompanied by a spirit of perfectionism and progress, the resulting reforms and modifications are governed by some elementary rules. One such rule is to preserve whatever does not pose an invincible obstacle to indispensable improvement. Another is that betterment must justify – and to justify it does not suffice to compensate for – sacrificing the tradition or even the prejudice that hinders the change. Another rule is to respect what may be useless, but which bears the mark of an epoch, and to only demolish what is truly harmful. A further rule is to replace provisionally insofar as possible, letting time take charge of testing the new material or form before consecrating or rejecting it. The last rule, rare and extreme, is to reform the institution in its original, oldest sense, seeking to preserve the primordial outline. According to these rules, one's duty is to demolish with the same loving care originally used to build in previous epochs. No explosives are allowed, because their effect cannot be predicted. One must demolish with a plumb bob and level, removing the stones one by one, just as they were originally placed.

However, what orients the spirit of progress is the spirit of reality, the practical, positive spirit manifested by the rejection of all things theoretical, *a priori*, tentative, logical, or which aim at perfection, finality, uniformity, symmetry. What corresponds to this spirit in the political order is the idea of growth: institutions have their habitat, like plants, their own latitudes and terrains, special conditions for acclimation, obstacles and hazards in transplantation. It does not suffice that experience recommend the reform, based on strong verisimilitude. The reform must have an affinity with the other institutions. This practical, positive spirit is the experience of utilitarianism, the spirit of creating and accumulating wealth, so characteristic of the English race. In utilitarianism, the reforms must have at least an economic advantage and be justified by algorisms. However, next to the utilitarian thrust there is an imaginative thrust, or that of a moral, national, religious ideal.

Manliness demands that the reformer not cause indirect casualties by holding individuals or institutions accountable for society's common mistakes, nor wash his hands of the crowd's injustices like Pontius Pilate, nor fawn to the downtrodden, then blame them for the intervention. In a word, the reformer must practice *fair-play*. Patriotism requires not allowing the party spirit to override one's responsibility to country. However, in England, what feeds, renews, and purifies patriotism is another kind of responsibility: that of man before God. The English sentiment only develops its maximum energy when the British pride and Christian conscience tremble together and join in one and the same cause. To a major extent, the inspiration for public life in England comes from the Bible. Politics and religion feel that they will always have great common cause, and that they both have the same practical objective, to raise man's moral condition. The effect of the latter and perhaps the principal element of the English spirit in relation to the reforms are to make the moral argument prevail over the utilitarian argument.

Taking the English spirit as I have just outlined it, what does it inspire in England in those who profess republican ideals, but who nevertheless submit as individuals to the collective conscience, the national instinct? There is an interesting page in *On Compromise*, a typical book of English intellectual casuistry written by John Morley. This page is the best illustration of what I said before on the kind of republicanism that can underlie the monarchist sentiment, and even give it a shine and warmth. Morley is an Englishman who is convinced that even a merely decorative monarchy tends to engender socially degrading habits. The republican's duty is to discard the monarchy and abstain from all public and private acts that may even remotely feed the spirit of servitude. "A policy like this," Mr. Morley tells us, "does not interfere with the advantages of the monarchy, such as they are asserted to be, and it has the effect of making what are supposed to be its disadvantages as little noxious as possible."[39]

I said that I had only a touch of this English spirit. However, on the issue of abolition I never swerved from it. Abolition was a reform that the English spirit placed before all others by order of sentiment. If abolition was enforced in Brazil without indemnification, partisan resistance was responsible, not the abolitionists. My original bill, in 1880, was for abolition in 1890 with indemnification. If at any moment a minister of the Crown had approached Parliament and declared: "Slavery can no longer be tolerated in Brazil, our degree of civilization repels it, and I have come to ask you to decree the immediate release of the existing slaves, allocating the necessary resources for the respective expropriation," could any abolitionist have wished to prolong slavery? None of us would have assumed such an odious responsibility. However, such a man never emerged among the statesmen of the Empire. They all thought either that abolition would ruin the country's agriculture and credit, or that Brazil could not afford to

---

39 John Morley, *On Compromise*, London, 1886. Located and quoted here thanks to the Gutenberg Project. T.N

pay for the moral liberation of its territory. Some abolitionists might have opposed indemnification, indeed some did, but could they have possibly voted against a law for immediate abolition? It was thus the responsibility of the parties, who committed themselves before the plantation owners to resist the movement, and who from even their own point of view would have done better by earmarking future budget revenues and expropriating the slaves before the non-indemnification principle prevailed in the Dantas bill and in the second law of September 28[40] [1885]. The only member of the Council of State who had this insight was my dear friend José Caetano de Andrade Pinto, but they paid him no heed. As for the law of May 13, by 1888 it was too late to propose equal indemnification in the face of a triumphant movement, when most of the slaves had already been freed by their owners and the rest were escaping, and especially since the law ensured the principle that slavery was irregular property, for which the legislator could set the expiration date with no burden to the state.

In relation to the Brazilian monarchy, my touch of the English spirit was sufficient to set a course from which I could never waver, even if I had so desired. It was an intellectual point of honor, a case of patriotic conscience definitively resolved in my spirit at twenty-three years of age. It had become clear to me that I would never support a policy to suppress our monarchy. I could just as well hurl a child into the sea or set fire to the Mercy Hospital, as ban or deport the Emperor. To break the tie, perhaps providential, that bound Brazil's history to that of the monarchy was as morally impossible for me as to surrender Pernambuco to foreigners with my own hands, as Calabar did.[41] I would have lacked the strength for such an intervention in my country's fate. I would have brought an attack of paralysis on myself, delivering myself a mortal blow. My courage retreated

---

40 A bill to free slaves over 60 years of age without compensation to their owners was introduced, at the instigation of the Emperor, by the Liberal Senator Manuel Pinto de Souse Dantas in 1884. It was twice defeated in Parliament. Under the Sexagenarian Law passed on 28 September 1885, the 14th anniversary of the Law of Free Birth, by a Conservative government, slaves over 60 were freed but forced to work for a further three years, at which point the slaveowners would receive compensation. L.B.

41 Domingos Fernandes Calabar (c. 1600–1635) was a smuggler and plantation owner who originally sided with the Portuguese against the Dutch in the struggle for control of Northeast Brazil in the early 17th century. For reasons never entirely elucidated, in April 1632 he defected to the Dutch, who subsequently inflicted serious blows on the Portuguese, thanks largely to Calabar's detailed knowledge of the local terrain. In 1635, the Portuguese ambushed some the Dutch troops, including Calabar, who was garroted and quartered. Calabar's name has historically been considered a synonym for "traitor" in Brazil. T.N.

before the mysterious line of the National Unconscious. Brazil had adopted the monarchist form, and I would not alter it.

What I saw in the United States merely served to further deepen the monarchist impression I brought from England. It was a second key, a security lock, which closed a door in my thinking that would never open again. The American political spirit, with certain modalities that I do not wish to belittle, but which I consider secondary, is a variety of the English spirit, which really deserves to be called the Anglo-Saxon spirit, because it is the common spirit of a race, of a great human family, overshadowing the forms and vicissitudes of institutions.

CHAPTER XIV

NEW YORK (1876–1877)

PERHAPS THE BEST WAY TO DESCRIBE what I owe to the United States is to reproduce some pages from my diary of 1876–1877. I arrived shortly after the visit by the Emperor[42] and was thus able to capture the echoes of the impression left by him. The year I spent in the great North American Republic was one of its most interesting political moments, because it was the year of Tilden's election. It is public knowledge that the Democrats won the elections in 1876, but that the Republican returning boards in some southern States manipulated the results to give their party the majority of the electors. Both sides claimed victory, and since the House of Representatives was Democratic and the Senate Republican, the prospects were that Congress would fail to reach an agreement by March, and that the United States would have two Presidents and all the likelihood of a civil war.

The practical spirit of transaction of the Anglo-Saxon race prevailed, and the House and Senate agreed to turn the ruling over to a special commission with members from both Houses of Congress and the Supreme Court. The difference between England and the United States could not be illustrated any better than by this case. The American ruling was like an English one, namely agreement rather than civil war, as in the latin countries. But in the United States, contrary to what would have happened in England, the commission failed to rise above the spirit of factions, and the votes were all strictly partisan. In other words, since the commission included five members from the Supreme Court, the highest court in the Union proved to be comprised of *politicians*. With English judges, the ruling might even

---

42 Emperor D. Pedro II visited the United States for the 1876 Centennial Exhibition in Philadelphia. For four months he then travelled the length and breadth of the country, showing a keen interest in industry, transportation, science and engineering, agriculture, education and prisons. L.B.

have turned out unfair, but it would never have been partial or issued with partisan political motives. The justices' votes could not have been counted ahead of time as if they were by members of Congress. In such a short time as I had, no comparative study of the two countries' education, seriousness, and political customs could have been as useful for me as this 1876–1877 election campaign and its outcome. The qualities and deficiencies of American politics were all visible and patent in this practical lesson. I had followed the parties' struggle to capture the Presidency with the greatest interest. I knew every *boss* by name, every Senator's background, every influential journalist's opinion, and every nuance in the two conventions.

Election year really is the best time for a foreigner to grasp political life in the United States at a glance. I had arrived in New York in time to become familiar with the issues, the allusions, and the political jargon of the formidable *canvass* that was shaping up and in which Reconstruction policy in the South was to be the central thrust. I was interested in the *Tammany Ring*, the *Whiskey Ring*, the schism of the Independents [Greenback Party], *Civil Service Reform*, the *Railroad Land Grants*, just as I was interested in the meeting between Gladstone and Disraeli on the issue of the East, or the struggle between Thiers and the Duke of Broglie. As the saying goes, when in Rome do as the Romans, and for more than a year I truly did in America as the Americans. It was the way I probed, understood, and felt the country's political pulse at will, and that was my reason for wanting to go to the United States.

My diary from that year records more my own thoughts than my impressions of America. There is very little politics in my diary, which shows that I lived in a very different atmosphere than that which party men breathe, even when they are abroad. I reproduce some of these notes here to show precisely that the North American environment had an effect on me that it often has on Americans themselves, namely to alienate them from politics, except as spectators. I lived those two years, 1876 and 1877, in New York society, as far away from American politics as if I had been in London or Paris. Still, the outer world that surrounded me everywhere, the street, the public square with its campaign posters and marches, the newspapers with the scenes of Congress and the torrents of eloquence from the *meetings*, could not fail to attract me like any grand and unique national spectacle, not to mention my intellectual curiosity in knowing how such a great country was governed and administered, the social forces and moral influences presiding over its colossal development. Here are some random samples of my notes.

October 22. Carl Schurz' speech delivered yesterday at the Union League Club illustrates the republican sentiment in its best light. The prime issue in the current campaign is becoming the Question of the South. As November 7 approaches, this point of view will become more important than all the others. The *bloody shirt* has fallen into complete discredit, but it is necessary to count on the fear that a united South, consisting of the former rebel States and where the candidates are all Confederate soldiers, may dominate the North so soon after the war, with the American government then represented by former separatists. This idea alarms those who place the Union above all else, even when it is necessary to reduce the impenitent States to territories subject to military despotism and handed over politically to the joint control of the *carpetbaggers* and the Negroes. This element will probably decide the struggle in favor of Hayes, which otherwise would have been easy for Tilden to win, because the situation in the South in recent years dishonors American politics.

January 1. I arrived in Washington, in Riggs House. I don my uniform for the first time. Off to the White House. Introduced to the President; later, off to the home of the Secretary of State, Mr. Fish. The so-called Grant dynasty, Mrs. Sartoris' daughter; the granddaughter receiving compliments on behalf of her grandfather. I go with Lieutenant Saldanha da Gama to visit the members of the Supreme Court: through the *terrapin* and *baked oysters* all day long, until at the home of the Secretary of the Navy a solemn *"The reception is over!"* signals the end of our *New Year's Day* pilgrimage.

I had met Saldanha at the Philadelphia Exposition, and we later became good friends in New York, where we lived in the same hotel, the Buckingham. He always laughed when he remembered *"The reception is over!"* Poor Saldanha! Born for the world, for love, for glory. Who could have imagined – seeing him then in New York – the fate he would meet? When he was still an adolescent the sphinx of life had given him one of its mysterious riddles to decipher, and destroyed his aspirations for happiness, and it reappeared to block his step precisely at the moment when he could have vied for the country's leading position.[43]

43 On Saldanha da Gama, see note 37 above.

January 11. To the home of Mr. John Hamilton, son of Alexander Hamilton. A man of the past, focused entirely on it. He tells me Brazil should preserve its monarchist system for as long as possible. This *Whig* does not believe that countries like ours can survive united under any other form of government. I am moved when he shows me the portrait of Louis XVI, a present to his father.

February 22. I attended a luncheon with Mr. Marshall at the Knickerbocker Club, today being Washington's Birthday, together with Mr. Manton Marble, former editor of the *World*, Mr. Appleton, the great editor, Mr. Stout, Mr. Robinson, Mr. Pell, and others. A *toast* was made to the Emperor, and since all the salutations were good-natured, I replied in kind with a touch of *humor*. I said we had feared that the Americans might decide to keep our Emperor, recalling what General Lafayette, a great authority for them, had said of the constitutional monarchy: "This is the best of the republics." But since they had allowed the Emperor to depart, I expressed my best wishes that the two countries would preserve their institutions, as a wager between the monarchy and the republic on perpetual freedom. As for President Washington, I expressed a proviso to his great work, namely that he had founded the nation's capital in what was certainly a very pleasant city, but which one visited at considerable sacrifice when one had to leave New York.

March 2. Today I went to Congress to see the wreckage from the day before. (Hayes had been proclaimed President by one vote.) There is no joy on the Republican side, and there is great disappointment among the Democrats. But in a short time, when the wound has healed and they can think of the future, this party will be happy that things transpired as we saw yesterday. General Banks, former *Speaker* of the House, gave me his seat on the floor of Congress (in session), later my minister came to sit in it, and we were introduced to several distinguished Representatives, including Lamar and Garfield.

March 8. The President has proposed a Constitutional amendment setting the Presidential term of office at six years, without reelection. This amendment stems from the fear that the Presidential elections will be so hotly disputed by the two parties that they will split the country in two, like last autumn, and that every three years of business will be followed by a fourth year of interruption and paralysis, as if everything were adrift, and as if anarchy, civil war, or perhaps even secession might follow a dubious election. Commercial and property interests will one day succeed in extending the term to six years, and since there will be fewer elections, they will tend to become more disputed, and there is no reason for the country to run a risk every six years that it does not want to run every four. Thus, the critical election of the head of state will be spaced apart as far as possible, and it is not inconceivable that the American Republic will come so close to the elective monarchies that it will realize the danger in the latter and prefer the tranquility of the long dynasties...

Curiously, the most perfect part of this democracy is the woman, who here in America is the most aristocratic being in the world.

April 2. Today's idea of government is entirely different from that of yesteryear. For example, let us take freedom of the press in the United States, which represented the new political education, and censorship in Russia. There is much to be said in favor of total freedom of thought and the inconveniences of repression. Yet it is true that forced respect for authority on the one hand, and its discredit on the other, form two diverse societies. The difficulty on the road of tradition is that no one wishes to sacrifice dignity or personal pride for grand moral results, and that men all consider themselves equal based on a feeling that is already indestructible. As an individual, I am certainly equal to any king, but since many good things come to society through the monarchist principle, I place myself on a lower level. This is not a breach of *human* dignity, even though one's personal pride has to *bow down*.

May 13. They say Tilden has refused to concede to Hayes as President. Some friend should read *Crito* to him. When Crito tries to convince Socrates that he should flee to avoid an unjust death, Socrates refuses on grounds that the sentence, unfair as it is, is still entirely legal. If the jury did wrong in issuing it, he would do worse in refusing to submit to the laws of Athens, because a citizen who enjoys the protection and rights offered by a city has a tacit agreement with it to respect its laws. Socrates refused life because it was illegal, although he knew that more good would come from his escape than bad for Athenian democracy. Should Tilden not reread this dialogue? Unjust as the ruling was against him, it was strictly legal, not in the sense that it was consistent with the law, but that the proper interpreters of the law issued it. He can only attract everyone's sympathy to himself and his party by submitting to the ruling, safeguarding his right to criticize the new President for the frauds by which the latter came to power.

June 13. Yesterday at the Manhattan Club the *swallowtails* gave a reception for the Democratic candidates who were elected or *counted out*. Tilden spoke for the first time after Hayes' inauguration, which he called 'the most portentous event' in the political history of America (by America he was referring to the United States, because in Mexico and Peru there are much more portentous events every day): *'Evils in government grow by success and by impunity. They do not arrest their own progress. They can never be limited except by external forces... A great and noble nation will not sever its political from its moral life.'*[44] All of this is true. Brazil is proof. Should the people participate in politics? A country measures its progress by the extent of the idea that politics is inseparable from society's most vital interests and thus from the interests of each individual. This idea has failed to take root in Brazil, due to our special conditions in terms of territory, population, slave labor, etc. Here in the United States, this idea is in everyone's head. What most surprised me at this Manhattan meeting was the fact that the Governor of New York – *de jure* and *de facto* –, Mr. Robinson, called the President of the United States a *fraudulent President* in public. After having said that they would not have to wait until 1880 to run Hayes out of the White House, he concluded as follows, referring to Tilden and Hendricks: *'Fellow citizens*, you had the first opportunity to greet the President and Vice-President of the United States after their election. I congratulate you and believe that this is but a foreboding of events that are sure to come.'[45] This speech by the Governor of the principal State of the Union, inciting rebellion, whether legal or illegal, is typical of the American political system and of the *laissez-faire, laissez-passer* treatment that speech enjoys in this country. Revolutions of the tongue and the pen are never a crime; they are a release. The mouth of the *politician* is a safety valve for the institutions. The United States is a country of automatic valves.

June 19. Today's newspapers published an interesting fact: the visit by Frederick Douglass to his old master, whom he left during adolescence to begin a life of adventures leading all the way to his position as United States Marshal in Washington and as the great spokesman for abolition. 'I came first of all,' said Douglass, 'to visit my old master, from whom I have been separated these 41 years, to shake his hand, and to contemplate his kind old face, bright with the infinite light, ready to step into the eternal unknown.'[46]

---

44 Quotation from Samuel Tilden's Concession Speech, 1876, on the website of the Rutherford B. Hayes Presidential Center, www.rbhayes.org/hayes/president. T.N.

45 It was impossible to locate the original quote by New York Governor Lucius Robinson, and therefore it was retranslated into English based on Nabuco's text. T.N.

46 The original quote in English could not be located and was possibly read by Joaquim Nabuco in a contemporary newspaper report, which he did not specify here. My back-translation is based on Frederick Douglass' account of his last encounter with Captain Thomas Auld in "Time Makes All Things Even", Chapter XVI of *Frederick Douglass, 1818–1895. Life and Times of Frederick Douglass: His Early Life as a Slave, His Escape from Bondage, and His Complete History to the Present Time*, Boston, 1892. T.N.

This scene gives us a more moving idea of slavery in the South than *Uncle Tom's Cabin*. The place is St. Michaels, Talbot County, Maryland. The master's name is Captain Thomas Auld. During this meeting Marshal Douglass learned his real age from his old master, whose record books listed 'Frederick Bailey, February 1818'. Thomas Auld probably failed to record any further events in Frederick's amazing career after the age of 18 (1836). This account, of all that I have read, is one of the most profound and striking descriptions of the complex moral fact of slavery, the bond between slave and master.

CHAPTER XV

MY DIARY OF 1877

I WILL NOW QUOTE SOME EXCERPTS from my diary in the United States. As I said, they are not so much impressions of America as my own personal feelings at the time:

June 20. Today, eleven criminals were hanged, members of an organization in Pennsylvania, the Molly Maguires. Just imagine eleven people hanged on one day in Brazil! How many speeches would this not have produced in the Chamber of Deputies? Here, it merely increases the circulation of extra newspaper editions.

June 8. There are two kinds of movements in politics: one, of which we are a part, believing that were are standing still, like the Earth's movement, which we do not feel; the other, the movement that begins within us. There are few people in politics who are aware of the former, but it is perhaps the only one that is not merely agitation.

July 8. The moral temperature of the future, judging by that of America, is likely to be quite low. Feelings get colder here by the day. England is a furnace by comparison.

June 26. France is like Ulysses' house, full of suitors fighting for Telemaco's fortune, waiting for Penelope to pick one of them. Each of them is certain that he is the favorite, and while she asks Minerva to rout her ruthless persecutors, they continue to devour the steers and lambs, repeating: 'Surely she is preparing to marry.' Unfortunately it looks unlikely that Ulysses will kill them and regain the palace.

This note is almost purely literary. Ulysses here was the Comte de Chambord, and the suitors were the political parties wreaking havoc in France after the national defeat, perhaps dragging it into civil war. I thought of writing an act entitled *The Suitors*, based on the idea of Ulysses' bow. Like the play I mentioned, it was a case where I lacked a combination of literary imagination and political sympathy.

There are other notes about the suitors:

July 16. The Comte de Chambord represents the theory that politics is a religious art, the reign of a kind of monument to the beliefs of an epoch. The concept that governing is a religious act, like confessing, and that it has a religious purpose, destroys all freedom of thought. A man can make his own life a form of art, but not the lives of everyone, who want to live in their own way. If politics is an art, it is not an ascetic or religious art, even in its hieratic period. As a religious art, politics turns the slightest act of individual freedom into a crime of sacrilege.

July 30. I was thinking about *The Suitors*. The respective candidate makes the *appel au peuple* to the frogs, and the royal test comes from another, who also appeals to them. They respond to it all the same: *couac*.

July 5. President Hayes has taken the most singular position ever seen in this country. He came to power through unprecedented electoral frauds, pushed into the White House by the ***carpetbaggers*** from the South and the ***wire-pullers*** in the Senate, after a campaign underwritten by the public servants. He thus owes his election, or rather his position, to countless ***politicians*** of all hues, ranging from the fabricators of false election returns to the Supreme Court justices that reviewed them. However, after reaching power he has become ashamed of it all and turned into the bulwark of administrative and electoral purity. As for the last ***carpetbaggers*** of the South, with the cutting of the ties that bound them to a President elected with them and by them, they have disappeared from the political scene forever. The politickers have been shooed out, the Senators ***snubbed***. The public servants, lords of the electoral machine that chipped in for the mutual election, have been forced to change their ways and not underwrite another ***cent***. The conclusion from all of this is that just as Hayes does not wish to be elected again, he understands that no one else should be elected the way he was. Few men could have made such good use of such poorly acquired power. This almost makes up for the lack of civic courage that made him accept the office.

July 19 and August 9. One cannot say that this country has an ideal. It is the practical country par excellence and has the admirable quality, for better or for worse, of governing itself. It does not lack **manhood**, but everything in it has a material purpose. The American is first and foremost a positive man in whose life metaphysics plays a minor part, recognizing every second that life is a **business**, that one needs a measure of reserve to avoid sinking in it. He considers art, science, culture, and the **polity** secondary to the essential, namely the **dollar**. Always forging **ahead** like a locomotive, treating his woman with the utmost respect, but as an **obstruction** in practical life, thus leaving her to her own devices, he aims above all at acquiring the wealth of a great Wall Street **operator**, and later the influence of a **boss**. Insensitive to envy, to ill will, to gossip, to everything that in other countries entangles, hinders, and sometimes ruins great careers. Never seeking pleasure for himself, but showering it on guests in his home, as toys are given to children. Aloof to all annoyances, somber in pain, calm in the death of his loved ones, and treating his own earthly demise merely as an insurance matter. '*Private life*' here is nothing but an expression that has survived in English. Every man is a public man, and entirely so.

These are the impressions of a simple passerby. Today I would no longer write that the United States is a nation without an ideal. I would say that it is a nation whose ideal is still taking shape. Just as the Englishman attempts to acquire fortune and independence before entering the House of Commons, one could say that the American nation is attempting to grow, to settle her immense territory, to achieve her complete development, *her full size*, in order then to speak of herself and ponder the name she should leave for posterity. So far the United States has lived a separate, self-occupied life. Still, a country that is becoming — if it is not already — the wealthiest, strongest, and best-equipped nation in the world necessarily has to bind its history to that of other nations, to join and struggle with them.

August 18. Gladstone, having settled the Civil War claims, is even more unpopular in the South than in England among the conservatives. However, for the foreigner, the time at which the Treaty of Washington was signed was one of perfect American unification. There is more than a political misunderstanding between the North and the South. There is a tacit underlying hereditary ill will, a state of latent war.

What makes the two great national parties accidental coalitions and prevents their respective unity of views is the divergence of interests between the States. For example, the Democratic Party has to rely on a negative formula to reconcile its policy for the Eastern States, with payments in gold and redemption of paper money, and that of the Western States, with *greenbacks*. Meanwhile the Republican Party has to reconcile Grant's policy of intervention with Hayes' policy of complete *self-government* for the Southern States.

July 25. The scenes of recent days (with the railroad strike) give one much food for thought. Victor Hugo says that the blame for the communists having set fire to Paris falls on those who failed to teach them to read. However, each of the incendiaries was probably a subscriber to *Rappel*. What a calm people, the Americans! The great excitement people talk about is nothing more than a private hotel *barroom* conversation. New York can be on the verge of a *riot*, and the authorities grant a park permit for the communists to hold their *meeting*. Everyone fraternizes: the troops with the *strikers* and the *citizens* with the *mob*, and nobody loses their calm. The French pessimist does not exist in this country of optimists who always say, "Nothing is going to happen." If something does, they respond, "It'll be over soon," and if it lasts, they say, "It could be worse." The old saying about your neighbour's beard[47] is not interpreted here from one town to the next, or even from one neighborhood to the next, but almost from house to house. Even those who lose everything feel powerless to complain, except about themselves.

September 1. Few men in politics prefer to take a fall for their principles rather than to gloss them over in order to remain standing. If a minister favors the preeminence of the Chamber of Deputies in principle, but the Chamber clashes with him, he will attempt to prove that it does not represent the country and will seek support in the Upper House. During the Empire, Gambetta would not have spoken of universal suffrage with today's enthusiasm, and no Bonapartist would submit now, as under the Napoleons, to an *appeal to the people*. In the end there are only two kinds of politics: government politics and opposition politics.

September 4. Thiers died yesterday. The news causes the same impression everywhere. 'Poor France!' people exclaim. The loss is irreparable. The helm is left without a helmsman. There is no one to receive the trust that all of Europe placed in the old counselor of France. The last of the great men of the past in France failed to name a successor.

---

47 From a popular saying, probably of African origin: "If you see your neighbour's beard on fire, water your own." Curiously, Nabuco quotes only the first half of the saying, which is unfamiliar to modern Brazilians, while the second half is an everyday household expression in Brazil: "soaking one's beard" means minding one's own business or taking a judicious step back from potentially ominous events. T.N.

September 8. Supreme Court Justice Bradley, who in fact made Hayes President, having been attacked by the Democratic newspapers and accused of changing his vote after meeting with the directors of the Union Pacific Railroad, felt it his duty to explain himself to the press. In this justification, admitting the possibility that during the case he expressed a different view to his colleague than his final vote, he claims that he drafted his reasons on the Florida vote first in one direction, then in the other, before reaching his final decision after great doubt and hesitation. This letter to a New York newspaper is curious in many ways. When a judge vacillates, reaching alternating conclusions for days on end, should he consider definitive the opinion that perchance prevailed in his spirit at the moment in which the vote was called? Is it not probable, or at least possible, that he will still change his mind again, after having cast what is now an irreparable vote? On the other hand, these doubts do not prove the sincerity of the logical process of investigation, and the judge could be required to form an opinion at the beginning of a case. Vacillation has less to do with distributing justice, which should always proceed from an unshakable and unshaken conviction, than with stubbornness, which is often a lack of perception and exclusiveness by the judge. As for the strength that subsequent reflection in his spirit has given to the vote he cast, this phenomenon involves acquiescence by the conscience, very common among judges. Having committed the error, the mind interprets it as the truth, because it is in the interest of the judge's good name.

September 11. Much has been said about the changes in Thiers. When one asks why this little Marseillais – born poor, without a family, and scorned by his aristocratic competitors – succeed in traversing so many and such diverse governments without ever losing his political importance, until in his extreme old age he became the Liberator of the Territory, one finds the explanation in these changes. When so many men of talent, character, fortune, and social prestige played their role in one regime and disappeared, Thiers was always counted in as a political force. His fate was to make and break governments, but he cannot be accused of having divorced himself from France at any of these moments. He always changed with the country. His grand final change from monarchist to republican coincided with his personal interest as first president of the republic, but it also coincided with the conversion of the middle classes, not to the republican principle, but to the idea that only the republic was possible. France, in its liberal movements, always found him by her side. During the empire, he waged a patriotic opposition that might have avoided Sedan and preserved the dynasty if they had not considered him an Orleanist. When he moved to place Louis-Philippe on the throne, the thinking was that a republican monarchy dispensed with the republic. The weakness of the 1830 monarchy was that the principle of hereditariness undermined it from the beginning. Louis-Philippe destroyed the divine right to rise to power, and later made use of it to last, transforming it into common sense, the principle of authority, etc. What produces the unity in Thiers' career is that he was always for parliamentary government, for the popular right represented in the legislative assemblies. Based on this principle he turned the presidency of the republic over to suspicious hands. The secret of his political fortune was that he always remained faithful to France.

A country often travels a long way only to return, tired and wounded, to its point of departure. France may still return to the legitimate monarchy, and if Thiers had lived long enough and the republic had brought new misfortunes to France, like the Commune, perhaps Thiers himself would have turned the country over to its sovereign heir. Even so, when France compares the two types of statesmen, Berryer, who never changed, either because of a constantly renewed monarchist conviction or a spirit of chivalry worthy of his character, and always stayed in the same place waiting for France to return there, and Thiers, who accompanied her in her vicissitudes, I believe that she will recognize herself in the man she always counted on as her counselor, who at times changed to remain by her side so that she could rely on his consummate experience, on days when she might need a sympathetic word.

Today, as I reread this page from my diary of 1877, I realize that my explanation for the unity in Thiers' political career is very similar to that published about Talleyrand several years ago, justifying himself in his *Memoirs* by the fact that he had only changed with France and because of France.

These excerpts show that in New York I was not under the American influence, but that the European influence continued in me and that I was an onlooker, as I had been in London, almost uninterested in politics, at least uninterested in any politics that could not be turned into a literary topic or a critical note or observation. I now proceed to describe my overall impression of the United States, which is now my idea of *democracy in America*.[48]

---

48 Nabuco's italics.

CHAPTER XVI

AMERICAN TRAITS

I ONLY SAW A LITTLE OF THE UNITED STATES, like England, so the impressions I reproduce here should be interpreted almost exclusively as those of New York and Washington. Due to fortuitous circumstances, I was able to stay in New York for nearly the entire time I worked in the Brazilian legation. My superior, the Baron Carvalho Borges, of whom I have the fondest memories, was in mourning and had thus left Washington and was living unobtrusively in New York City, unlike many of his colleagues, whose flashy appearances at Fifth Avenue balls and receptions were criticized in vain by the Washington press. Besides the two great capitals of the Union, the political and the cosmopolitan, I only visited Philadelphia during the Centennial, Saratoga during a National Convention, and Niagara and Boston, and as a result missed Newport. However, my impression is that whoever has seen New York and Washington has seen everything that there is to see in the United States, except for the few cities that one can call historical towns, which bear the mark of their own traditions. Whoever has seen Buffalo, St. Louis, San Francisco, or Chicago has not seen New York, and whoever has seen Saratoga has not seen Newport, while Boston and New Orleans have no equals.

For the engineer, the inventor, the architect, anyone who loves to save time and work or admires this century's industrial genius above all others and the improvements it has introduced in human tools, the United States is a country to visit and scan from coast to coast. It is perhaps the country where one can best study material civilization, where dynamic power at man's service appears greatest and within everyone's reach. In a certain sense, the United States is a successful Tower of Babel. However, on the intellectual and moral level, including art, the United States has nothing to show. Meanwhile, any given cultural order, nearly every higher culture, need not acquire any American component to be perfect and complete.

My overall impression of American politics was that of a struggle without the impartiality, elevated patriotism, or delicate manners and honest procedures that make the political career in England, for example, acceptable and even attractive to the most distinguished spirits. What characterizes this struggle in the United States is the raw publicity to which everyone who enters it is exposed. As I said before, there is no private life in the United States. Newspaper reporting respects no dividing line between public and private life. The opponent is subject to unlimited and unscrupulous investigation, and not only he – everyone connected to him. If a Presidential candidate ever enjoyed even the most trivial adventure in his youth, he will experience the displeasure of seeing it photographed, proclaimed on the streets, splashed on posters, and sung in the *music halls* by all the modes and inventions that ridicule suggests and are most likely to captivate the electorate. The campaign against Tilden was waged with a disclosure that he once misrepresented his personal income to the internal revenue service. The politician is served up mercilessly to the reporters, whose sole obligation is to rip his reputation apart in any way possible, to tear it to shreds, then wallow in the muck with him. In order to achieve this purpose, there is no artifice that does not appear legitimate to the partisan press. No espionage, bribery, or interception of personal correspondence or confidential information is unjustified if success is at stake.

Such a system's effect may be to moralize private life, at least that of would-be political contenders, if indeed there is any morality in the terror wreaked by one of these formidable campaign exposés, which the French would call *chantage*. Political life, however, has no moral side. The American public conscience is far inferior to the private, as are its state morals to family morals.

Of course, in the United States, the so-called *rings*, which we would call gangs, the public pilfering, and the administrative syndicates are all denounced and investigated as perhaps they would not be in any other country, and the American takes no pity on his adversaries, deeming himself obliged before his own party to reduce them to the most humiliating condition and to expel them from public life one by one if he can. But since corruption reigns in both parties and both have well-known skeletons in their closets and compromising connections in their dealings, all the campaigns for administrative purity display a large dose of insincerity, simulation, and convention, which does not happen with the inquiries into private life. The latter, indeed, are unanimously echoed by the country's unity of sentiment and religious education. The conscience in vogue among the *politicians* obeys its own special logic.

This does not mean that American politics has nothing other than the *politician*, or as they used to say, the demagogue, or that next to such elastic consciences – jaded by all manner of fraud, corruption, and chicanery as the inevitable ills of democracy – there is no honor, decorum, or spotlessness. There are men in politics who are respected all over the country, and towards whom both parties deem themselves incapable of the slightest indelicacy when it comes to their personal honesty. Yet there is not one such man in activity and in the party struggle in whom the people acknowledge the necessary character to repudiate or condemn any of his own coreligionists, even when the latter may have employed the most deplorable devices. The man with the purest reputation in the American Senate will always vote the *party line* whenever the party's general interest is at stake.

I saw nothing in the United States that gave me the impression of its institutions' superiority over those of England. American politics definitely had a more loaded moral atmosphere. The class of men that politics attracted was inferior, that is, it was not the best class in society, unlike England. On the contrary, the most scrupulous side of American society naturally shies away from politics. The struggle is not waged in the terrain of ideas, but in that of personal reputations. Individuals are discussed and the struggle is waged with Roentgen rays, as it were. The candidates' doors are flung wide open and their entire homes are exposed, as if on an auction day. With such a regime, subject to the summary executions of slander and lynching in newspaper headlines, naturally all those who are unwilling to appear in a boxing match in the public square, to play a part in a *big show*, tend to avoid politics altogether.

The show put on by the United States is all the greater, the lower the professional politician's level. The degradation of the country's public customs, coinciding with its fabulous development and culture, with its accumulation of wealth and energy, with its unlimited resources, simply means that the American nation does not care if its affairs are managed poorly, because it does not have to time to keep tabs. It is like a farm with a bumper crop whose absentee owner turns a blind eye to the administrator's dilapidations, writing them up as profits and losses, inevitable in any kind of business. The Americans let themselves be treated by their **politicians** just like the kings of France by their *fermiers-géneraux*. Whether due to ignorance and incapacity or to corruption and bribery, every administration is bound to suffer losses. To prevent such losses would demand an inspection system that would be ruinous to the country, not only because of its outrageous cost, but because it would require diverting the country's best business leaders and other professionals.

What could be worse than turning the country over to political parties that organize themselves as mutual aid societies and that deduct a percentage of the national revenue for that very purpose? A tax increase? Why should an American care about paying a few more **cents** on the dollar and not being bothered with politics? Have the **politicians** involved the country in a foreign war? The danger is highly problematic, and the American men do not fear that the politicians will involve the country in a war unless the people want it and find it legitimate or advantageous. The American knows that there is a public opinion in his country, so long as each American has his own opinion. It is a latent force, overlooked, in repose, which does not rise up without sufficient cause, (which rarely happens), but it is a force with incalculable energy that would toss into the air whatever resisted it: parties, legislatures, Congress, the President.

It is a big show in this sense. The government has limited capacity to do harm. The portion of influence and profits that the nation leaves to the political class is limited by a moving scale, that is, proportional to the public revenue, which grants the political profession growing and progressive advantages, but limited nevertheless. The nation allows itself to be divided into parties, lines up and maneuvers in political fields, and – despite the mass abstentions – accompanies the bad administrators of its interests. Yet everyone knows that public opinion can suddenly change, become unanimous, and acquire the force of an irresistible impulse, destroying everything in its path. Government in the United States is not as important as in countries where it actually governs. Government in America is pure business management, practiced poorly or well, honestly or dishonestly,

Aerial view of Massangana, the sugar plantation in Pernambuco where Joaquim

Nabuco spent the first eight years of his childhood. *Family collection*

Portrait of José Tomás Nabuco de Araújo, Nabuco's father, by Victor Meirelles, 1869. *Family collection*

Photograph of Ana Benigna de Sá Barreto, Nabuco's mother, 1874. *Fundação Joaquim Nabuco Collection – Recife*

Portrait of Joaquim Nabuco, aged seven, by an unknown artist, 1856. *Family collection*

Photograph of Nabuco, aged fifteen, 1864. *Fundação Joaquim Nabuco Collection – Recife*

Photograph of Nabuco as a deputy for the province of Pernambuco, aged 29, 1879. *Fundação Joaquim Nabuco Collection – Recife*

Nabuco, aged 54, in Nice, France, 1904. *Fundação Joaquim Nabuco Collection – Recife*

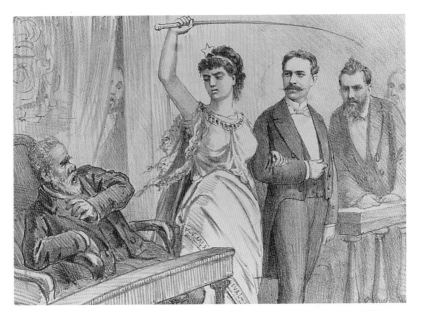

Nabuco arriving in Parliament, with the province of Pernambuco punishing the leader of the slaveowning interest. Angelo Agostini, *Revista Illustrada*, 1885. *Fundação Biblioteca Nacional Collection*

Nabuco addressing an abolitionist meeting, *Revista Illustrada*, 1887. *Fundação Biblioteca Nacional Collection*

Lithograph by E. M. S. Gouveia of Nabuco as abolitionist, 1886. *Fundação Biblioteca Nacional Collection*

Lithograph by Angelo Agostini on the cover of *Revista Illustrada* celebrating the abolition of slavery on 13 May 1888. *Fundação Biblioteca Nacional Collection*

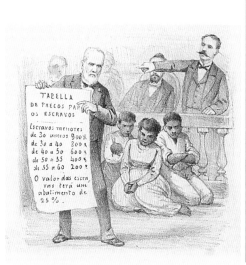

Nabuco points accusingly at a list of prices for slaves: "Female slaves subject to a 25% discount." *Revista Illustrada. Fundação Biblioteca Nacional Collection*

The cover of *Charivari* (Porto, Portugal) celebrating the abolition of slavery in Brazil, *Revista Illustrada*, 1888. *Fundação Biblioteca Nacional Collection*

Portrait of Dom Pedro II, 1882, supportive of the abolitionist movement. *Museu Histórico Nacional Collection*

Portrait of Princess Isabel (1880s), who as Regent signed Brazil's Abolition Act of 13 May 1888. *Museu Histórico Nacional Collection*

Abolitionist beer label with image of Nabuco. *Fundação Joaquim Nabuco Collection – Recife*

Gold medal given to Nabuco by "the people of Pernambuco", 15 December 1885. *Family collection*

Title page of the first edition of *Minha formação*, Garnier, 1900. *Family collection*

Front page of *Minha formação*, with a list, in Nabuco's handwriting, of family, friends and colleagues who were to be sent a copy. *Family collection*

Brazilian legation in London, 1901.
From left to right: Graça Aranha, Silvio Gurgel do Amaral, Joaquim Nabuco (minister),

Domício da Gama and Oliveira Lima.
Fundação Joaquim Nabuco Collection – Recife

Nabuco's children, London, 1902.
Left to right: Mauricio, Joaquim Filho,
José Thomaz, Maria Carolina, Maria Ana.

Fundação Joaquim Nabuco Collection – Recife

Nabuco's wife Evelina, London, 1903.
Family collection

Joaquim Nabuco, first Brazilian Ambassador
to Washington, 1905-10. *Family collection*

Joaquim Nabuco's funeral in Washington,
January 1910. *Family collection*

Photograph by Augusto Malta of the arrival of
Nabuco's coffin in Rio de Janeiro, 9 April 1910,
en route for burial in Recife. *Family collection*

with the tolerance and knowledge of the big capitalist that delegates it. Thus, political corruption in the United States, as I once quoted Boutmy, is a simple skin eruption, while in other countries it is a deep, visceral disease.

The fact is that I retained no impression of the United States that was on a par with my impression of England, not even that of individual freedom. Of course the American, compared to the Englishman, has a stronger feeling of individual pride, because he bows to no class or hierarchy. The Englishman worships position, class, and birth. The American does not, and this means naturally that he considers himself more independent than the Englishman. It is undeniable that when democracy introduces the idea of perfect equality into education, it raises man's feeling of self-pride. The question, considering the overall results, is whether old societies like England, where traditional influences have not been completely erased, but have been artificially maintained, do not produce with the class limitations a personal dignity that is morally superior to this pride of equality. One should not forget that for the American, human equality is circumscribed by race. Without mentioning the Chinaman or the Negro – who would be classified on an order different from that of man if the American spirit had its way – no one would ever convince a free citizen of the United States, as he calls himself, that his neighbor from Mexico or Cuba or the illiterate and indigent immigrants that he turns away from his ports are his equals. For them, his feeling of pride becomes the deepest disdain that one human being can feel for another.

I would not wish to deny the higher inspiration in the feeling of equality in America, as in ancient Israel and ancient Greece, where it was a breath of liberty, heroism, and independence, a source of the most perfect types in art and religion. On this path, it is England that is obviously moving to catch up with the United States, not the United States backsliding to meet England. No one who knows the American type, all the way from the *newsboy* shouting the headlines on the streets to the *king* of some monopoly or capital venture, railroads, coal or silver mines, or cotton or wheat futures can ignore the American's prime characteristic, namely his conviction that there is nobody better in the world. The raw material for the speeches to the crowds and the campaign propaganda is all contained in this phrase, which I heard by one of the speakers at a *monster meeting*: "In the United States (as always, the speaker actually said '*in America*'), every man is a king, and every woman a queen." It might sound paradoxical if I say that the effect of such a feeling may be none other than to spawn unbridled pride, and that such pride will lead to a backlash – if not of inequality (since equality can become embedded in the blood of the race) – at least of servility. Has this not happened with the freest of all races and the proudest of all democracies? Nevertheless, the feeling of equality before the law and before the courts, whatever the feeling of equality of condition, is greater and more solid in England than in the United States. The *groom* of the Marquis of Salisbury is more likely to obtain justice against his employer than a cashier in a large New York establishment against his boss, if the latter has any influence in City Hall.

In the United States, it would be unnecessary to advertise today: "Wanted: An Aristocracy". The aristocracy already exists, or at least it is taking shape as quickly as everything else there: aristocracy of birth, aristocracy of fortune, aristocracy of intelligence, aristocracy of beauty. What distinguishes this aristocracy – with no titles or noble pedigrees, all made of convention, but an aristocracy nonetheless – from the world's other aristocracies is that it is not political, but the result of political abstention. Second, and this is the most delicate point in American society, the idea that has captured women in this very closed circle is that the English *gentleman* is a superior type in relation to their countrymen, even of greater culture and distinction. Of course, fewer American women prefer to marry foreigners in order to join the most exclusive European aristocracy as compared to those who marry their compatriots, but the aristocracy in itself is a minority, and the minorities-within-the-minority best represent the overall spirit. In my opinion, this American woman's preference for the foreigner spells disaster for the American man's feeling of equality. If the result, and of course the effect does not come from any other cause, is to create an aristocracy in which man is considered below woman's level and less apt than an English lord or *honorable* to inspire her love and to betroth her, that feeling of equality will have failed disastrously at the highest level of society.

On this point, no high society could suffer such a depressing ill as the American man's awareness that his young countrywoman, beautiful and often a millionaire, considers the English duke or the French count superior to him. It is not necessarily the title that constitutes the advantage for the foreigner who telegraphs back to London or Paris with his *veni, vidi, vici,* just days after landing in America. In part, it is the prestige, the seduction of the European world and the idea that the American man would only exceptionally be attuned to English, French, or Italian society, as she, the American woman, is attuned. Yet it is mainly the aristocratic type of man that exerts this fascination on her, so desolating for her male compatriots. There are patrician families in the United States, and there will be more every day, whether due to their immense wealth, like the Astors and the Vanderbilts, the diplomatic roles they have played, like the Adams, the Hamiltons, and the Jays, and the generations of distinguished and socially prominent names they represent, and it is evident that in this aristocracy, which tends to have its class spirit, the idea of marriage to a foreigner or of the foreigner's superiority can only be the exception. But in a society one must consider the sentiment of the group that attracts the most public interest, and there is no doubt that in the highest echelon of American society, the English nobleman with his prestige, the fine Frenchman with his titles, and the Italian prince prevail over the national competition. The country's protectionist genius is impotent against such a terrible state of affairs. The only compensation one could imagine would be a ***drawback*** in favor of American men who happened to marry into European high society or finance. An aristocracy suffers from an imbalance in ideals between the two sexes when the most ambitious women – the most beautiful, the wealthiest, the most seductive – find the foreigner more on their own level as compared to their male compatriots when it comes to love or marriage. It is only fair to assess societies by their finest flower, by their elite, by what they admire most deeply in themselves and by what the world admires in them.

CHAPTER XVII

THE INFLUENCE OF THE UNITED STATES

I COULD NOT HAVE LIVED IN THE UNITED STATES for almost two years as I did without having changed somehow under the American influence. Europe is one thing, and the United States another. Analyzing the Americans as one single moral person, their mettle, basic human experience, and touch of life are entirely Anglo-Saxon. The United States, like Australia and Canada, cannot hide its origins. The Anglo-Saxon background, to a greater or lesser extent, reveals itself in the courage and tenacity, in the toughness and impenetrability, in the entrepreneurial spirit and independence of the race, but also in the brutality and cruelty of the grassroots instinct, in the blood feuds, in the drinking, in the lynchings, in the unquenchable thirst for money, as well as in other traits like the need for physical and moral cleanliness, the spirit of national conservation, emulation, self-esteem, religion, respect for women, and the capacity for free government.

Yet how different the American is from the Englishman! The molds diverge so greatly that in order to explain the difference one would have to admit a stronger modifying influence than that of social institutions, such as a regional influence, whereby over time each great region in the world produces its race, different from the others. Institutions modify a people's character, but it has never been proven that they modify its type and physical temperament. What would be the difference between a Greek from the time of Miltiades and another from the time of Alexander or Trajan? What would be the difference between a Neapolitan from the time of Alphonsus the Great and that of King Umberto, or between a Portuguese from the time of King Manuel and one of today?

A comparison of the political and social machinery in the United States and England is almost entirely favorable to the latter. The English political and legal institutions, both public and private, are more dignified, more serious, and more respectable. In the House of Commons, *lobbying* is unthinkable, there is no *spoils system* in the English administration, no one would conceive of *squaring* in an English court, and there is no piece of English territory in which the citizens only trust in the justice they make with their own hands, like the American *lynchings*. For anyone who has to deal with the administration and depends on justice, the American system offers less protection and many fewer guarantees of equity than the English system.

In addition, whoever enters public life in the United States has to seek the good graces of very different individuals from those who open the political doors to newcomers in England. He also has to learn through a much more slipshod catechism. The influence of the great thinker, the great writer, and the skilled man is felt much more keenly in England than in the United States, where the masses obey influences that have nothing intellectual about them and which lack any kind of appreciation for mental elaboration. In fact, everything superior bears the mark of individuality, while disdaining the wisdom of the masses. For the Americans, political genius of whatever stripe is rife with rebelliousness. The single citizen is worth less in the United States than in England. In order to count in American politics, the individual has to join a party and renounce his personality from that day onward. There is no such partisan slavery in England. Like the United States, England is ruled by two alternating and counter-balancing parties, but the English parties are parties of opinion, not *machines* like the American ones, in which a handful of *bosses* rule, calling all the shots.

Nevertheless, considering the individual man, unrelated to the political machinery, who depends on neither the administration nor the courts and who also renounces his own right to misgovern his compatriots, the United States is the quintessential free country. As a nation, the Americans would like to live without government, and thank their governors for acknowledging their wish. Hence the popularity of the American Presidents:

they do not cast a shadow over the country, nor do they weigh on the nation. The pressure from the top down, from government on society, to which humankind has become accustomed since time immemorial, such that it can not live without it, is felt less in the United States than anywhere else, including in England, where government protection is ubiquitous. The burden of authority weighs lighter on the American's shoulders than on those of any other people. His breathing is the freest, longest, and deepest. Government may be better or more perfect in England, but what does the American care, if he wants increasingly limited government action, if he wants to feel it less and have less to do with it? The question is whether the burden of authority, which is now so light in the United States, will not one day become the heaviest of all. Granted the difference in epoch and progress, the American system may well represent the personal freedom that peoples have always enjoyed to a greater or lesser extent when they have unlimited room to extend into sparsely settled surroundings in a new country. In the final analysis, this extreme freedom is a form of individualism, isolation, life apart, and complete responsibility as man in society. Taken alone, as I said, the American will always be the freest of all men. However, as a citizen, his contract with society is not cloaked in the same guarantees as that of the Englishman, for example. The authority weighing on his shoulders is lighter, but human solidarity is also feebler in his conscience.

One thing American government is not: it is not the government of the best man, as the ancient democracies intended. Presidencies may be personal government, or at least they were accused of having been. Still, one cannot identify the one great man of influence in the United States, the American Gladstone or Gambetta. The nation dispenses with tutors, directors, counselors, rejects all that appears *patronizing*, that puts on airs of protection or condescendence. In the eyes of the American, what makes a worthy statesman is the sum of trust he merits, the reflection of satisfaction he causes for **Uncle Sam**.

The American's main source of pride is the idea that his government is the strongest in the world and the one that most spares and disguises its strength. Between European militarism and the unarmed democracy of the United States, a conflict may one day break out which now appears almost paradoxical. But until the United States experiences a great foreign war, as it tasted a great domestic rebellion, America's durability and flexibility cannot be considered superior to those of the old European fabric.

What can be said is that the United States has still not been forced to fight against the same perils as Europe. The government that changes every four years may be the strongest in the world, but it has not been tested under the same conditions as the others, for whom, as governments armed and in constant surveillance against the hazards of foreign coalitions, it is like the magnificent transatlantic ships, with vast illuminated parlors, high ceilings, and roomy and airy staterooms, veritable floating cities as compared to warships.

The Union, compared to England, is like the American *prairie* compared to the inner courtyard of a Norman castle. In the former, open space unveils on all sides in an infinite plain. In the latter, high walls close in on the viewer, always telling him the history of other epochs. The past weighs on the present in England and limits it, while in America there is no hindsight. For the American, all this results in a feeling of independence, which, as it did for the Greek, would make him feel half slave if they gave him a king, even if the effect of the royalty were to increase his actual share of rights and his influence in the community. This is the gist of American "freedom": the feeling of hierarchical equality between the governors and the governed.

I ran no risk of acquiring this American idiosyncrasy. It was evident to me that it resulted from the conditions under which the United States had grown, and that if Independence had been won with an English prince, as ours was with the heir to the throne,[49] the United States, in a century of progress and advancement, would have developed the same feeling as the English, of *loyalty* to the royal house. Given that during the same period the royalty in England underwent a metamorphosis from the reign of George IV to that of Victoria, in the United States the monarchy would have enjoyed an even greater transformation. *Mr. King* or *Mrs. Queen* would have been a much more popular person than *Mr. President*, and would have received more crushing *shake-hands* and friendly mail. In Brazil, the monarchy was – as we witnessed it – a purely popular government. Why would it have been any different in the United States, where the active

49 D.Pedro I, first Emperor of independent Brazil, son of D. João VI, king of Portugal, Brazil and the Algarve. L.B.

ingredient, the acid strength of democracy, is even more energetic? The monarchy in New England would probably have exerted a greater influence on the old European monarchies than the great Republic did, and another kind of influence on the rest of America.

After the reception and hospitality that Dom Pedro II received in the United States in 1876, it was no longer thinkable to doubt that for the country's cultured intelligentsia, the constitutional monarchy, represented by a dynasty like that of Brazil, was a far superior government compared to the so-called republics of Latin America. It may not have been convenient for the speaker to say such a thing to every American audience. At times he might have claimed that the worst of republics represents progress over the best of monarchies, but in my opinion such a statement would be the privilege of an irresponsible demagogue. It was not the feeling of the Washingtons, the Hamiltons, the Jeffersons, or of those who sought to follow their traditions. The effect of American republicanism on me could only have been to correct the superstitious side of my monarchism, to eliminate from it whatever appeared as divine right or super-human consecration. I saw no opposition between the two spirits, the English and the American, as there is no opposition between the two peoples or the two societies. Nothing was easier than to understand and reconcile the admiration with which Gladstone speaks of the United States and the admiration of the most respectable American writers for the English Constitution.

Although none of my political ideas changed in the United States, no one can breathe the American air without finding it more alive, lighter, and more buoyant than others, seeped in tradition and authority, convention and ceremonial. This impression does not disappear during one's lifetime. Whoever once took a deep long breath will never mistake the American air for that of anywhere else. Its composition is different from that of all others.

As for me, I was treated with such kindness and I enjoyed such a generous welcome in the United States that to this day I take comfort in the fond memories. My overall impression of America is that of crispness, where everything is sharp, with a perfect, precise contour, like an old medal. The English make everything solid, the French, elegant, while the Americans endeavor to make things sharp, *clear-cut*. This can be recognized in any American design. There is a perfection of its own which is the American perfection, distinct from the final touch that the English or French put on things, real, undeniable perfection, like the Japanese. One may prefer the European way of seeing, or rather way of looking – art, after all, is nothing but a way of looking, a matter of visual angle – as compared to the American, and to a great extent this is also a matter of race, but there is no doubt that the American stroke has achieved its own perfection. Everything I saw appeared to be designed and made with this stroke, which I would not mistake for any other. What distinguishes it is that it does not express, like the others, a state of spirit or aspiration of a purely aesthetic order. It does not express a resolution, a will, or a character. If it were not for my historical aspiration, which I could not and would not forego, no place of residence, no life, no spectacle would have seemed as fascinating as that of New York. I don't know if the New York sky seemed like the most beautiful one in the world to me. I do know that it spills waves of light and joy with life and courage on the most amazing procession of youth and human beauty that has ever passed before my eyes, flowing back and forth every afternoon and morning between Fifth Avenue and Central Park.

The American – I am speaking of the man, not the woman, and the man who does not belong to the country's elite – lacks what has come to be called the manners, or the touches or signs, unknown to the uninitiated, by which the initiated in worldly secrets recognize each other. This merely means that Americans are a race growing in the most perfect equality and earning their living through breakneck competition. Meanwhile, no school in the world can match the United States for learning what at least from now on will be the most important lesson in life, namely the art of self-reliance. American children – and when one says children in the United States, one includes both boys and girls – are immersed from their most tender infancy in a chemical bath that gives every fiber of their determination the toughness and temper of steel. Whatever the value of culture, no parents would prefer to give their children a purely intellectual upbringing rather than the powerful American *pick-me-up*, a bracer that prevents one from getting upset even in the face of the direst moral challenges. The game of life in modern times – and all the more so in future centuries, when competition will be even fiercer – looks nothing like the minuet figures or country outings of the last century, as we see in a Boucher or a Goya. It is like the so-called *roller coaster*, an unceasing performance at breakneck speed, trains careening along the tracks, disappearing over ravines only to reappear further down the horizon, and for this constant feeling of giddiness it is primarily the heart that needs to be fortified. By all likelihood, the United States will come to a stop one day, and then it will have time to produce its cultured society, like the old countries of Europe. Portions of society in the United States are already stopping and attempting to remain in repose. They form the first hint of an aristocracy which some day will become a great power within the Union, a great historical or artistic influence.

In an interview he granted several years ago to an American reporter, Herbert Spencer concluded with the following prediction about the future of the United States:

> From biological truths it is to be inferred that the eventual mixture of the allied varieties of the Aryan race forming the population will produce a more powerful type of man than has hitherto existed, and a type of man more plastic, more adaptable, more capable of undergoing the modifications needed for complete social life. I think that whatever difficulties they may have to surmount, and whatever tribulations they may have to pass through, the Americans may reasonably look forward to a time when they will have produced a civilization grander than any the world has known.[50]

Such may be the biological law of the Aryan mixture, but to this day no American branch from the European trunk has proven that it can produce the same blossom of civilization as the old stock. American civilization may one day be greater than any the world has ever known, but for the time being I consider it dangerous for Europe to delegate humankind's work to the United States. If such a task were limited to the current American elements, much noble inspiration would likely be lost forever and the genius of the human race might never flourish again. The United States apparently has the only educational system that is not conventional, not simply the galvanization of states of spirit from past times, of classic and literary ideals that men living in libraries force on those who lack the time to read. Ideas play a much smaller role in life in the United States than in

---

50 *The New York Times*, October 20, 1882. T.N.

other countries, where everything is written and turned into rules, and of whom one can say, inverting the famous phrase, that nothing touches their senses that has not inhabited their intelligence first. The Americans are inventing life on a grand scale, as if nothing had existed before today. All this suggests great future innovations, but there is still not the slightest sign that the design of human fate or a higher revelation to man has to pass through the United States some day. The nation's mission in history is still totally unknown. If the United States suddenly disappeared, one cannot specify what essential thing humankind would lose, what ray would be extinguished from the human spirit. It would still not be as if France, Germany, England, Italy, or Spain had disappeared.

CHAPTER XVIII

MY FATHER

WHEREVER I TRAVELED, whatever the influences I experienced from the country, society, art, and authors, I was always affected by a more powerful inner force, which was strange in a certain sense, but which appeared to act on me from within, from a hereditary background, and by means of the heart's best impulses. That influence was always present, no matter how far I was from it, dominating and modifying all the others, which were invariably subordinate to it. Now is the time to speak of it, because it was not exactly an influence of childhood, nor of the first bloom of youth, but of the growth and maturation of the spirit, and destined to grow unceasingly and to reach its full flower only after his death. The influence was that of my father.

When I saw him for the first time, in 1857, he was 44 and had just left the Ministry of Justice. The Paraná-Caxias cabinet (1853–57) had been the longest ever in the Empire, and it turned out to be the most brilliant school of statesmen in the kingdom. The group of *youths* that the Marquis of Paraná gathered around him illustrates how astutely he read men and the future. Paranhos, Wanderley, Pedreira, and Nabuco were all destined to play leading roles in politics. This cabinet became known as the Ministry of Conciliation. It reflected the thinking, accepted by the Emperor after the shock of the Empire's last civil war,[51] of opening up politics to the banned liberals without changing the conservative spirit of its policy. Before joining the cabinet, Nabuco had been the one who best defined the scope and limits of this new policy, which he carried on virtually alone for a considerable time after the death of Paraná. I will quote an excerpt from his speech in

---

51 This is a reference to the *Revolução Praieira* in Pernambuco in 1848, which was not exactly a civil war but a rebellion by Liberals, after a Conservative cabinet took office. The rebellion was limited to Pernambuco, and the rebels were defeated with the help of the central government. R.S.

1853 as a simple Deputy, a platform speech one might say, because it was so frequently interpreted and invoked after he was named to the cabinet, and because this excerpt suffices to give an idea of his way of introducing a new approach into people's spirits, a different direction from that which had prevailed.

His speeches included the so-called *golden bridge*.[52] Nabuco's contemporaries always referred to his speeches by some creative or comprehensive phrase or image he had used to describe the situation, or by the meaning and scope ascribed to them by his adversaries. "I understand," he said, speaking of the idea of conciliation, which was in the air, "that it is necessary to make some concession in the sense that progress and experience demand, in order even for pride and self-esteem not to become entangled in the idea of an apostasy; in order for the transformation to be explained by the new principle, by the modification of ideas. Conciliation as a coalition and fusion of the parties, in order to merge the platforms, in order to erase the traditions, is impracticable, and even hazardous, and by all principles inadmissible, because having destroyed the barriers of political antagonism by which opinions oppose each other, having placed conservative and radical[53] ideas on common ground, the latter will inevitably absorb the former. Liberal ideas are bound to triumph over conservative ideas. Liberal ideas per se have enthusiasm, while conservative ideas have only reflection. Enthusiasm draws more followers, while reflection pertains to a few. Liberal ideas seduce and coerce, while conservative ideas convince. History teaches us that in these coalitions, liberal opinion gains more than conservative opinion." And he proceeds, "I heard with repugnance an idea defended in this house, that the parties should reconcile with each other of their own accord. I defend the opposite view, that conciliation should be the work of the government, not of the parties, because in the current state of affairs, if the parties reconcile themselves on their own, it will be out of hatred and spite for the government, and such a transaction, in relation to the principle

---

52 This is a reference to a famous speech in July 1853 in which Nabuco de Araújo, then a Conservative, defended the idea of a Government of Conciliation which should incorporate moderates from both the Conservative and Liberal parties. See note 2 above. An opposition politician Ângelo Muniz Ferraz claimed that in his speech Nabuco de Araújo had built a "golden bridge" by which he had distanced himself from his fellow Conservatives, had escaped from isolation and had been invited to join the Paraná cabinet as Minister of Justice. R.S.

53 In the original, the term Nabuco uses for "radical" ideas is *exageradas*, literally "exaggerated". T.N.

of authority, cannot fail to be utterly grievous to the public order and the country's future."

For Nabuco, those four years in the cabinet were extremely toilsome, but equally fruitful. My father's work as both a judge and member of the Chamber of Deputies had given him a solid reputation as a legal expert, which he consolidated as Minister of Justice. I will not attempt to summarize his work here, having recompiled it extensively in *Um estadista do Império* (*A Statesman of the Empire*).[54] I merely choose several traits to help illustrate his individuality and influence. First, it was his task to finish eliminating the slave traffic, which his predecessor, Eusébio de Queirós, had mortally wounded, but which refused to disappear except slowly.[55] The slightest hesitation on the part of a future administration would make it reemerge with a redoubled impetus to ride out the storm, because the slave trade infrastructure remained intact in Brazil and Africa. As an extreme recourse, Nabuco de Araújo proposed that repression of the slave traffic no longer be left to local juries. This sounded to liberal ideologues like an enormous blow against the "popular institution" of a trial by peers. Still, he sustained his position on grounds of absolute moral and social necessity. He said to the Chamber:

> In 1850, you know quite well, the great slave market was on the coast. That was where the big warehouses were located, where everyone went to buy. With this new law of September 4, 1850 [the Eusébio de Queirós Law], the circumstances have changed, and the slave traders have changed tactics. As soon as the Africans are loaded off the ships, they are smuggled away to the hinterlands by impenetrable paths and obscure trails. Given these new circumstances, what can the government do with the law of September 4, 1850, whose enforcement is limited to the coast? If we sincerely want to repress the slave traffic and not merely gloss over it, we must track down the slave traders[56] with their new tactics. The government does not demand such measures in order to abuse power, because if it wished to do so it already has sufficiently powerful means at its disposal. Unless a government ignores its mission, it cannot, through love for one interest, jeopardize

54 Joaquim Nabuco's three-volume biography of his father (Rio de Janeiro: Garnier, 1897–8). L.B.

55 On 4 September 1850, in the face of intense British diplomatic and naval pressure, a Conservative government, although allied with landholding and slaveholding interests, had decreed a ban on the international slave trade. The Brazilian Parliament had already passed a similar ban in 1831, also under British pressure, but the trade had continued – illegally – on an unprecedented scale for the following twenty years. R.S.

56 The term Nabuco uses for slave trader in the original is *africanista*, literally "Africanist". T.N

society's other interests. The great challenge in public administration is to reconcile all the interests. I said that the government sincerely wishes to repress the slave traffic and not gloss over it: would it not be sophistry to allow a jury to try this crime? Can we not expect the slave traders to unload the Africans in places where public opinion is favorable to the traffic? Will they not cart the Africans away to wherever they find a safe haven, where the jury, the accomplices, the vested interests, the connivers in the crime can try the case?

The government triumphed, and the Chambers passed the proposed bill. Having dared to revoke the jury's powers when the slave traffic was expiring was the courage of a true statesman, whose motto should be Caesar's *nil actum reputans*. There was no real glory in repressing the slave traffic after the blow by Eusébio, who had trumped both his predecessors and successors. All that remained for those who came after Eusébio was simply the duty to enforce the law. In order for the higher principle of the social interest to prevail, more than once my father had to confront those who claimed that the jury was untouchable. He was alarmed by the statistics on impunity, and among the causes of this state of affairs my father identified the power of the vested interests in the hinterlands that controlled the juries and thereby expanded their vassalage and kept it in obedience. As a solution, he proposed that jury trials be held in places with a sufficiently large population to ensure impartial rulings.

That was his principal quality as a politician, to adapt the means to the ends and not allow a single doctrine or claim to jeopardize the greater social interest. Just as he acted in relation to the jury, he acted as a judge before the court system. The administration of justice was one of his greatest feats in government. For him, a good, efficient, learned, and respected court system was the solution to half of our problems. To improve the judge's calling by all means at the state's disposal would be a compliment to his other *desideratum*: to improve the religious calling, to train a clergy in whose hands one could entrust the Ten Commandments, as a repository for morals and customs. Meanwhile, he was the main advocate of compulsory retirement for judges with lifetime appointments. It was he who made a maxim for the government, an aspiration for statesmen, from the words of an old French chancellor, who said: "I would prefer a thousand times over to be tried by a dishonest yet capable judge, rather than by an honest yet ignorant one, because a dishonest judge will not fail to administer justice except in cases in which he has an interest in doing so, while an ignorant judge only issues a good ruling by mere chance."

He took the same approach to the clergy. As Minister of Justice, my father strongly encouraged education for the clergy and proposed the creation of theological seminars. He issued the decree granting bishops power *ex informata conscientia* over their priests, without which it would have been impossible to passively recruit the ecclesiastic militia. Meanwhile, it was he who interrupted the monastic novitiate in Brazil. His thinking, far from suppressing the religious orders, was to regenerate them, restore them to the desired purity, or as he said in a phrase that stuck in the memory of Pius IX, "to raise a bronze wall between the new and the old clergy". He also served the monarchy with loyalty and impartiality. When he was still young, a student in Olinda, he raised the first cry that echoed throughout the North against the republican tendencies of April 7, yet the monarchism found no greater bulwark in Brazil than his liberal spirit heavily imbued with the constitutional principle. Typical of the way he viewed his position as state counselor was the frankness with which he sustained the maxim before the Emperor himself: the king reigns but does not govern.[57]

From 1868 to 1871, when the Viscount of Rio Branco embraced the idea and turned it into law, my father was the main proponent for the emancipation of future generations [of slaves]. In 1866 he had voted for this reform in a cabinet dispatch, and in 1867 he was its strongest advocate in the Council of State, as rapporteur for the bill that later became the law of September 28.[58] Sharing the laurels on the day of triumph, Francisco Otaviano paid him this tribute: "Glory is also unquestionably due to the honorable Sir Nabuco de Araújo for the dedication by which in the Council of State, in discussion with the plantation owners, and at the rostrum by means of eloquent speeches, he made the idea mature and acquire the proportions of a national aspiration."

This was the reform to which he devoted his greatest interest and love. Since 1866, too, my dream, my ambition for him, was that his name be associated with the Empire's first emancipation act. I wrote many

57 *Le roi règne et ne gouverne pas*, attributed (c. 1830) to Louis Adolphe Thiers, French statesman and historian, President of the Third Republic, T.N.

58 The Law of Free Birth (1871).

letters from law school (and fortunately he kept them, as he did with all his correspondence, so I later found them), expressing my inner hope that he would become the Brazilian Lincoln! And no trait in his career is more precious to me than the one I reconstructed faithfully in his *Life* and that made him the Cobden of that first abolitionist movement, just as [the Viscount of] Rio Branco was the Robert Peel. Thus, when I entered the Chamber of Deputies in 1879, if he had still been alive, although his presence in the Senate would have greatly modified my freedom of action, on one issue I am absolutely certain that my role would have been the same, or even stronger: slavery. On this point, he would not have corrected or restrained me. His attitude, like that of Rio Branco if he had participated in one more legislature, would have been fully favorable to abolition. If they had both lived, the revolutionary nature of the movement might have been avoided, because both parties would have had members (afterwards it was too late) who identified with the [abolitionist] propaganda, thus preventing the liberal human aspiration from becoming political ferment in the future. I have no doubt, thank God, that he would have taken this stance. In 1879, as a Deputy, all I did was continue from the point where he had left off, standing in for him – with the natural difference between my youth and his old age – and further developing the opinion in favor of the existing slaves that he had indicated as a national duty by drafting and debating the law that liberated the future generations.

Towards the end of his life, his liberalism had acquired a sharper tone, but he always dealt with freedom in practical terms. Thus, he was specifically preoccupied with legal guarantees for individual freedom. He had a certain number of constitutional formulas and political maxims that comprised his loyalty to both the monarchist cause and the liberal cause. A Conservative during his youth and throughout the part of his career in which life expanded and emulation inspired him, only in his declining years did he break with the party of tradition, which in his view had become an oligarchy, taking the form of a triumvirate.[59] He was now a Liberal leader, but one who still preferred the manner, pace, and composure of the old school to the hullabaloo, backslapping, and indiscipline of his new camp.

---

59 On the *Saquarema* triumvirate at the head of the Conservative party, see note 5.

These few brush strokes would suffice to portray the statesman: he had a liberal nature, with a highly pronounced imaginative impulse, focusing clearly on his political ideals, but pursuing realities rather than mirages, preferring a little freedom that he could leave as a legacy for his children, a relative state of well-being, rather than magnificent but illusory rights that could not be enjoyed or grand reforms in the political machinery that would do nothing to improve the country's condition. He based his idealist foundations on inflexible principles, but always tempered by a clear intuition of the law's practical effects. As a party leader he was alien to petty politics, meaning that he exercised a kind of moral authority that both friend and foe sometimes compared to the spiritual power of the ancient Mikados.

Living in the midst of a truly noteworthy elite of statesmen, orators, and legislators, the richest of the two reigns in parliamentary talent, political tradition, and administrative expertise, for a long time he played the widely acknowledged role of oracle. He rarely spoke in his declining years, and an invincible sadness mingled with his patriotic divinations. Reading him, one would say today that the demise of the liberal institutions cast its shadow twelve or fifteen years into the future and that he saw it encroaching on the Senate rostrum.

Many years after his death, as I studied his life, meditated on what he left of his thinking, perused his vast archives, his political correspondence, the testimony, the controversies triggered by his individual action, and the consequences attributed to it by coreligionists and adversaries, I finally grasped my father's political personality. In my youth I could never have understood him fully as I later did. I would have lacked the proper faculties and the necessary calm to admire what only speaks to reason, systematic spirit, and constructive genius. But while I could only measure and assess the statesman at a later stage in my development, never in my life did I experience such a direct and positive influence as my admiration for the man himself. I knew quite well, I could see, that his greatest knowledge came from within, not from the books, which were literally no more than authorities on which he drew for the sake of the public, judges, and colleagues. Even more than his knowledge, what overwhelmed me was the visible harmony of his mental and moral fiber, manifested by an unparalleled serenity and gentleness.

In 1860 my father moved from Catete to Flamengo Beach, where he lived until his death. The house was one of those solid buildings from the good old days of Portuguese construction in Rio de Janeiro, with the interior proportions of a palace or convent. There, in those drawing rooms and spacious bedrooms, he was in his medium, he had the inner space and – with the sea lapping at his doorstep – the outer variety and movement that a bookworm needs. Rio de Janeiro society came to his parties and receptions. The neighbors came on Sundays to the mass said in his oratory. When the Chambers were in session, deputies from Pernambuco came to visit, and always his close friends, like the Marquis of Abrantes, Quaraim, his old colleagues. These and his trips by carriage to the Senate or the office were all the distraction he had outside of his study. His life was exclusively cerebral, and he never had time (perhaps not a day in his entire lifetime) to interrupt, to suspend this ceaseless toil, which was all forced labor. None of it, not the most insignificant portion, was of his own choice or inclination. This way of life, cloistered within the high walls of books, only leaving his cell to join his family in greeting visitors whose friendship or loyalty drew around him, resulted in that captivating kindness that was his principal trait.

Today, I feel profound regret and contrition for not having made my main mission in life to quench my thirst for him, have my full of him, make my spirit a copy, a duplicate of all that I had printed and engraved of him, at the very least of the notes I had kept, but which I allowed time to erase. I will never be able to fill some of the gaps. I am thinking of the great bound volumes that kept him company in the exile of his study, like the old copies of court rulings and legal articles. It was a collection of the journals that he had written for or edited in Recife. Twenty years of his life were right there. This entire collection has scattered, vanished. Why did the profound, incomparable interest that all this later awakened in me not coincide with the period when I lived by his side? This desire to gather up the slightest vestiges of his thinking and the most fleeting traces of his reflections – which was always, in the sphere where he produced it, personal, creative, and transformational in relation to the topic at hand – only dawned on me when I could no longer turn to him to ask for clarifications, to have him relive for me that magic dust of life that only he possessed, to give me the key, the spirit of the time, the character, the scope, the real truth of what was depicted there, and for which only he knew the limits, the scale, the definitive pattern for interpreting it all. Not to mention the characters he had known, with whom he had lived! Why didn't I parade before him, without tiring or forcing him, the gallery of his contemporaries in order to capture the traces that had remained from each and every one? And yet, so much I neglected to talk about with him! My greatest joy for years on end were the hours he gave us every day, when I soaked up his words and gazed on him even more. I now regret that when I still could have, I did not aspire to be the one to merely receive and conserve as much of him as possible, and whose constant presence by his side would have gathered and recorded the reminiscences, the points of view, and the representative images that fifty years of intellectual activity had imprinted in his thinking.

Having made this act of contrition for whatever I failed to assimilate from my father during my own formative years, and for whatever of his intellectual legacy that I allowed to disappear, the truth is that for a long time, no moral influence was as strong as my awareness of the relationship that bound me to him. I was always prepared, at a word from him (but which he never pronounced), to renounce my aspirations in favor of his, or to forego the role I pursued in favor of that which he might assign to me. As I said, only much later, twenty years after seeing him for the last time, I finally appreciated what I now call his political genius and felt all the conscious, objective admiration for him of which I am capable. But even so, in his time I had an instinctive feeling of his superiority. Far removed from him, in my independent intellectual world, I expressed many opinions different from his and overstepped the limits of the line he practiced, but it was unthinkable that I would fail to cede to the slightest pressure he deemed necessary to exert on me or some attempt to persuade me on an issue. My youthful pretentiousness, drawing inspiration only from itself and decreeing its own infallibility, because it only saw the things within its grasp, would have vanished without hesitation at an appeal from his gentle demeanor, from a touch of his superior reason. Had God so willed it, such a request would have come in the early years of my insatiable intellectual curiosity, when I first learned of the *terra incognita* inscribed on the map of faith as the limit of imagination itself.

More than any other influence, my father's devotion helped keep my own belief intact for years. My convictions were shaken seriously, but that predominant impression from my father always made me treat what I felt was essential in religion as the highest sphere or prime source of human inspiration. Occasionally, however, thinking of him and his great authority over me, I could not fail to feel the advantage that emancipated spirits ascribe to themselves as compared to those who have never left the faith. It was during the time when I was asking myself whether a man, even having the genius of a St. Thomas Aquinas, could be called superior if in our century he had no intellectual horizon other than revelation. Perhaps, by way of consolation, I believed that my father also had doubts that he kept from surfacing, or that he had returned to the faith as a finished synthesis of human life in all its relations after having attempted in vain to construct one of his own. Only later was I able to understand that the mind can work to the very end, entirely alien to the grave religious problems that confuse the thinker who attempts to solve them by reason, if no outer shock has come to disturb the solution received in childhood. Doubt is not a sign that the spirit has achieved greater perspicuity, and sometimes it is merely discontentment with life. A life occupied by grand works may not have a moment to spare for religious doubt. Although it would be incorrect to claim that doubt never helped any great genius of humanity to plan or improve his work, it has certainly aided fewer as compared to those who did not require a breath of denial to inspire them and who succeeded in creating while believing. At least one thing is certain, that the creative faculties must be built solidly in order for doubt not to make them produce a less considerable or less beautiful work than would faith. Doubt may be the sign of a new human fate, the outline of a future intelligence, but it will take a long time to achieve a greater meaning than that of religion. Fortunately, my ideas on what constitutes intellectual superiority have changed since the time when I sought pretexts for attributing it to spirits devoid of the faculty of doubt, but which otherwise caused me great admiration, like my father. I thus sometimes considered a literary expert or writer superior to one of these coarse thinkers whose ideas can only be grasped after breaking their hard protective covering. It is as if the flower that blooms for just one morning were the ultimate creation in the plant world rather than the millenary cedar, father of the forest.

CHAPTER XIX

ELECTION AS DEPUTY

MY POLITICAL TRAINING PER SE lasted until 1878. The following period, from 1879 to 1889, featured the role that befell me. The end – and now I view all the rest as such – has witnessed the damping of my political interest and its replacement with other concerns, perhaps even more unreal and chimerical, but in a sense more fitting for the twilight of life, when the spirit begins to hear the final bugle call from afar. During the ten years I have retold in the previous chapters, I was no more than an inquisitive man enticed by travel, by the character of the different countries, by new books, the theater, and society. An enviable life for me at that time would have been to watch from the wings the great events of the time, to rub elbows with the main characters, and as a distraction from the present, to have the right of entry to the excavations of Athens or Rome. At the end of my phase of intellectual dilettantism, when I was elected to Parliament for the first time, I needed a new source of inner sunlight. I no longer needed dilettantism, but human passion, a live, palpitating, absorbing interest in the destiny and condition of others, in the fate of the unfortunate, to dedicate my life to some work of national mercy, to aid my country, to put my shoulder to the task of my time in some noble undertaking. Given the conditions I have described, no partisan political cause could have sparked this sort of enthusiasm in me or inspired such fascination. Inevitably, politics would have been mere partisan emotion: uncertain, negative, at the risk of constructing with shoddy materials on shaky ground. There had to be a universal human interest. The task had to be unerringly absolute, involving finality, certainty, the divine, like the great redemptions, the revolutions of charity or justice, the auroras of truth and conscience in the world. In the year I began my public life I still had such an interest, with all this power of fascination for feeling and duty, likewise impulsive and unlimited, capable of the *fiat*, whether the matter was the fate of single creatures or the nation's character. Such an interest could only be that of emancipation. Fortunately for my time, ever since childhood and adolescence I had the interest, the compassion, and the feeling for the slaves, the seed that would produce the only flower in my career.

The fact that launched me in politics was my father's death in March 1878, the year in which I was to be elected Deputy for the first time. Before his death he had guaranteed my election through a deal with the Baron of Vila Bela, the political boss of Pernambuco. After my father died, Sousa Carvalho went to great lengths to oppose my candidacy, complaining to Vila Bela: *Sublata causa, tollitur effectus*. However, friendship and loyalty were like a religion to Domingos de Sousa Leão, and Nabuco's death, rather than relieving him of his commitment, reaffirmed it as a point of honor. My personal desire at that time was to continue in diplomacy, but my mother insisted on seeing my father's wish fulfilled, to see me enter politics, to replace him one day, to occupy his seat in the Senate, just as he had occupied that of my grandfather, who himself had not been the first Senator Nabuco, since he had been preceded by his uncle José Joaquim Nabuco de Araújo, the first Baron of Itapoã. I would thus represent the fourth generation of the same family in Parliament, which had not happened to anyone else [in Brazil's history].[60] Martim Francisco III was the son, grandson, and great-grandson of members of Parliament, but in his case there were really only three generations of politicians, since his grandfather and great-grandfather, Martim Francisco the Elder and José Bonifácio, were brothers.[61]

My election did not cost me anything. However it did entail a cost in the court for Vila-Bela and for provincial president Adolfo de Barros – who passed through politics like a perfect *gentleman* – in order to make

---

60 Senators were appointed by the Emperor for life. José Joaquim Nabuco de Araújo, baron of Itapoã, great uncle of Joaquim Nabuco, was a senator from 1826 to 1840; José Thomaz Nabuco de Araújo, brother of José Joaquim and grandfather of Joaquim Nabuco, was a senator from 1837 to 1850; and Jose Thomaz Nabuco de Araújo Filho, Joaquim Nabuco's father, was a senator from 1858 to 1878. L.B.

61 The Andradas were one of the most influential families in 19th-century Brazilian politics. Three brothers – José Bonifácio de Andrada e Silva (1763–1838), Antonio Carlos Ribeiro de Andrada Machado e Silva (1773–1845) and Martim Francisco Ribeiro de Andrada (1775–1844) – played a central role in the early years of Brazilian independence. Martim Francisco Ribeiro de Andrada Filho (1825–86) was the son of Martim Francisco Ribeiro de Andrada and Gabriela Frederica, the daughter of his older brother José Bonifácio (and therefore his niece), and the father of Martim Francisco Ribeiro de Andrada III (1853–1927). L.B.

sure I was included on the slate. My name crowded out several party old-timers, like Aprígio Guimarães, popular in academic circles for his republican liberalism and speaker's eloquence. I had no reason to regret this arrangement, *fata viam invenient*. I was not the only newcomer that trumped seniority. The slate was full of new names. I represented a tradition of services to the party – those of my father – just as worthy as those of anyone else, and I was confident that once in the Chamber I would make good on my expeditious promotion. Although this election cost me no effort, since it was all arranged by the party and with its official backing, there was an incident in it for me nevertheless. During a student meeting on August 2, in the Santa Isabel Theatre, when I was making the opening speech from the chairman's box, I was received by shouts and protests from a large group that soon became the majority and that later moved its *meeting* of outrage against me to one of the city squares. In my impromptu speech, responding from the stage to the barbs and diatribes launched against the government, I had claimed that the great issue for Brazilian democracy was not the monarchy, but slavery. I can safely say that I occasionally tasted the sweetness of popularity, but nothing can match the speaker's pleasure when he faces such a storm and feels himself in possession of the truth, at the service of justice, and foresees that those who attack him at that very moment will join arms with him the next day. I allowed that rabid, foaming wave to pass, having been launched against my candidacy through intrigues that exploited the weaknesses that were typical of democracy in Pernambuco at the time, with bitter memories of the *Praieira*[62] and based on unfamiliarity with me or with the role I would come to play. I knew that there would be a complete recanting and that the *mal-entendu* created between the people of Recife and myself would be undone, as soon they realized the purpose for which I aspired to a term in Parliament. The general opinion about me in the Popular Party, zealous of its forums and traditions, did indeed change during the first session in which I took the floor in the Chamber. From that day onward, an affinity was created between Recife and myself that was never broken, and that I am certain remains unchanged even to this day, when I have completely retired from politics, because it was like the meeting of two

62 See note 51 above.

opinions that gazed into each other's depths and mutually acknowledged their underlying sincerity.

The year 1879, when I made my parliamentary debut, witnessed unparalleled activity and growth in my life. I took the podium every day, participated in all the debates, all the issues. The kindness and respect I received, the applause from the floor and the galleries, and the attention people paid me could easily have gone to a newcomer's head. How different it would be today, and how pointless it all seems to me now as a source of personal pleasure! Today, my thirst is only quenched by the pristine drop seeping from the bedrock of the ideal – the hidden wellspring we all have inside us – but not by the grand fountains and aqueducts in the public square. At the time, however, any topic served my purpose for a speech. I spoke on the Navy and immigration, on public lighting and income tax, on leasing the Xingu Valley and direct elections. I had the speaker's heat, the movement, and the impulse. I ignored the "Is it worth while?" of the observer who restrains himself at every step. The public, the great audiences, were for me what my wastebasket is today or the flame that consumes one's superfluous intellectual outbursts. Only much later did I understand why those who preceded me shrank back, while I pressed forward. For many it was a sense of satiety, a hint of disgust. Some were trading their aspirations for another more utilitarian order of interests. For others, it was their conscience that was reaching maturity, a love of perfection. Of all the speeches credited to me in the Parliamentary Records of 1879 and 1880, I would not go to the trouble of salvaging a single one, except perhaps one or another that might contain some intimate, personal note. However, I would save those delivered in the Chamber during the momentous week in May 1888, and the ones at the Santa Isabel Theater in Recife in 1884 and 1885. They were the best speeches of my life.

When I say that the period leading up to 1879 was that of my political training, I only mean that it was the time when I acquired the tools for my subsequent political trade. Even so, the chronological limits are not all that precise, because it was in politics itself, in the Chamber, under the impact and determinism of the role I chose, that my true training took place, that is, in which the contradictions were reconciled, the outbursts and biases were suppressed, the essential affinities took shape, and the harmful inner frictions, vacillations, attractions, and repulsions were eliminated.

Once I knew my fate, this knowledge created my calling, and the job itself produced the means.

Indeed, when I entered the Chamber of Deputies I was entirely under the influence of English liberalism, as if I were following orders from Gladstone. This was essentially the result of my political education. I was an English liberal – with radical affinities, but with *Whig* loyalties – in the Brazilian Parliament. This definition fit me precisely throughout my career, because the English liberalism of Gladstone and Macaulay persisted in me forever as the irreversible vassalage of my political temperament or sensitivity. Meanwhile, after my first term, the partisan political trappings became secondary, subordinate, replaced by my human identification with the slaves, the personal characteristic in which and by which everything was shaped. In this sense, emancipation was the true formative change for me, that which merged the isolated or divergent elements from my imagination, the extremes of curiosity and intellectual sympathies, the contrasts, the antagonisms, the variations in sensitivities to truth and beauty that opposing systems tend to pit against each other, and shaped the mold in which not only my political aspiration was cast, but also my thinking and imagination, my very dreams and chimeras.

As I said before, however, my interest in the slaves dates back to my childhood. Perhaps it would be appropriate to tell this story now in these memoirs.

CHAPTER XX

MASSANGANA[63]

L IFE'S ENTIRE JOURNEY IS TRACED OUT in a childhood drawing that the man later forgets, but which he embraces forever, unknowingly. I for one have never transcended my first four or five impressions. My first eight years thus formed my definitive instinctive and moral background. I spent those early years, so remote and yet so present, on a sugarcane plantation in Pernambuco, my native province. The land was among the broadest and most picturesque in the Cabo area. This backdrop from my early childhood will never disappear from sight, as the last great yonder of my life. The populace of this little domain, entirely closed off to any outside interference, like all the other fiefdoms of slavery, consisted of slaves, distributed among the various quarters in the *senzala*, that great black pigeon coop next to the plantation house, and the tenants, bound to the landowner by grace of the mud-and-wattle shacks that sheltered them and the little crops he allowed them to plant on his property. In the center of the slave quarters stood the master's residence, looking out on the cane mills, and in the background there was a rise in the terrain with a chapel dedicated to St. Mathew. The sloping pasture was dotted here and there by trees whose impenetrable parasols shaded little herds of sleepy cattle. The cane fields extended out across the plain, traversed by a tortuous alameda of old *ingá* trees draped heavily with moss and vines, shading the little Ipojuca River from bank to bank. The sugar was shipped off to Recife from the broad white sandbars on this sluggish water. Near

---

63 The reason I decided not to begin this book with my childhood years is that when these pages were first published, they had a political air that they gradually lost, because even as I wrote them, politics was already losing its interest and appeal for me. The original idea was to write about my monarchist background and then expand on that to my literary political (or political literary) training. Finally, I intended to examine my human formation, so that the book would go hand-in-hand with another I had written on my religious reawakening. It was from the latter book, of a more intimate nature, composed in French seven years ago, that I now translate this chapter [into Portuguese] to explain the reference to my relationship to the slaves. Author's note.

the plantation house, the river fed a huge fishpond, famed for its abundant catches and surrounded by alligators, which the Negroes hunted. Still farther away began the mangroves that reached all the way to the coast at Nazaré. The sweltering afternoon heat brought naptime, with the ever-present aroma of molasses simmering in the great copper caldrons. The sunset was spectacular, turning vast stretches of the plain into gold dust. Dusk, the hour of the four-o'clocks and nighthawks, was pleasant and balmy, followed by the deep majestic silence of the starry skies. None of these impressions will ever die. Children of fishermen will always feel the sand scrape beneath their feet and hear the breakers roar in the distance. I can sometimes feel myself stepping on that thick carpet of crushed cane stalks surrounding the sugar mill and hear the far-off squeaking of the great wooden oxcarts...

Emerson believed that the child's education should begin a hundred years before his birth. My religious education certainly followed this rule. I feel the idea of God in the remotest part of myself, as a dear, loving sign passed down from many generations. On this particular, the chain was never broken. There are spirits who would break all their chains, preferably those that others have created for them. I, however, would be incapable of entirely breaking the smallest of the chains that once bound me, that helps me withstand the most vexing bondage, and all the more so since it was passed down to me as an inheritance. It was in the little chapel in Massangana that I was bound to my chain.

My lasting childhood impressions illustrate quite well how deeply our first foundations are laid. Ruskin wrote the following variant on Christ's thoughts concerning children: "Childhood often holds a truth with its feeble fingers, which the grasp of manhood cannot retain, which it is the pride of utmost age to recover."[64] The toys I held in my hands as a boy were all the symbolism of the religious dream. Among my recollections, I constantly find miniature images with such *avant la lettre* freshness that they must date back to these first selections of the soul. These indelible images are so perfect that one can only imagine the impression they made on me. Thus, although I later saw Michelangelo's creation in the Sistine Chapel and Raphael's in the *Loggie*, no matter how I ponder, neither gives

---

64 John Ruskin, *Modern Painters* [1847] (London , 1906), pp. xxxi-xxxii. T.N.

me the inner relief of the first paradise that passed before my eyes in a vestige of an old folk mystery. I later heard the lost notes of the *Angelus* in the Campagna Romana, but the inner *muezzin*, the peal that echoes in my ears at prayer time, is that of the little bells the slaves heard with their heads bowed, murmuring "Praise Be to Our Lord Jesus Christ". That is the inalterable Millet painted inside me. I have crossed the ocean many times in life, but if I wish to remember it, I can always summon before my eyes the instant image of the first wave that rose before me, green and transparent like an emerald curtain, on the day I crossed a huge coconut grove behind the raft fishermen's thatched huts and found myself on the beach, with the sudden, fulminating revelation of a liquid, moving earth. That wave, developed on the most sensitive plate of my little boy's retinal **Kodak**, became my everlasting embodiment of the sea. Only under such a picture would I dare to inscribe: *Thalassa! Thalassa!*[65]

Nearly all the shapes of my ideas and feelings date to that time. The grand impressions of adulthood lack the magic wand to make me relive them, unlike the little five or six-page notebook in which the first sketches of my soul appear as fresh as if they had been drawn this very morning. The enchantment of these scribbled, naïve childhood *eidoli* is simply a feeling that only they can preserve from our first erased sensations. They are the loose yet still-vibrant strings of an instrument that no longer exists inside us.

As with religion and nature, the same was true for the great moral facts around me. I plunged into the abolitionist movement, and for ten years I sought to extract from everything – from history, from science, from religion, from life – an argument that would convince the monarchy [to declare abolition]. I witnessed the slaves in all imaginable conditions. I read *Uncle Tom's Cabin* a thousand times, in the original living and bleeding pain. However, for me slavery will always be portrayed by one unforgotten childhood image, a first impression, which I am certain decided my life's subsequent direction. One afternoon I was sitting on the landing of the outside stairs to the house, when a young black man about eighteen, previously unknown to me, hurled himself upon me, clutching my feet, begging me, for the love of God, to have my godmother purchase him to

---

65 A reference to the cry of the Greek soldiers when they saw the Black Sea (*Thalassa! Thalassa!* The sea! the sea!) after their defeat by the Persians in 401 BC, as related by Xenophon in *Anabasis*. L.B.

serve me. He came from the vicinity, desperate to change masters, because his owner, as he told me, punished him mercilessly, and he had fled at the risk of his life. This unexpected turn of events unveiled to me the nature of an institution that I had always taken for granted, never suspecting the pain it concealed.

Nothing better than slavery itself demonstrates the grip of this initial feeling, so powerful that my determination and thinking never resisted its impact, and where I found no true respite except by giving in to it. I thus fought slavery with every breath. I repelled it with all my conscience, as a utilitarian deformation of human beings, and when I witnessed its demise, I believed I could also claim my own emancipation, proclaim my *nunc dimittis*, for having heard the most joyous tidings God could send to the world in my time. Yet today, now that slavery has been abolished, I experience a singular nostalgia, which would shock a Garrison or a John Brown: a longing for the slaves.

That is, both the master's side was unwittingly selfish, and the slave's side was unwittingly generous. Slavery will remain as Brazil's national trait for a long time to come. Across our vast hinterlands it spread a great gentleness, far and wide. Slavery gave the country's virgin nature its first and definitive shape. Like a natural, living religion, slavery peopled Brazil with its myths, legends, and spells. It filled the country with a childlike soul: sadness without grieving, tears without bitterness, silence without concentration, joy without reason, happiness with no worry for tomorrow. Slavery is the indefinable sigh that our nights of the North breathe to the moonlight. As for me, I absorbed slavery in the black milk that nursed me. It enveloped me like a mute caress throughout my childhood. I aspired to it in the dedication of the old servants who viewed me as the presumed heir to the tiny domain to which they belonged. There must have been a continuous exchange of sympathy between them and me that resulted in a tender and familiar admiration that I later came to feel for their role. In contrast with the mercenary instinct of our time, I saw their role as transcending the force of human nature, and on the day slavery was abolished I felt that one of the most absolute forms of neglect the human heart has ever shown would no longer find the conditions that had allowed it.

I cannot think back to slavery during my childhood without feeling an involuntary sorrow. Just as I felt it around me, it remains within me as the remembrance of a gentle yoke, the master's outer pride, but also the slave's inner pride, something like the dedication of an animal that never gets upset, because the ferment of inequality never affects it. I also fear that this particular kind of slavery only existed on a few very old plantations, administered for generation after generation with the same spirit of humanity, and where a long legacy of fixed relations between the master and the slaves had turned both into a sort of patriarchal tribe, isolated from the outside world. Such proximity between such unequal situations under the law would have been impossible in the newer, wealthier plantations of the South, where the slave, anonymous to the owner, was merely a harvest tool. The sugar mills of the North were mostly poor industrial enterprises, existing merely to preserve the master's status, whose importance and position were measured by the number of slaves he owned. Thus one also found there an aristocracy of manners that time later erased, a decency, a discretion on matters of profit, proper to classes who do not engage in trafficking.

I recently mentioned my godmother. Of all my childhood memories, that which eclipses all the others, and the dearest of all, is my love for the one who raised me as her son until I was eight. Her image, or her shadow, is so etched in my memory that I could turn it into an oil portrait if I had the least talent as a painter. She was massively corpulent, invalid, walking with great difficulty, constantly sitting – on a broad leather bench that the servants carried from one room to another in the house – next to the window that looked out on the sugar mill's main yard, with the stable, the corral, and the little house that had been built for my teacher and that served as my school. She always wore her widow's black mourning dress. My godfather, Joaquim Aurélio de Carvalho, had been famous in the province for his luxury and openhandedness, of which the local people tell various tales to this day. Even after so many years I can still picture the furniture in the vestibule where my godmother used to spend the day. On the walls were some colored engravings depicting the story of Inês de Castro,[66] between the birdcages with the famed *curiós*, the songbirds for which my godmother's deceased husband used to pay whatever price people asked. Next to her, a glass cabinet contained the little Portuguese editions of devotional books and the novellas of the time. My godmother always sat at the head of a huge work table, where she played cards, handed out the sewing and embroidering to the numerous servants, tasted the homemade sweets, examined the elixirs for the infirmary, distributed the silverware to her godchildren and protégés, and received the friends that flocked to her every week, attracted by her generous table and hospitality, always surrounded, adored by all her people, putting on a serious air that never fooled anybody when she had to scold some slave girl who had dropped her bobbins and lacework to prattle in the women's quarters, or some spendthrift tenant who had turned to her lending purse once too often. Her greatest joy was to exchange part of her surplus for gold doubloons, which she saved, unbeknownst to anyone except her freedman confidant Elias, to hand down to me when I came of age. She referred to this trust fund as her "invisible". When her most trusted servant died, she wrote the following hand-delivered letter to my mother:

> Good lady, I regret to inform you and my *compadre*[67] that my trusted Elias has died, and that he will be sorely missed in my business affairs. He took stock of everything, and always with an unparalleled goodness and humbleness. My house was always in order with him, as in my husband's time. He will be missed not only by me, but also by our little son, who loved him like no other. Although I have a family, I entrusted the lad to Elias, so that if I were to die he would be sure to deliver to you, good lady, the inheritance I left for the boy. But what can I do, if God has so willed it?

---

66 Inês Pérez de Castro (1325–55), Galician noblewoman, lover and posthumously declared lawful wife of King Pedro I of Portugal and thus Queen of Portugal. Inês came to Portugal at fifteen years of age as maid to Princess Constance of Castile, who was recently married to Prince Pedro, then heir to the Portuguese throne. The prince fell in love with Inês. Following the death of Constance in 1349, king Afonso IV first banned Inês from the court and then had her murdered. Pedro rebelled against his father, causing a civil war in Portugal in 1357. Pedro announced publicly that he had married Inês, thus making her the lawful queen. He had her body exhumed and forced the entire court to swear allegiance to her. Pedro and Inês are buried side by side at the Monastery of Alcobaça. The story of Inês de Casto is immortalized in numerous plays and poems, including 19 stanzas in Camões' *The Lusiads*. T.N.

67 Literally "co-father" or "co-parent", used as a form of respect, recognition, and affection to designate or address the biological father of one's godchild. Also used inversely by the biological parents to address their child's godparents. Thus Ana Rosa Falcão de Carvalho, Joaquim Nabuco's *madrinha* or godmother, would have been addressed as *comadre* or "co-mother" by his parents. T.N.

Later, in another letter, the last one I still have, she returns to the death of Elias:

> ... my Elias, whom I miss so sorely, as does my little [god]son, because he took such good care of him, and because of the parties the boy enjoyed so much and always went in his care. God grant me life and health until the boy has grown older, when I can give him something invisible. As your dear departed *compadre* used to say, we only had Elias for this mission, although he is survived by his brother Vítor, whom I also trust entirely.

Ah, dear and blessed memory! That treasure accumulated parcel by parcel never reached my hands, nor could it, as an inheritance lacking the necessary legal provisions, as perhaps thou[68] mightst have foreseen. And yet to imagine thee, year after year, in this pleasant task of thy elderly days, gathering together for thy godson – whomst thou hast called thy son – a nest egg to pass on to me when I came of age, or to entrust through others to my father, hadst thou died leaving me still a minor. To accompany thee in thy conversations with thy faithful servant, in this loving concern during thy last years, will always be such an indescribably sweet sensation that it alone wouldst suffice to wipe away any bitterness in life.

The night my godmother died is the black curtain that separates my childhood memories from the rest of my life. I was sleeping in my room with my old nanny when I awoke to litanies and moaning, announcing the terror that had gripped the house. In the hall, tenants, freedmen, and slaves were kneeling in prayer, weeping and wailing. It was the sincerest consternation one could imagine, the scene of a shipwreck. This entire little world had taken shape for two or three generations around a center that no longer existed after her. My godmother's dying breath had shattered that world to pieces. To change masters was the most terrible thing that could happen in bondage, especially if the ownership was to pass from a saintly old woman, who by then was nothing more than a nurse to her slaves, to the hands of a strange family. And as with the slaves, so, too, for the tenants, the poor, all the *gens* she supported, to whom she distributed the daily rations, the succor, and the medicines. I too had to leave Massangana, for my godmother had bequeathed the plantation to another heir, her

---

68 Nabuco employs the archaic second person singular in this paragraph as if to address his godmother directly, as a sign of affection and respect. T.N.

nephew and neighbor. She left me one of her other sugar mills, with a dead fire,[69] that is, with no slaves to work it. To this day I can still picture what seems like the day after her death, with the new owner's oxcarts arriving. It was my ousting… I was eight years old. My father soon sent for me through an old friend, coming from Rio de Janeiro. I parceled out all my belongings among the people of the house, including my horse, the animals I had been given, and my personal items. "The boy is happier now," wrote the friend who came to escort me to my father, "since I assured him his nanny would be going with him."[70] What grieved me the most was to part ways with those who had protected me in my childhood, who had served me with the same dedication they showed my godmother, and above all, among them, the slaves who literally dreamed that they belonged to me after she died. I felt all too harshly the counterblow of their dashed hopes on the day they wept, as they watched me leave, despoiled – perhaps they thought – of my ownership over them. Who knows, perhaps for the first time they felt all the bitterness of their plight, tasting the dregs.

A month and a half after my godmother died, I thus left my lost paradise, but belonged to it forever. That was where my innocent little hands dug the unfathomably tiny well of childhood that refreshes life's desert, making it an eternally enticing oasis. The parts of my being that I have acquired, and that I owe to various influences, are sure to scatter in different directions. However, what I received directly from God – my true inner self, crafted by His hands – will be bound forever to that piece of ground wherein lies she who gave me my start in life. Thanks to her the world received me with such a sweet smile that all the tears imaginable would never make me forget it. Massangana survived as the seat of my innermost oracle: to impel me, to hold me, and to be precise, to retrieve me, the voice, the sacred flutter, would always come from there. *Mors omnia solvit…* death dissolves all things, except love, which it binds forever.

---

69 Refers to defunct sugar mills, with no slaves to stoke the fires for boiling the cane juice down into sugar and molasses. The same term, *Fogo morto* ("dead fire"), later became the title for a novel in 1943 by José Lins do Rego Cavalcanti (1901–57), a native of the neighboring Northeastern state of Paraíba. T.N.

70 Gilberto Freyre, in his classic *Casa grande & senzala* (1933), refers to this passage and the importance of Nabuco's testimony for his own study of patriarchal society in Brazil: "When his godmother died, that 'scene of shipwreck' which he has evoked in the most deeply moving passage of his book, his one great consolation was the old Negro nurse who continued to serve him as before… On this subject, the relations of white children with their 'Negro mammies', the personal data I was able to obtain through interviews with distinguished survivors of the slave-holding regime serve to confirm the statements of Joaquim Nabuco and Sílvio Romero." Quoted here from the English translation by Samuel Putnam, *The Masters and the Slaves: a study in the development of Brazilian Civilization*, New York, 1946, pp. 371–72. T.N.

Twelve years later I returned to visit the little St. Mathew's chapel where my godmother, Dona Ana Rosa Falcão de Carvalho, was laid to rest in the wall next to the altar, and through the tiny abandoned sacristy I entered the little fenced-in graveyard where the slaves were buried. Crosses, which may no longer exist, on mounds of stones hidden by the nettles, were nearly all that remained of the opulent *fábrica*, as the plantation's body of slaves was called. Below, on the plain, the great green sugarcane fields glistened as ever in the sun, but the mill now huffed and whistled with a new steam, announcing a new life. The old *almanjarra*, the great wooden wheel turned by yoked oxen to crush the sugarcane, had vanished. Free labor had replaced most of the slave labor. On the side of the river "port", the sugar mill had the appearance of a settlement. Not a trace was left of the plantation house. The sacrifice of the poor Negroes who had incorporated their lives into the future of that property no longer existed, except perhaps in my memory. Beneath my feet lay all that was left of them, in front of the narrow chapel's vaults wherein slept those they had loved and freely served. Alone, I invoked all my memories, called out to many by their names, breathed in the air laden with scents exuded by the wildflowers on their graves, the breath that filled their hearts and inspired their unfailing joy. It was thus that the moral problem of slavery was laid out for the first time before my eyes in all its clarity and with its obligatory solution. Not only had these slaves never complained of their mistress, they had blessed her to the end. The gratitude was on the side of those that expressed it. They had died believing themselves debtors. Their affection would not have allowed the slightest suspicion that the master might have some obligation towards them, those who belonged to him. There, God protected the slave's heart, like that of a faithful animal, from contact with anything that might cause him to rebel against his sense of dedication. The slaves' spontaneous forgiveness of the master's debt struck me as the amnesty for countries that had grown up in slavery, the means for escaping one of the worst retaliations in history. Oh, the black saints! They would be the ones to intercede for our miserable land, which they drenched with their blood, but blessed with their love! These thoughts all raced through my mind as I stood among those graves, all of them sacred to me, and thus, right there, at twenty years of age, I resolved to devote my life, if I should be granted to do so, to the service of this most generous of races, among all those whose unequal condition had made them gentle rather than bitter, and through their sweetness in suffering, lent a spark of goodness even to the oppression they endured.

CHAPTER XXI

ABOLITION

W HEN THE ABOLITIONIST CAMPAIGN was launched, there were still nearly two million slaves in Brazil, and their children under eight years of age and all those still unborn, as *ingênuos*,[71] were subject to a regime that was the equivalent of bondage until the age of 21. This was the immense stone block I attacked in 1879, in the belief that I might spend my entire life without completely sculpting it. Ten years later only dust remained. The outcome had many causes. First was the historical period in which the idea was launched. Humankind was too advanced for anyone to still defend slavery in principle, as they had done in the United States. The Latin race lacks such courage. The feeling of being the last nation with slaves humiliated us, tarnished our sense of pride and emulation as a new people. Next, there was the weakness and gentleness of the Brazilian national character, to which the slaves had contributed with their kindness, as had slavery itself with its easy-going nature. On this point, suffice it to compare slavery in Brazil and the United States. In Brazil, slavery was a melting of the races. In the United States, it was a war between them. Our owners emancipated their slaves by the hundreds rather than banding together to lynch the abolitionists, like the Kentucky breeders and the Louisiana planters. The abolitionist cause exerted its seduction on youth, the press, and democracy. It was a categorical imperative for judges and priests. It had deep affinities with the workers and the army, recruited preferentially among men of color. It acted like a dissolvent on the mass of

71 According to the Rio Branco law of 28 September 1871 newborn children of slaves were thenceforth defined as *ingênuos*, or "freeborn", but the same law stipulated that they would remain with their masters until they reached the age of eight at which point they could be freed provided compensation were paid or remain in semi-slavery until the the age of twenty-one, prompting Nabuco to denounce that "every year , slave women give birth to thousands of *slaves for twenty-one years* to their owners. By a legal fiction, they are born *free*, but in fact under the same law they are worth 600 *milreis* each at *eight years of age*. A slave woman born on 27 September can give birth in 1911 to one of these *ingênuos*, who will thus remain in provisional bondage until 1932." *O Abolicionismo* [1883] Petrópolis, 1988. T.N.

the political parties, whose rivalries it challenged on grounds of the honor it could bestow on the statesmen who embraced it. Meanwhile, the cause inspired the dynasty itself to the indispensable sacrifice for success.

Five different acts or factors contributed jointly to the final outcome: 1) the motor force of the spirits that created opinion through ideas, words, feelings, through the Parliament, *meetings*, the press, the universities, the church pulpits, the courts; 2) the coercive action of those who proposed to materially destroy the formidable apparatus of slavery, snatching the slaves from their owners' power; 3) the complementary action of the owners themselves, who loosened their resistance as the movement advanced, releasing their slaves in droves; 4) the political action of the statesmen, representing the government's concessions; and 5) the monarchy's action.

The first two categories formed concentric circles consisting largely of the same members. The bulk of the Abolitionist Party, the leaders of the movement, belonged to these circles. A keener judge than myself would be needed to place each figure on the level he deserves, with his respective importance. Having witnessed each of the veterans in this campaign, in the struggle and effort, I could never forgive myself for the slightest involuntary injustice to any of them. Profound disagreements separated me from many of them after the victory, but the spirit of impartiality I harbor for each of them is still based on the loyalty I believed to have maintained intact during abolition for all those who aided it, from the first to the eleventh hour. Nor will I include a special tribute to any of the large Brazilian landowners in this list. However, among the political leaders, I can highlight three statesmen who made decisive contributions to the movement at different times: Dantas, who first placed at the campaign's service one of the country's constitutional parties, namely the Liberal Party, a contribution on the order of that made by Gladstone to the Irish cause; Antônio Prado, who removed São Paulo's veto against abolition, thus breaking what had previously been solid resistance by the South, the wealthiest part of the country; and João Alfredo, who led the Conservative Party to submit the bill for immediate elimination of slavery, a highly daring act even at the time, and which due to the general political atmosphere and disposition could only have been proposed by it. I would also include José Bonifácio, whose adherence to the idea was an event equal to the liberation of [slaves in] Ceará, Cristiano Ottoni, Silveira da Motta, and others in the front line of antislavery propagandists.

It is nearly impossible for me to speak about abolition now except by quoting outstanding incidents and figures. Everything I say is subject to the proviso that I would have much more to say. When I utter a name, it is only one in a long history. The ranks were full on all sides. Who could write the history of his contemporaries impartially, fairly, and completely, unaffected by political passion, sectarian bias, or personal sympathy and friendship? No one, of course, which means that various histories will be written in the future. I inevitably contribute to the subject based on my own memory and through some fragments of certain facts in which I was involved or of which I had direct knowledge. I only hope that God may grant me the time and means for this task, to discharge this duty as my personal testimony, as planned. It would be a sort of key to the period that drew an end to the monarchist era.

Among those with whom I worked most closely in 1879 and 1880, and who formed a homogeneous group with me, our own little congregation, the principal figures were André Rebouças, Gusmão Lobo, and Joaquim Serra. The adjoining congregation was that of José do Patrocínio, Ferreira de Meneses, Vicente de Sousa, Nicolau Moreira, and later João Clapp with the Abolitionist Confederation. If I were writing at this moment on the work by the abolitionist movement from 1879 to 1888, I would already have mentioned Jerônimo Sodré, who was the first to pronounce the *fiat*, and I would cite my fellow Deputies in the Chamber: Manoel Pedro, Correa Rabello, Sancho de Barros Pimentel, and others, because the movement began in the Chamber in 1879, and not as has been claimed in the *Gazeta da Tarde* of Ferreira de Meneses, dating it to 1880, nor in the *Gazeta de Notícias*, where José do Patrocínio was then writing the weekly political section, always supporting us, but still without having guessed his mission. Of course Luís Gama and others had already been working for the slaves even before the 1871 act, as did all those who helped pass this law. However, the abolitionist movement of 1879 to 1888 had its own line, its own distinct background, whose beginning and pace are easy to verify. It was a fluvial system in which the headwaters, volume of water and the value of each tributary, the falls, the rapids, and the estuary are all known, and this movement began, without a doubt, with the speech by Jerônimo Sodré in 1879 in the Chamber. The speech was prepared in Bahia and struck the Chamber like a burst of water, suddenly. There had been absolutely no hint of it. Jerônimo Sodré's act relates chronologically to my stance several days later. Rebouças, Patrocínio, Gusmão Lobo, Meneses, and Joaquim Serra joined later. This is not meant to date the first abolitionist writings by each of these protagonists. Mine, for example, dated back to law school. It means to claim for the Chamber of Deputies, for Parliament, the initiative that some have attempted to deny it on this issue, crediting it to the grassroots, republican element. It is purely a matter of dates. As long as one has the proper date for each fact, one will verify the above-mentioned *autem genuit*. I acknowledge that in the order of events, my name comes after that of Jerônimo Sodré. The others, however, came after mine.

Perhaps it was the grassroots movement that nourished the parliamentary seed, not allowing it to die in the subsequent sessions, but the fact that the seed came from Parliament, that the *liber generationis* began in 1879 with Jerônimo Sodré, can be proven by the documents themselves, even those that intended to prove the opposite, as long as they are authentic. After all, the issue of who took the first initiative is entirely secondary, especially since the idea was in the air and the spirit of time agitated it everywhere. Nothing is more difficult than to assess the relative importance of the various factors in what has become a nationwide movement. The last of the apostles can become the first of all, like St. Paul, in both service and conversion. Everything in abolition was interconnected, and one cannot write its history while eliminating any of its links. A fact that should be remembered is that the compensations always far outweighed the setbacks, and thus the latter even favored the cause. Thus, when Ferreira de Meneses died, Patrocínio took over the *Gazeta da Tarde*. The abolitionist minority of 1879 was not reelected, but the Abolitionist Confederation emerged. When Ceará completed its work, Amazonas launched its own. When the president of a province (Teodureto Souto) was dismissed, a president of the Council (Dantas) was named. When the police crackdown was organized, the agitation began in the Army. The abuses committed against slaves in Paraíba do Sul and Cantagalo were followed by the struggle in Cubatão.[72] When José Bonifácio died, Antônio Prado took his place in São Paulo. When

---

72 There was intense abolitionist activity in the Baixada Santista on the coast of São Paulo, including Cubatão, with the formation of *quilombos*, or havens of escaped slaves. Various clashes with the police led to numerous casualties R.S.

the Chamber repelled José Mariano, Recife defeated the Minister of the Empire. When the Liberal Party wavered, the Conservative Party moved. When the Emperor left, the Princess stayed. In the end, nobody knows who did more for abolition, whether the propaganda or the resistance, whether those who wanted everything or those who wanted nothing. Nothing is more illusory than sharing the laurels. Legends will always survive, like rays of light in the accumulated darkness of the past, but their beauty lies not in their truth, which is always limited, but in humankind's effort to retain some episodes of a life so vast that no memory can possibly encompass it.

I can only give some random impressions, and I am thus not embarrassed if I skip some names that should be included in any summary of the abolitionist propaganda, no matter how brief. The two groups I mentioned met, worked together, and mingled, but the dividing line was clear: one represented political action, the other revolutionary action, although they occasionally reflected their mutual influences. This was at the time in which the idea was being launched, because the movement soon became widespread, when the provinces joined in, with Ceará, Amazonas, Rio Grande do Sul, Pernambuco, Bahia, and São Paulo emerging as propaganda hotbeds. The abolitionist movement did in fact have two quite distinct periods: the first, from 1879 to 1884, in which the abolitionists struggled alone, confined to their own resources, and the second, from 1884 to 1888, in which they saw their cause adopted successively by the country's two main parties. The Liberal Party converted to the cause in 1884 and the Conservative Party in 1888. The campaign's purely abolitionist phase was the former, as opposed to the political phase, which could just as well enter the history of the two rival parties.

Of all the abolitionists, the one with whom I established a veritable communion of feeling was André Rebouças. My life and that of Rebouças were one for ten years. For a long time, our friendship was the fusion of two lives in a single thought: emancipation. Rebouças embodied, like no one else among us, the antislavery spirit: the entire, systematic, absolute spirit, sacrificing everything, without exception, that was contrary to it or suspect, not being content with tackling the issue from one side, but considering it from all sides, *triangulating* it, according to one of his favorite expressions, socially, morally, and economically. The people saw no great gift in Rebouças in terms of his speech, style, or actions. It might be said that in a movement headed by orators, journalists, and popular agitators, there was no outstanding role for him. Nevertheless, his job was the most important of all. Characterized by strictly internal psychological action, it involved the most essential (though hidden) function of the motor force, providing inspiration to all. He almost never appeared in the foreground, but all those in the public eye looked to him, felt his influence, and were governed by his gestures, which remained invisible to the crowd, knowing that only he had the conscience to solve all the problems in the cause, only he entered the burning bush and saw the Almighty face to face. It is as impossible for me to sum him up in one stroke as to draw an infinitely long line. After abolition, he always felt a foreboding that slavery would bring some terrible misfortune on the monarchy, as it had caused Lincoln's assassination. His greatest love was perhaps for his students at the Polytechnic, but all his memories of "the School" turned into so many other torments when he witnessed them singing praise to November 15, which he interpreted as revenge for May 13![73]

From his room in the Bragança Hotel in Petrópolis, where for years he recorded our common pulse in his diary, to the cliff at Funchal, what a line André Rebouças drew! He was the courtier of *Alagoas*,[74] a republican to whom fell the role – at that bitter moment – of beloved disciple to the old, exiled Emperor. Rebouças was a man of industry, a bold and successful engineer, who ended up practicing Tolstoyism. He was a mathematical genius, an alchemist who reduced all his science into a serpentine coil in which he distilled abolition from everything. His center of gravity was truly sublime. Nor can I speak of him in relation to me, because that would give an incomplete picture. I prefer to describe him in relation to the Emperor. The following is one of his quick self-portraits, where those who knew him will recognize his countenance, with all the mobility of his expression and inalterable human affection. I found this letter by chance:

---

73 André Rebouças, Joaquim Nabuco and various other abolitionists, especially those who were monarchists, partially interpreted the proclamation of the Republic on November 15 1889 as an attempt to regroup the pro-slavery forces and/ or as revenge against the monarchy for having abolished slavery on May 13 1888. This was not exactly the case with the students at the Polytechnic School, but Rebouças believed that their adherence to the Republic had the effect of encouraging pro-slavery or anti-monarchist groups. R.S.

74 *Alagoas* was the ship on which Rebouças accompanied Emperor Dom Pedro II when the latter departed Brazil into exile on November 17 1889. T.N.

Cannes, May 13, 1892.
My master and Emperor,

The third anniversary of the Liberation of the African Race in Brazil will not pass without André Rebouças having born witness, once again, to his filial gratitude for the sublime martyr of abolition.

I feel fortunate for having been chosen by the Good Lord to represent the devotion of the African Race to Your Imperial Majesty and to the Princess Redeemer, which I take joy in repeating unceasingly.

It is now gratifying to recall the *synthesis* of our life, as my good master said on the *Alagoas* when we celebrated your 64th birthday.

It all began in Petrópolis, in 1850, 41 years ago, studying arithmetic when I was still a schoolboy, and continued almost daily in the lessons and exams at the Military, Central, and Preparatory Schools at the fort in Praia Vermelha until December 1860.

The years 1861 and 1862 were devoted to practical studies of the European railways and ports. The first *Treatise*, written with Antônio and dated Marseilles, June 9, 1861, was dedicated, and rightly so, to our good master and Emperor. Whenever Your Majesty would meet our father, your first words were, 'How are the boys? Where are they now? Remind them to always study and work hard.'

We returned to Brazil in late 1862 and launched into practical life with the military construction projects in Santa Catarina, in the wake of the *Christie* incident.[75] On December 28, 1863, I parted ways for the first time with my brother Antônio. The industrial phase of my life began from that point onward.

Your Majesty and my father did not want me to follow any inclination beyond my tranquil life of science and teaching, but the Viscount of Itaboraí, who also treated me with fatherly devotion, said, 'André! I want you to succeed Mauá!'

Your Majesty knows all too well how I suffered with the petty political oligarchy and slave-owning plutocracy of those toilsome times. I now have only one consolation, that I planned and built the Pedro II Docks, designed and headed the Conde d'Eu Railway and its beautiful Cabedelo maritime station.

Your Majesty enjoys recalling that together in Uruguaiana, thanks to our aversion to bloodshed, we saved seven thousand Paraguayans and hundreds of Brazilians. With my current aversion to militarism, I only remember the projects in Itapiru and Tuiuti.

75 On December 31 1862, following several minor incidents involving British sailors, the British minister William Dougall Christie declared a blockade of the port of Rio de Janeiro and the seizure of several Brazilian ships. In January 1863 the Brazilian government broke off diplomatic relations with Britain – which were only restored in September 1865. L.B.

The abolitionist propaganda began in 1880. We, the inflamed orators, had only one certainty and one hope: the Emperor. In 1871 Your Majesty had granted your favorite daughter the role of freeing the newborn slaves, with Paranhos, Viscount of Rio Branco.

In 1888 the initiative came from her, who could no longer stand to see the tears or hear the sobs of the poor, the misfortunate, the slaves, in the holy love of the martyr of original Christianity, aspiring less to glory on Earth than yearning for worthiness in heaven, next to Jesus, Redeemer of redeemers.

In a word, I believe that we can faithfully await God's judgment, because we have kept his greatest commandment by toiling for the progress of humankind.

Now, all that remains to say is that since November 15, 1889, I have lost the dividing line between my father and my master and Emperor, and that I sign with the greatest outpouring of love, from the bottom of my heart, **André Rebouças**.

Consider also the following route that he drew up for me, for slaves to escape from São Paulo to the North, a pure figment of his imagination, but so full – for all of us – of the traces of his originality, touches of his almost impersonal generous sensitivity:

UNDERGROUND RAILROAD from the UPPER SÃO FRANCISCO VALLEY TO FREE CEARÁ

First stop: São Paulo, next to the tomb of Luís Gama.

Second stop: Pirassununga.

Third stop: Cachoeira de Moji-Guaçu.

Fourth stop. In the high hinterlands, headed towards the Northeast; the sun should rise on the right and set in late afternoon on the left.

Fifth stop. Piumhi, headwaters of the São Francisco, always following the banks of that beautiful river, full of fish and lined with delicious fruit trees.

Sixth stop. On one side, free Goiás, on the other, the hinterlands of Bahia, where there are no slave hunters.

Seventh stop. At Vila da Barra, where the great waterfalls of the São Francisco begin.

Eighth stop. At the portage trail between the São Francisco and Parnaíba Rivers.

Ninth stop. In Paradise: Free Ceará.

Mathematician and astronomer, botanist and geologist, industrialist and moralist, hygienist and philanthropist, poet and philosopher, Rebouças was perhaps the only native-born Brazilian who was universal in both spirit and the heart. We have others who are universal in spirit and others in the heart, but only he was capable of reflecting the universality of both knowledge and human sentiments. Perhaps he was the reflection that broke the mirror! "Standing ovation from my students," he wrote in his diary on May 15, 1888. "I had announced my project for a Moral Triangulation and Census of Brazil. Vote of praise from the student body. Another ovation. Carried on my students' shoulders all around the courtyard."[76] He was the greatest of all in the abolitionist movement, not because of his outward action or direct influence on the movement, but because of the force and stature of his intelligence, the dizzying sweep of ideas and sensations around the burning, all-consuming axis, which for him was the slaves' suffering. It was a cosmic fire burning inside him. If Rebouças was viewed in his own time as a star of the second order, it was because he was far ahead of all the others. Among the evangelists of our good tidings, he had the eagle's keen eyesight. Much of his style and temperament reminded one of St. John. An idealist to the core, he wrote almost entirely through symbols. The island of Madeira was the Pathmos of a revelation unfortunately lost, because he wrote his final pages facing the South and seeing the stars and constellations as if they were letters.[77] Yet his legend survives, and there is no danger that it will be forgotten: that of his exile and friendship with Dom Pedro II.

I also collaborated closely and exchanged views with Joaquim Serra. From 1880 until abolition he never let a day pass without a few lines on the subject. Wracked by a merciless illness, each morning he salvaged enough happiness to smile with the hope of the slaves, which he saw grow day by day during those ten years, like a delicate plant he himself had cultivated. When abolition was a fact, when the flower blossomed, he died. And what a death! What sorrow for his wife and two children, his beloved little daughter who did not want to leave his side for a minute!

76 The "Moral Triangulation and Census of Brazil" is a metaphor for the need to survey, open up, and settle the country's territory, with a particular emphasis on small farms, following the moral imperative of eliminating slavery. Rebouças was extremely popular with his students at the Polytechnic School, and all the more so just two days after abolition. R.S.

77 An allegorical comparison between the island of Madeira, where in 1898 Rebouças, in profound depression and looking South toward Brazil, committed suicide by jumping off a cliff, and the island of Pathmos in the Aegean Sea, where St. John the Evangelist is believed to have written the Book of Revelation. T.N

Serra fulfilled his task with unswerving dedication and discipline, never missing a day, and with a perfect spirit of abnegation and loyalty. Shunning the limelight, he nevertheless demonstrated an increasingly keen vision and clear expression worthy of a true leader. I myself, believing that I knew him well, was surprised by his daring maneuver when he once promised all our hope to the Baron of Cotegipe – we answered for each other – if the Baron would make concessions to the movement. Unlike Rebouças, Serra was a political spirit, but above his party, in which he had been the lowliest aide during the opposition, and promoted our common cause with an inner sincerity beyond all suspicion. "The great Joaquim Serra has passed away," wrote Rebouças in his diary on October 29, 1888, "my law classmate in 1854 and comrade in the abolitionist struggle from 1880 to 1888, the propagandist who wrote most extensively against the slave-owners." "No one contributed *more* than he," wrote Gusmão Lobo following his death, "and who did so *much*?"

Gusmão Lobo was another figure from our inner circle. Some of those who struggled together tirelessly during the first five years of the campaign, which were the years of political and social ostracism for the cause, realized that their task was greatly relieved, but not complete, on the day when a great party in government, with its cadres, its influence, its constituency, its press, took up the cause for which they had been the only supporters until then. Among these was Gusmão Lobo, who would not have laid down his pen in the struggle if he had not seen the banner that protected it pass triumphantly from the hands of the agitators to those of the Presidents of the Council. But at the turning point in the movement, that in which the impetus had to be created to make it stronger than the resistance, that is, in which the campaign was virtually won, his contribution was inestimable. He alone filled the *Jornal do Commércio* with news on emancipation in the editorial column, where he used all sorts of skills, artifices, and subtleties, and thanks to the good will of Luís de Castro, succeeded in focusing constant attention on the issue. His talented writing style – graceful, perfect, prismatic, one of the most beautiful and spontaneous of our time – was truly inexhaustible. He found a solution to everything, he had the resources and the finesse, and he had the art of expression. All his work was anonymous and thus might have gone unnoticed by subsequent generations without the unanimous testimony of those who worked with him. He played an awesome variety of roles in the press, and his presence and advice were priceless in our meetings and later within the confines of the Dantas cabinet. His name was inscribed on the walls of all the catacombs in which nascent abolitionism lived its first five years, like a tiny persecuted church, but it appeared less and less as the new faith became an official religion. It was one of the riddles or our time – a national riddle, because it was linked to the issue of the rapid withering of the country's entire flower – namely, how such a talent could later suddenly forego all ambition.

I do not mean to list the hall of fame of abolition, but since nostalgia has already made me provide two or three sketchy biographies of friends, I will also pay my tribute to José do Patrocínio. He represented the revolutionary spirit which – together with the liberal spirit and the government spirit – brought abolition about, but which was stronger than they and ended up absorbing and dominating them. Without the government spirit of men like Dantas, Antônio Prado, and João Alfredo, a peaceful solution would not have been reached, and not as soon. Without the humanitarian spirit, free of hatred and political tendencies, abolition would have degenerated into a war between the races or a clash between factions. Without the varied, inestimable work of each of the provinces, writing their own pages in History, like Ceará with João Cordeiro, São Paulo with Antônio Bento, and Pernambuco with João Ramos, all these individual names representing collective groups, the result would have been different and perhaps disastrous. Yet Patrocínio represented the *fatum*, the movement's irresistible thrust. He was a mixture of Spartacus and Camille Desmoulins. Those who struggled only against slavery were like the liberals of 1789, blind men of good will, merely the volunteers that revolutions employ to open the first breach in the wall. Patrocínio was the revolution itself. If, on the day after the triumph of abolitionism, the movement scattered and part of it joined the large landowners against the monarchy (which the movement had urged to make the sacrifice), it was because the spirit that roused it most deeply was the revolutionary spirit that a stunned society allowed to slip into the first crack in its foundations. Patrocínio was the essence of his time and in a certain sense its most representative figure.

CHAPTER XXII

NATURE OF THE ABOLITIONIST MOVEMENT; AND THE MONARCHY'S ROLE

ABOLITION WOULD HAVE HAD A DIFFERENT MORAL SCOPE if it had been launched from the altar, preached from the pulpit, pursued by successive generations of the clergy and educators of the conscience. Unfortunately, the revolutionary spirit had to complete a task in a few years that had been neglected for a century. In order to please God, a great social reform requires that the reformer's soul be purified first. These are the first fruits he struggles for, with his eye on the prize. Even for the most noble and beautiful undertakings, it makes a great difference whether we pursue them with the spirit of true Christian charity or merely devote to them a kind of personal stimulus that secular morals refer to as love for humankind. The reformer never triumphs, based entirely on the concept of justice that his proposal contains. The outcome of the victory depends on the degree of charity that inspires the germination. Politics is the art of choosing the seeds, while religion is that of preparing the earth.

The antislavery movement in Brazil was humanitarian and social rather than religious. It thus lacked the moral depth of the abolitionist movement in New England, for example. It was a party comprised of heterogeneous elements, capable of destroying a social state built on privilege and injustice, but not of planning the future building on new foundations. Naturally, the task thus ended with the elimination of slavery. The movement's triumph might have been followed, as it indeed was, by political upheavals, even revolutions, but not by complementary social measures in favor of the freed slaves, and never by an inner impulse to renew the public conscience and expand the stunned noble instincts. Freedom itself is fertile, and in time a more just society will be built on the ruins of slavery, with more open ideas. Furthermore, this new society may claim, as its founders, those who merely stopped the oppression previously ruling over births, the sighs that signaled the appearance of one more social stratum in Brazil. However, the truth is that the abolitionist movement stopped on the day abolition was decreed and retreated the day after.

During the abolitionist campaign, during one of the elections in which I ran for office, a slave, who had appeared to be happy and contented, committed suicide on a plantation in Cantagalo. The mistress told me years later that in his last dying words, when they asked him why he had taken his life, or whether he had some grievance, he replied to the owner that he did not, but that he only wanted to kill himself because I had not been elected Deputy. I am convinced that if a fair and clean referendum had been held, the black race would have spared their defenders the slightest displeasure, and that deep down, when they think of the early morning hours of November 15, they still somewhat regret their May 13. They could not have experienced such generosity and dedication without having been affected by it. On the side of the monarchy, which had a throne to offer, no one who took part in emancipation will ever regret it. One does not regret the emancipation of a race, the immediate transformation of the fate of a million and a half human lives with all the prospects that freedom promises for future generations. There are no ungrateful races. "Mr. Rebouças," said the Imperial Princess on board the *Alagoas* that took them together into exile, "if there were still slaves in Brazil, we would return to free them."

Alas, the monarchy fell, and many things followed that might cause me to think back with some regret on all those years of perfect illusion. But no, that was the way it had to be. The consequences, the deviations, and the strange and alien aberrations cannot tarnish the perfect beauty of a task completed, can no longer alter the course of a historical cycle, once ended. The day the Imperial Princess decided on her grand stroke of humanity, she was fully aware of the risks at stake. The race she was about to liberate had nothing to give her except its blood, and she did not want that blood to guarantee the throne for her son. The entire slave-owning class threatened to adhere to the Republic, her father was reported to be dying in Milan, a change was likely in the reign during the crisis, and she did not hesitate: an inner voice told her to fulfill her mission, a divine voice that makes itself heard whenever a great duty needs to be met or a great sacrifice accepted. If the monarchy could survive, abolition would be its endowment; if it succumbed, it would be its will and testimony. When a person, especially a woman, has the ability to do a great universal deed, like emancipation, she should not balk in the face of forebodings. Her duty is to deliver herself entirely into God's hands. And who knows? The impression – when ones looks back from posterity, from the historical perspective – is that the monarchy's national role had been too beautiful to last forever, uninterrupted. There are no vast spaces for happiness in human things. If the historical thrust had been prolonged, it would have ended in a disastrous demise. This dynasty had only three names. The founder led the independence of the young American country, dismembering the old European monarchy to which he was heir. His son, at fifteen years of age, found the Empire weakened by anarchy, ripped apart by the tip of the Rio Grande, and founded national unity on such a strong basis that the Paraguay War tested it and left it immune to any domestic or foreign pressure, and did all this without touching the country's political freedoms for fifty years, as a *noli me tangere*. Finally, his daughter virtually renounced the throne to hasten the liberation of the last slaves. Each reign, counting the regency of the princess as the embryo of a reign, was a new national coronation: the first, that of the state; the second, that of the nation; and the third, that of the people. The column was thus perfect and harmonious: the base, the shaft, and the capital. My spirit tends to take the definitive point of view. From this perspective, November 15 was not a fall, but a rise. By a stroke of fate, the Brazilian monarchy was snatched away before its decline began, before it ran the risk of forgetting its tradition. Of course the Emperor's exile was sad, but it also gave his figure the majesty in which it is now cloaked. No, nothing can make me look back on my activist phase in politics with any feeling other than the most perfect gratitude. I owe the dynasty no reparation. I set no trap for it. In the humble role that befell me, what I did was beckon the monarchy to the glory, immortality, and perfection of its place in History. No one can claim that the monarchy would not have fallen if it had turned its back on abolition. At any rate, abolition was its duty, and it received the glory for the act. It released us of our debt...[78]

What would have become of the Brazilian monarchist legend if the Republic and Abolition had been proclaimed on the same day? Indeed, I owe and will always owe the monarchy infinite gratitude for May 13, but never reparation for a harm I did not cause.

---

[78] In the original: "*deu-nos quitação*", literally "gave us remission", in the sense that by proclaiming abolition on May 13 1888, the monarchy released Brazil from its historical debt to the slaves. T.N.

CHAPTER XXIII

MY PASSAGE THROUGH POLITICS

O H, WHAT GOOD THINGS I RECEIVED in those years of struggle for the slaves! How the sacrifices I inspired were greater than my own! I had the fame, the rostrum, and the political career. True, I received no other compensation, but that was the best a young man could hope for if he was avid for fame and the sensations of triumph. It was my name that emerged victorious from the ballot boxes in those elections that electrified the entire country's liberal spirits, bringing me blessings from afar from the old *Quakers* of the *Anti-Slavery Society*, and even good wishes from Gladstone on one occasion. Yet those who contributed to the victory were fated to vanish in the anonymous list of the forgotten. The names of even the main protagonists failed to echo outside the province. Amongst them, only José Mariano was known nationwide and considered the electoral arbiter of Recife. But who knew Antônio Carlos Ferreira da Silva, then just a lowly company bookkeeper in Recife, but who nevertheless guaranteed all my elections on the abolitionist platform? He was the true spirit that moved everything in my favor. Everything would have taken a different direction without him. This is the best proof of the spontaneous, natural, popular nature of my successful elections in Recife, namely, that it sufficed to have a man like him, sincere, dedicated, intelligent, loyal, skillful, with all his heart and enthusiasm (under the mask of a cold misfit), but with no position in society, no fortune, no political status, no party strings, a simple abolitionist, never appearing in public, and to top it off, a self-professed republican. This fact alone demonstrates the sincerity, the modesty, and the naiveté of the entire movement of

1884–1888. He was my advocate. The many people who contributed to the success of the common cause, or to my personal triumph, as occurred with so many, will understand my feeling when at least once I reveal the secret of my relationship with Recife, saying that Antônio Carlos, who was nothing and did not want to be anything, was the true author. I have not forgotten anyone, beginning with Dantas, who practically forced me to go north to claim one of the voting districts in the Pernambuco. Of course I could never forget Ermírio Coutinho and Joaquim Francisco Cavalcanti, both of whom dropped out of the race and thus facilitated my unexpected election from the fifth district (a week after my claim to run in the first district had been denied),[79] an electoral move that surprised everyone in the Chamber and in which Antônio Carlos was greatly assisted by his friend Coimbra. Nor can I forget José Mariano, with his unswerving loyalty to me under circumstances that would have put to the test the emulation and susceptibility of another spirit, prone to envy or jealousy, or the gentle countenance, a pure Carlo Dolci, of his sweet and loving wife Dona Olegarinha, departed so prematurely, who on the eve of my election – for which José Mariano had taken personal responsibility, against the minister of the Empire – pawned her jewels to finance the struggle, a fact which I only discovered the following day when the party reclaimed them and had them returned to her. I forget no one, none of the liberal bosses and centurions, Costa Ribeiro, João Teixeira, Rego Barros, or Silva da Madalena, Faustino de Brito do Peres: I would have to list a hundred, two hundred. Nor any of the group of abolitionists who received me with Antônio Carlos: Barros Sobrinho, João Ramos, Gomes de Mattos, João Barbalho, Numa Pompílio, João de Oliveira, Martins Júnior, the entire group.[80] I never forget the brilliant articles by so many distinguished journalists, above all

....

79 In December 1884 Nabuco narrowly lost an election in the first district of Pernambuco (the city of Recife) to the Conservative candidate Joaquim Pires Machado Portela. Because of disturbances and irregularities the election was declared invalid. In a second election in January 1885 Machado Portela chose to abstain and Nabuco won unopposed. In May, however, the result was overturned in the Chamber of Deputies. In June, there was an election in the fifth district of Pernambuco (Nazaré da Mata and Bom Jardim) and two Liberal politicians Joaquim Francisco Cavalcanti and Ermírio Coutinho stood aside to allow Nabuco to become the Liberal candidate and win the seat. L.B.

80 Antônio José da Costa Ribeiro, João Francisco Teixeira, Francisco Barros Rego, Luís Gonzaga do Amaral e Silva (Silva da Madalena), Faustino de Brito do Peres, Antônio de Barros Sobrinho, João Barbalho Uchôa Cavalcanti, Numa Pompílio, João de Oliveira, José Isidoro Martins Júnior, João Ramos and Manoel Gomes de Mattos were lawyers, journalists and politicians in Pernambuco who supported the abolition of slavery. Many belonged to the *Clube do Cupim*, a secret abolitionist society whose objective was to free slaves by any means. To ensure their anonymity, members adopted "war names" based on the provinces of the Brazilian empire. For example, Barros Sobrinho was "São Paulo", João Ramos, the Club's President, "Ceara", Silva da Madalena "Pernambuco" and Numa Pompílio "Mato Grosso". L.B.

Maciel Pinheiro, Castro Alves' friend, austere, gleaming, talented, a figure that reminded one of Velázquez' brushstrokes, at once both somber and luminous. And these are just the first names that come to mind. Others, many others, are equally present in my spirit, like Aníbal Falcão and Sousa Pinto, the intellectual leaders of the youth.

I doubt that I ever experienced a greater revelation or outer impression that acted on me for so long as that of the elections from 1884 to 1887 (the election in 1889, when abolition was already a fact, scarcely interested me). The elections put me in direct contact with the neediest part of the population, and in more than one poor home I received such a striking and moving *lesson in life*, on the selflessness of those who possess nothing, that the mere memory of what I witnessed will always have the power and the effect of challenging my conscience. I visited the voters from house to house, knocking on every door on some streets. Some of these dwellings were so poor and the family's political faith so intense that I sometimes gave up going farther. It hurt me to see how dearly these credulous people paid for their political loyalty. Numerous such episodes are engraved in my heart. Once, for example, I entered the home of a worker, an employee at one of the Armories, to ask him to vote for me. His name was Jararaca [Pit Viper], but his name was the only terrible thing about him. He was ready to vote for me, and he sympathized with the cause, as he told me, but if he did he would be fired, he would sacrifice his family's bread. He had been given a *coffin ballot* (rigged with a dead voter's name, thus identifying it during the returns), and if that ballot failed to turn up in the box, his fate was sealed that very day. "Just look, sir," he said to me, pointing to his four children, who stared at me indifferently, perfectly unaware that they were the crux of the matter, or that their next day's meal was at stake. And then, turning to another little child, lying on a rickety old bench: "To top it off, two months ago my wife found this little creature on our doorstep, nearly dying of hunger, gnawed by ants, and now we have another mouth to feed! Still, I'm ready to vote for you, sir," he continued, giving in to his liberal temptation, "as long as you bring me a request from Brigadier Floriano Peixoto." He was probably the first *Florianist*[81] in the country. "The Brigadier can send me

---

81 A follower of Floriano Peixoto, first Vice-President of the Brazilian Republic, who had taken power in November 1891 on the resignation of Deodoro da Fonseca. Floriano served as president until November 1894. With an iron fist and the support of loyal followers, the *florianistas*, particularly young military officers, he crushed monarchist opposition and was responsible for consolidation of the Republic. R.S. See also note 37 above.

a telegram. He's on his sugarcane plantation in Alagoas. And whatever he asks of me, whatever it costs, I'll never refuse to do. Send him a telegram." "No, that's not necessary," I replied. "Vote as the government wishes, and don't forget to take your *coffin ballot* with you. Don't risk the daily bread of all these little creatures that are staring at me. The day will come when you can vote for me freely, but until then, it's as if you had. I can't give you an excuse to do what you're suggesting, to invoke the intervention by your protector." And I left, urging his wife, pleading with her, not to let him change his mind and vote for me.

In other homes, the head of the family had been unemployed for years just because he had voted for the opposition party. They were in abject poverty, almost destitution, but they were all proud to be suffering for their party loyalty. And it was just as true for the conservatives as for the liberals. They were coherent in their misery, in their total deprivation. This spectacle would no doubt have been extremely encouraging for a selfless optimist. He would have been certain that he had discovered the hidden refuge of true human nature. However, for the candidate it was terribly moving to capture the agony of dignity like that. As for me, I can say that I would never again have dared to run for an office that cost so much suffering, had it not been to serve the cause of others even more unfortunate than these victims of the poor man's pride, the people's political passion and illusion. Today, who knows, in any case I might lack the strength or courage to suggest that the good, the credulous, the naïve make such personal sacrifices for a cause that was not directly theirs. I would proceed with everyone as I had done with the good man Jararaca. I would advise them not to sacrifice their families. But that is precisely what the fight for justice is all about. It sacrifices entire generations for the right sometimes of a single person, to remedy an injustice done to the oppressed, perhaps to a stranger. Of course I feel no remorse or regret. I will not profit personally from all the abnegations practiced in my name. I did not capitalize on the suffering of so many selfless souls. I am consoled by not having personally received anything from abolition except some memories of the speaker's stand and fame, nothing more than youthful vanity. Thank God for this inestimable favor, that I received no direct or indirect material profit from the ideas that persuaded me, and with which I persuaded others.

Still, what I did receive was priceless. Only God himself can tally the figures, He who witnesses the proud suffering of those who pass unnoticed through the crowd. I am a slave to Recife. A person who never accompanied one of the candidates from house to house, from the sands of Brum to the canals of Afogados during the abolition campaign, cannot appreciate what it cost those densely populated communities, living in utter destitution, to welcome me into their homes. I reached the Chamber on the shoulders of those who had nothing but the sweat of their brow and who ran the risk, for themselves and their families, of showing up for work the next day only to find that they had been fired and evicted after voting for me. What I retain from this entire episode, the only one in my political career, is an overwhelming feeling of bankruptcy. My only asset is gratitude. My liabilities are infinite. There were thousands who offered me everything they had, and since they had nothing, it was what they were, what they might become, and I accepted on behalf of the slaves. Many of them will have pulled themselves up by the bootstraps again and gone on their way on the trails that have been blazed since then, but which all appear to lead to the same searing mirage on the horizon. They will have gone, or are going, poor souls, from illusion to illusion, from sacrifice to sacrifice, from loyalty to loyalty. It does not matter. What does matter to me is that during that stage in my life I asked for and accepted absolute abnegation by many for the cause I defended. Of course it was the noblest, the most magnificent of all causes, but in actual practice I was the one representing it, and to a major extent the dedication and sacrifice were for me, just as the triumph, the career, and the political future were mine.

My lasting impression of politics, except for this painful context of naïve sacrifice by the lowly, the righteous, those who suffer, those who rise up, reminds me of an enchanted Oriental garden, in which everything consisted of otherworldly, petrified lives, waiting for the magic word to release them, where the rose, which never bloomed, expressed the hidden presence of a stubbornly undeclared passion, where the alabastrine marble of the fountains symbolized the immaculate body from which continuously flowed the pure blood of martyrs for love and truth, and where the warbling nightingales were lovers forbidden from seeking each other in human form. Everything there was permanently suspended, transposed to another scale of being, another order of sensitivity and feeling. It was the same fact, but with different aspirations, a different conscience, a different will, and where, for that very reason, time stood still, as if in a dream. The political scene for me was also pure make-believe. Under the guise of the parties, cabinets, Chambers, and the whole system presided over by the old white-bearded man from São Cristóvão, the Brazilian genie had embodied and cloaked the drama of tears and hopes that was playing out in the national unconscious, and it befell my generation to pierce that vast simulacrum at the moment in which the signal, the call for redemption, was about to be issued, when it would all crumble in order for human reality to take its place, suddenly called to life, restored to freedom and movement. That is why I harbor no disappointment towards politics, no bitterness, no resentment. I passed through it all during the metamorphosis.

CHAPTER XXIV

AT THE VATICAN

I WILL NOW RELATE ANOTHER EPISODE in the story of abolition, my
journey to Rome in early 1888, because it became a link in my life, a
subtle touch of awakening in parts of my conscience that had long
become numb.

I had always been critical of the Brazilian clergy's neutrality towards
slavery, its indifference in dealing with the issue. However, the voice of
the bishops rang out in what I saw as a moment of inspiration. On the
occasion of the sacerdotal jubilee of Pope Leo XIII, nearly all of the bishops
published pastorals calling on their congregations to honor the Holy Father
with emancipation papers for their slaves as offerings. This appeal by the
prelates provided the Abolitionist Party with an opportunity to ask the
Pope to intervene for the slaves, and I decided to seize the moment.

I had just been elected Deputy from Recife, defeating the minister of
the Empire, and my election sounded like the death knell for the proslavery
resistance. In the few remaining days of the 1887 Parliamentary session,
I came to Rio de Janeiro to take my seat in the Chamber, but my main
purpose was to seek (and indeed I was successful in obtaining) a moral
pronouncement by the Army against slavery, establishing a clear legal
separation between the public armed forces and the slave-hunting patrols.
To occupy the Parliamentary recess, I hesitated between this journey to
Rome and a visit to the United States, where the welcome I would receive
from the old abolitionists would give great repercussion to our cause
throughout the Americas. I opted for Rome, convinced that a statement
by the Holy Father would touch the religious sentiment of the Princess
Regent.

I was certainly justified in turning to the Pope, or to any other moral oracle that might inspire the Princess by speaking to her ideals and duty. For ten years my only aim was to capture the monarchy's interest and awaken the country's conscience. I considered international public opinion a legitimate weapon on an issue that affected all of humankind, not only Brazil. To seize that weapon I had gone to Lisbon, Madrid, Paris, London, and Milan, and I was now going to Rome, and if slavery had persisted longer I would have gone to Washington, New York, Buenos Aires, Santiago, or anywhere else that new sympathy for our cause might appear, focusing the prestige of civilization on it. If there was some lack of patriotism in traveling abroad to stir an opinion that would later reach us spontaneously through the grand voice of humankind (considered not as a material power, but as a universal moral mirror, which it is for us), then I cannot deny my guilt. It was the same crime as that of W. L. Garrison journeying to England to arouse the British against slavery in the United States, or the same error as the delegates of the various international antislavery congresses. It is never forbidden to seek out human conscience or sympathy for oneself and to place it at the service of one's country or the cause one defends.

Reaching London in December, I departed for Rome in January with letters from Cardinal Manning, which the Anti-Slavery Society and Mr. Lilly of the English Catholic Union had obtained for me. In Rome I also found equally useful support from our diplomatic representative, Sousa Correa, an old colleague and friend of mine. He immediately contacted the Cardinal Secretary of State, who gave me an extremely kind reception. Pilgrims had flocked to Rome for the jubilee, and the Vatican was full of work, but I still managed to open the doors to meet with the Holy Father. On January 16 I submitted my petition to Cardinal Rampolla. I would have worded it differently today, but now I no longer have the propagandist's zeal. I quote a few excerpts from this supplication to illustrate how my plea was not only for the slaves in Brazil, but for the entire Negro race, for Africa, where the awesome figure of Cardinal Lavigerie would soon appear:

Almost without exception, the Brazilian bishops have issued pastorals declaring that the most dignified and noble way of celebrating the sacerdotal jubilee of Leo XIII would be for the slaveholders to free their slaves and for other members of the congregation to contribute to emancipation papers in lieu of any offerings they might make to His Holiness.

The morally unanimous plea by our prelates could not fail to exert great influence on the abolitionist movement, which was already persuading public opinion, and a great national and religious outcry soon followed whose magnitude proves that there is no longer any disagreement among the political parties concerning abolition in Brazil.

With the emancipation of multitudes of slaves in the Holy Father's name, his jubilee will promote hundreds of new Brazilian families to freedom.

Of the all the offerings placed at the feet of Leo XIII, Brazil's tribute in the form of these freed Christians, partaking from afar in his universal glorification, is perhaps the only gift that will have moved the Holy Father to tears of recognition.

Here, Your Holiness, is a splendid occasion for the sovereign pontiff to intercede, to intervene, to ordain in favor of the Brazilian slaves. Leo XII can take these emancipation papers deposited at the foot of his august throne and transform them into the seed for universal emancipation. A word from Your Holiness to the Catholic masters on behalf of their slaves, Christians like they, would not be limited to Brazil's vast territory, but would have the same scope as that of religious faith, reaching like a divine message wherever slavery still exists in the world. The Pope has just canonized Pedro Claver as the Patron Saint of the Negroes.[82] Despite the advanced stage of civilization in which we live, there is still enough bondage in the world for Leo XIII to add to his other titles that of Liberator of the Slaves.

Several of his illustrious predecessors spoke out against slavery. Since the only source of slavery is slave traffic, it is included de facto in the papal bulls condemning the slave trade. Still, those immortal pontiffs spoke before our time, when humankind had still not made efforts to eliminate its centuries-old crime against Africa, whose hapless race appears doomed to suffer the fatality of its color under various forms of prejudice. An act by Leo XIII – benevolent, fervent, and inspired by the generosity of his soul – against the curse that weighs on that race would be an inestimable blessing.

---

82 Pedro (Peter) Claver, Catalan Jesuit priest (1581–1654). From 1610 to his death in1654 in Cartagena Claver baptized and instructed in the faith tens of thousands of slaves (hence "the apostle of the negroes"). He was beatified by Pope Pius IX in 1850 and on 15 January 1888 canonized by Pope Leo XIII, who described him as "the saint whose life most impressed me, next to Christ". L.B.

No political thinking influences my plea to the leader of the Catholic world in favor of the most unfortunate of his children. I ask for nothing more than to place his Holy Father's heart in direct communication with theirs. This contact between charity and martyrdom can produce nothing else but the wave of mercy for which I hope. The jubilee of Leo XIII will thus go down in history as a date of human redemption wherever the Negro race can be deemed orphaned from God.

On February 10, His Holiness granted me a private interview. I wrote the news about it that same day for *O País*. Among the old papers that form the *pieces of my life* (the expression is from a letter from the Emperor, another paper among my keepsakes), this one will always be one of the most treasured. The emotion it contains can never be repeated and increases as the years pass. That is why I reproduce it now:

— The Pope and Slavery —

Today I had the honor of being received by the Pope in a private interview, and since this meeting was granted in relation to a political matter that had brought me to Rome, I dare not delay in reconstructing the conversation I had with His Holiness and which I brought back from the Vatican in shorthand, photographed in my memory. It was an outstanding kindness by His Holiness to grant me such an audience when his every moment is scheduled for the bishops, archbishops, and prominent Catholics who are bringing him some offering to celebrate his jubilee.

The Pope is constantly receiving numerous influential delegations from all over the world, and addresses each of them with a lively allocution. This additional work above and beyond his daily concerns leaves the Holy Father no time for rest, and his 78 years and the majesty of the tiara have begun to weigh on him. Nevertheless, it is during these hours of repose that His Holiness himself receives the noteworthy men of the Catholic world and converses with them at length about their respective topics of interest.

I, however, was an unknown, and brought not an offering for the Pope, but a request. I had never provided any service to the Church, and my matter required that His Holiness read a series of documents beforehand and meditate in some way on the serious reply he would give me. This in itself was an effort, and given the special circumstance of the jubilee, the attention bestowed on me by the highest of all human individuals is an act to which I ascribe even greater appreciation and recognition, knowing that through my humble person, Leo XIII meant to receive the slaves of Brazil and invite them before his august throne, symbolically the highest of all places of refuge.

The Pope receives such visitors in a private audience, with no witnesses whatsoever. No one is in the room except His Holiness and the person to whom the interview is granted. A secretary and officer of the guard remain in an adjoining room, but once the visitor enters the little chamber, he finds himself behind closed doors in the presence of Leo XIII alone. The Pope, who was reading a book of Latin verses when I was announced, ordered me to take a seat by his side and asked me in which language he should address me. I preferred French.

My impression throughout the entire interview, which lasted less than three quarters of an hour, was nothing like the feeling caused by the presence of one of the world's great sovereigns. The Brazilian throne is an exception. Never has Brazil had such an accessible man as the Emperor, nor a house as open as São Cristóvão. But the monarchs in general are educated and grow up – because their station is superior to that of all other men – in the belief that they are *better* than the rest of humankind. Beyond all the papacy's other advantages as a monarchist institution, one must especially add its electiveness – the Pope's superiority over the other sovereigns, who are born, live, and die on the throne, while the Popes only attain royalty in their latter years, that is, when they have lived their entire lives as men and merely crown their careers on the throne. This *human* side of the pontifical royalty is the principal reason for its prestige, just as its electiveness is the condition for its unlimited duration, and the religious spirit for its moral selection. I would even say that being alone with the Pope reminds one more of the confessionary than the steps before the throne, except that something in the Holy Father's frankness and calm immediately rules out the impression of a confessor interested in unveiling the depths of his interlocutor's soul. The predominant impression is rather one of absolute trust, as if within those four walls everything that could be said to the Holy Pontiff assumes the nature of an intimate conversation with God, whose interpreter and intermediary is immediately present.

The words from the Holy Father's lips are recorded indelibly in my memory, and I do not believe they will ever be erased, nor do I believe I will ever fail to hear the voice and firm tone with which they were pronounced. The Pope began by observing that he had delayed somewhat in receiving me in

Rome, but that he had numerous duties at that moment, to which I replied that my time could not have been spent any better than by waiting for His Holiness' word. "I was going to the United States," I said to Leo XIII, "where most of the Negroes in the Americas are, but when our bishops began to speak with deliberation and common accord concerning Your Holiness' jubilee and to request the slaves' emancipation as the best and noblest way of celebrating it in Brazil, I felt that first and foremost I should come to Rome to ask Your Holiness to complete the work begun by those prelates, by condemning slavery in the name of the Church. If we receive this grace from Your Holiness, we abolitionists will have obtained a fulcrum in the country's Catholic conscience, which will be of the utmost importance for the complete fulfillment of our hope."

His Holiness replied to me, "*Ce que vous avez à coeur, l'Eglise aussi l'a à coeur*. Slavery is condemned by the Church and should have been eliminated long ago. Man cannot be slave to man. All are God's children, *des enfants de Dieu*. I felt deeply moved by the bishops' gesture, which I approve completely, for having chosen, together with Brazil's Catholics, my sacerdotal jubilee for this great initiative. It is necessary now to take advantage of the bishops' initiative to hasten emancipation. I will speak in this sense. Whether the encyclical will appear next month or after Easter, I still cannot say."

"What we would like," I noted, "is that Your Holiness speak in time for your voice to reach Brazil before the Parliamentary session begins in May. Your Holiness' word will have the utmost influence on the government's disposition and that of the small portion of the country that still chooses not to join the national movement. We hope that Your Holiness will say a word that will seize the conscience of all true Catholics."

"*Ce mot je le dirai, vous pouvez en être sûr,*" the Pope replied, "and when the Pope has spoken, all the Catholics will have to obey."

The Pope repeated these last words two or three times, always in the impersonal form, not "when I have spoken," but always "when the Pope has spoken."

I believe that I was absolutely honest towards my adversaries in my description to His Holiness concerning the current state of the abolitionist issue in Brazil. The Pope asked me several questions, each of which I answered with the complete allegiance I owed first to the Pope, then to my compatriots. I described the abolitionist movement in Brazil as having become principally a movement of the slave-owning class itself, and as was only fair, I gave the selfless eleventh-hour participants the greatest share in the definitive solution to the problem, which would have been unsolvable without their generosity.

I referred to the brilliant work by Antônio Prado and to the moral effect of the noble pronouncement by Moreira de Barros as facts of the greatest importance. I explained how world history knew no other example of humanity in a great class equal to that of the Brazilian masters when they gave up their slave ownership titles. I said that this was the real proof that slavery in Brazil had always been a *foreign* institution, alien to the national spirit, which was further confirmed (although this I did not say to the Pope) by the fact that of all the congregation, foreigners in Brazil were and still are those who showed the least sympathy towards the emancipation movement. As for the Imperial family, I repeated to the Holy Pontiff that whatever has been done by the law in favor of the slaves has been at the Emperor's initiative and imposition, although it has still been too little. "A dynasty," I added, "has material interests that depend on the support of all the classes, and cannot provoke the ill will of any, much less the most powerful of all. However, the papacy does not depend on any class, and its point of view is thus one of absolute morality, a stance no dynasty could assume without destroying itself." Speaking of the current president of the Council, I said to His Holiness that he was a man to whom the Church in Brazil owed a great deal, since he was the principal author of the amnesty that put an end to the conflict in 1873, but that on this particular issue we had no reason to suppose that he wished to go beyond the current law, which was absolutely contrary to the nation's unanimous wish. "However, I do not ask Your Holiness for a political act," I added, "although the political consequences that the nation will derive from the act that I request of you are indisputable. Fortunately, in Your Holiness' position, you do not see the parties, but the principles. What we request is a moral commandment, a lesson by the Church on man's freedom. No government in the world can harbor the pretense that the Pope, when he establishes a principle of universal morality, stops to ponder whether the principle agrees or clashes with that government's political interests. Even now, a Brazilian priest has been arrested for sheltering slaves. All over, we abolitionists shelter slaves. We do what the bishops did with the serfs in the Middle Ages. The nation's opinion, this I can assure Your Holiness, is *unanimous*, and the word of the Church's leader will find no one to dispute it."

The Pope then repeated to me that his encyclical would be full of the Gospel spirit, that the cause was as much his as ours, and that the government itself would realize that it was good policy to acknowledge the freedom to which all children of God have the birthright, and that the Pope would speak not only of freedom but of the need to provide religious education to this mass of the unfortunate, theretofore deprived of moral instruction.

Cardinal Czacki had also spoken to me of the duty to provide moral education to the freed slaves, and that the Catholic Church in North America and the Antilles apparently intended to make a great effort in this direction. Sympathizing with the principle of our abolitionist propaganda and highlighting the responsibility that we abolitionists had embraced, Cardinal Czacki had placed his finger on the wound of the Negro race, perhaps even more degraded than oppressed, and had told me that from the Catholic point of view there was no other way of making moralized men out of yesterday's slaves except to spread among them the religious education they had never enjoyed. I answered the Pope just as I had the Cardinal: "Before the abolitionist movement began in 1879," I said to the Holy Pontiff, "the Liberal Party, to which I belong, due to the struggle with the bishops in 1873, a struggle in which the conservatives declared an amnesty, was focused primarily on measures to secularize civil affairs, nearly all of which Brazil still entrusts to the Church. These measures led to a state of war between liberalism and the Church. However, ever since the abolitionist movement began, all other issues have been swept aside, and for nine years literally no other business has been discussed in the country. A veritable truce has been established between God and men of all spirits and philosophies concerning the other issues. The first member to speak out in the Chamber for immediate abolition, Deputy Jerônimo Sodré, is a prominent Catholic. The co-owner of the abolitionist newspaper in Pernambuco, which supports my policy, is Gomes de Mattos, the president of a Catholic society. The bishops and abolitionists are now working in common accord. Thus far, the truce has lasted without any setbacks, and I hope that it will last for a long time to come. Once slavery has been abolished, the freed slaves will have to be protected. Nothing prevents the Church from competing for worshippers among the race it will have helped to rescue. We abolitionists would not think of hindering an approach between the new citizens and the only religion capable of winning them over to civilization. The country's eyes will be turned on other issues to improve the people's condition and enhance Brazil's domestic life, a process in which the truce, or rather the alliance, can and should persevere. If the Church succeeds in winning the recognition of the enslaved race by contributing to its liberation, the abolitionists will certainly not counsel ingratitude on the part of the former slaves."

The Pope listened to me throughout the interview with the greatest sympathy, and pardoned me for having requested more than Cardinal Manning had considered reasonable. His Eminence, in fact, had advised me to ask that the Pope reissue the bulls of some of his predecessors, but I was asking Leo XIII for a *personal* act. "Circumstances change," the Pope said to me, "and the times are no longer the same. When these bulls were published, slavery was still strong in the world, but now, fortunately, it is finished."

"The gesture by Your Holiness," I said, concluding, "will become a page in the history of Christian civilization that will illustrate your pontificate. Your encyclical will rise as high in the world's eyes, encompassing the abolitionist movement, as Saint Peter's dome over the Campagna Romana."

This was a basic account of the long private audience that Leo XIII paid me the sublime honor of granting, and which His Holiness brought to a close with a special blessing for the cause of the slaves. I had previously sent Under Secretary of State Monsignor Mocenni the recent pastoral by the bishop of Rio de Janeiro, and I apologized for not having found the issues of *O País* in which the other bishops' pastorals had appeared. Even so, I had the good fortune to find clippings of the pastorals by the bishops of Mariana and Rio Grande do Sul and the archbishop of Bahia, all of which were sent to Cardinal Rampolla. Unfortunately I was unable to locate the admirable letter by the bishop of Diamantina, to which I referred specifically when I spoke with the Pope. Together with his encyclical, now promised and announced throughout Europe, these pastorals would make a beautiful book on human brotherhood.

My delay in Rome prevented me from returning by way of the United States, because I would no longer have had enough time for any of the activities for which I wished to visit that great Republic. But I was satisfied. The Pope's word was bound to have a greater impact on all Catholics than any other manifestation on behalf of the slaves. No one in sound conscience could deny the supreme leader of the Christian faith the right to speak out on a fact like slavery, which establishes a bond between the master and the slave, the equivalent of eternally interweaving their souls and responsibilities. I found nothing in the Pope's words to suggest the least vacillation or the slightest attempt to twist the moral teaching to adapt it to the political circumstances. All I saw was his moral conscience shining like a beacon whose light was indifferent to the ships that might wreck by failing to guide their course by it.

Rome, February 10, 1888.

Cardinal Czacki was certainly correct when he told me that I was handing the Pope a veritable golden opportunity! Unfortunately diplomacy got entangled in the issue, and the conservative cabinet became alarmed by the Pope's announced intentions and managed to postpone the encyclical's release. The short delay was sufficient for his pronouncement not to appear until after slavery was already abolished in Brazil. The time was so short between the fall of Cotegipe and abolition that the beautiful work by Leo XIII was only published when there were no longer any slaves in Brazil. However, the Holy Father's blessing for our cause, the word that he had intended to pronounce sometime after late February, with the Cotegipe cabinet still in office, became public knowledge in the country through my revelations. Leo XIII was so pleasantly surprised by total emancipation that as a postscript to his superb letter on slavery he sent a Golden Rose to the Imperial Princess.

My role was a very modest one, as described above. As a simple bearer, to Cardinal Rampolla and Monsignor Mocenni, of the letters of introduction by Cardinal Manning, all I did by presenting Leo XIII with the bishops' pastorals celebrating his jubilee was to offer him a topic with all the respect he deserved. The Pope immediately grasped the grandeur of the service he could pay to humankind, an incomparable theme for his writings. If I can flatter myself for something, it was the fact that I connected the cause of the slaves in Brazil to that of Africa, as a common aspiration. Just a few months after the pronouncement I had supplicated from the Holy Father, Cardinal Lavigerie came to Rome, where the Pope invested him with the African crusade that was his life's noble coronation. In a letter from the Anti-Slavery Society, Mr. Charles Allen honored me by confirming that I had prepared Cardinal Lavigerie's way with the Pope. In the speeches by the great apostle of Africa, in what he said so many times *ex abundantia cordis*, one realizes that when Cardinal Lavigerie arrived in Rome, Leo XIII was possessed, dominated, inflamed with antislavery fervor. My part was simple: on the occasion of the Pope's sacerdotal jubilee and the canonization of St. Pedro Claver, so favorable for the unveiling of this and other generous initiatives and aspirations, I had the good fortune of attracting the great spirit of Leo XIII, disputed by so many solicitations, to the problem most capable of fixing his attention.

I returned from Rome with a strong impression. In late April, unsure of how far the reform announced by the new João Alfredo cabinet would go, I attended the celebration of the mass emancipation of slaves at a coffee plantation in the Paraíba Valley, and the marvels of the Vatican immediately came to mind on the occasion. What grand emotions sprang up with abolition! How everything merged in a single, mysterious, and intimate note, as if at those moments we had the hearts of slaves rather than our own! The following is an excerpt from my description of that emotion at the Bela Aliança plantation[83]:

> Three months ago I had the good fortune of attending a Papal mass at the Sistine Chapel. At the time, I did not expect the hour of abolition to ring so soon, and suspecting that the Regency was a vice-reign and that the vice-reign belonged to slavery, I had journeyed to Rome to ask Leo XIII for a word that would touch the Princess' religious sentiment. How wrong I was, as were so many others, beginning with the president of the Council! During that mass, in which everything was new to me, and when the Pope held everyone's attention among the Cardinals in the Sistine, with the music, listening to which one realizes that the human voice is the only instrument that rises up above the Earth, I could scarcely take my eyes off the ceiling, the most beautiful page ever inscribed by man. What a unique opportunity this ceremony was, and to accompany it by rereading Michelangelo's Bible and memorizing his poem of Creation! Later, the mass at the Bela Aliança plantation renewed that infinite emotion of the Sistine. It included other touches of grandeur. There was no Holy Pontiff, children's choir, or frescos by Michelangelo. But there was the Pope's representative, blessing the reconciliation of the two races in his name. All the eyes were filled with tears, anxiety, and apprehension for both those who were giving and those who were receiving freedom. For me, the gentlest of all possible sensations was to witness the cloud of slavery retreat from the countenance of a race,

---

83 Bela Aliança was a large coffee plantation in the province of Rio de Janeiro belonging Anna Clara de Moraes Costa ("Dona Nicota"), niece of the Breves brothers, among the biggest slaveowners in Imperial Brazil, who had married a Russian nobleman, Maurice Haritoff. The date inscribed on the invitation to celebrate the emancipation of their slaves was 22 April 1888, just three weeks before the abolition of slavery. The event was one of numerous mass releases of slaves by owners who, on the eve of abolition, were attempting to anticipate emancipation in order to negotiate some permanent form of labor on their plantations. T.N.

the great *fiat lux*, to see yesterday's shapeless clay, the slave, awaken as a man, like Michelangelo's Adam in the morning light of Creation. My thoughts turned back nearly four centuries to the first mass said in Brazil, baptized then as *Terra de Santa Cruz*, Land of the Holy Cross. Four centuries transpired for the cross to recover its true meaning as the symbol of redemption and for the mass to signify God's sacrifice for man! Seeing before them the woman to whom they would soon owe their freedom, next to the statue of Our Lady of Mercy in the altar niche, the slaves, mixing their two great sources of gratitude, must have imagined the rubies – like tears of blood from the splendor of the Mother of God – descend for a moment on the head of their redeemer, kneeling as she was in prayer.[84]

Oh, the times in which one wrote like this! When the heart, and only the heart, dictated the words, and so quickly that the pen could not keep up. The abolitionist campaign would have moved me much less deeply if I had not kept this page from my journey to Rome to reread, this reencounter with the sympathy and fervor of Leo XIII. Why did I make this plea so late, when perhaps it should have come first? I am convinced that although abolition came so suddenly, it was all in due time. The memory of my visit to Rome – followed so suddenly by the end of slavery and the monarchy's demise, the forced ending to my political career – could not have failed to grow in the void of my finished task and the impossibility of taking on another challenge of such magnitude. A new life began for me with those religious impressions, absorbed in the fire of a struggle that was to bring my activist life to a close and epitomize it. A new layer in my formative years was sketched subtly through this brief contact with Leo XIII – or perhaps another more primordial layer began to unveil itself after so many dormant years, and the mother lode of childhood reappeared. Whatever the theological truth, I believe that God acknowledges the usefulness of our lives in some way, and as long as slavery existed, I believe I could not have made better use of my own existence than to struggle for abolition. I know fully well that this outer life cannot replace the inner one when the spirit of charity or human love encourages us to persevere in our task. No matter

---

84 The lady to whom I was referring is a countrywoman of ours who had married a young and elegant Russian in Paris. There is a beautiful life-sized portrait of her by Richter. The gentle, sweet countenance of Madame Haritoff, known affectionately as Dona Nicota, lent her an expressive beauty all of her own, with her long black hair, her large, glowing eyes, her olive-brown skin, and her graceful body, with a special, distinctly Brazilian charm for foreigners. Author's note.

The portrait was painted by the German artist Gustav Richter (1823–84). It is to be found in the Museu Nacional de Belas Artes in Rio de Janeiro. L.B.

how humble one's station, the satisfaction at having done good for others, of shedding at least a ray of hope on dark and oppressed lives like those of the slaves, is a source of intense joy that erases the memory of personal privations and protects one from envy and disappointment. Everyone who participated in the abolitionist movement surely shared in this joy. As long as slavery lasted, I believe that for me religion would not have transcended the latent state of humanitarian action. It is often difficult for religion to distinguish itself from the ordinary task of life, and it is only when this task is finished or interrupted that self-examination begins, that one wishes to penetrate the mystery, that one feels the need for a belief that explains life. Until then, the role we play suffices. The critic does not appear from underneath the actor. Doubt does not distract one from the continuous outer action. As long as we are simple instruments, no matter how small the circle drawn around us, our imagination is enclosed within it, and inner life does not even reach our conscience. Action is a distraction. It is only when the task is completed that higher affinities speak out in certain spirits. For those who succumb in this phase, I would like to believe that the good they may do eliminates part of the impurity they carry in their moral or religious conscience, which amounts to the same, and even worse. I cannot think back today to my sojourn to Rome in 1888 without believing that the seeds forgotten in the earliest fields of my boyhood were revived, only to germinate later under the heat of other influences. From the point of view of my religious feeling, I had not gone to Rome in vain.

CHAPTER XXV

BARON TAUTPHOEUS[85]

N O OTHER SINGLE PERSON left as strong an impression on me as my teacher, the old Baron of Tautphoeus. His imagination exuded history, and during my fiery liberal years he used to call me Alcibiades. He certainly represented the Socrates type for me. Although he had not borrowed Silenus' mask from the great Athenian, even physically, and especially in his old age, he had many of Socrates' traits: cold courage, imperturbable calm, resistance to fatigue, a taste for the lecture, for intellectual conversation, for the company of youth, complete self-abstraction, modesty, the joy of living as a spectator of the universe, while always reserving the best place for others, strong spiritualism, indifference to ridicule, and respect for the social order, whoever embodied it. His youth is still somewhat cloaked in mystery, and nothing would be more interesting than to unearth the facts about it. What I heard more than once from my brother Sizenando – who admired Tautphoeus enthusiastically and had more contact with him than I, although the Baron saved the best of his last days for me, his final afternoons – is that the young Tautphoeus fled into forced exile from Bavaria due to a revolution, accompanied King Othon to Greece, and later moved to Paris around the 1830s, where he hung out with the liberal crowd from *Journal des Débats* before emigrating to Brazil.

Extremely nearsighted, he had a square eyepiece that he used almost automatically because of his constant reading habit, although he was even more attached to his cigars than his monocle. Always with a thick German tome under his arm, he paced for hours on end on the same floor, oblivious to the outer world. He was a man who knew everything. Although his conversation was inexhaustible, he rarely led the talk himself. No topic

85 Joseph Hermann de Tautphoeus, Baron Tautphoeus (1814–90), was a German scholar who emigrated to Brazil and was Nabuco's tutor at his school in Nova Friburgo. L.B.

was beyond him, and until the very end, year after year, day after day, he was never without curious interlocutors ready to hear him expound on the points that most interested them. He was literally like a dictionary that someone consulted every second, or an encyclopedia that one opened to such subjects as Babylonia, the Invasion of the Huns, Adam Smith, Luther, hieroglyphs, the Amazon, Gothic architecture, free experimentation, Greek roots, paper money, tropical crops, Albrecht Dürer, or the Divine Comedy, all at random. All one had to do was turn on the switch, pose the question to the machine, and wait for the answer to roll out, as if he were Meyer's *Lexicon* or Cesar Cantu's *History of the World*. He spoke evenly, with no emphasis, no flare, even without any expression, but he was an endless fountain of science and erudition, as if he had just been studying the topic that very day. Nothing could have been more different – as compared to the frivolous ostentation with which so many people take pleasure in dumbfounding the hapless listener who inadvertently offers them a subject within their reach – than the scientific, ***up-to-date*** dissertations Tautphoeus delivered to his disciples, who to him were all eternal journalists, professors, ministers of state.

His conversation contained an awesome abundance of general ideas, provocative points of view, and food for thought. The man never wrote publicly, at least in Brazil, but published more essays, historical dissertations, and other treatises than all our writers put together, because he issued countless editions with just a handful of copies each that vanished like his words, that is, when they were not transformed into somebody else's authorship. What did he care? He was devoid of ambition. This respecter of hierarchical order and social pragmatics never worried if the powers-that-be considered themselves his superiors or if last-minute nobles looked down their noses at his hereditary title, because he was a teacher to boys, a Greek scholar, practicing the philosophy of Ecclesiastes with pagan spirit and integrity: *Vanitas vanitatum...* He had long since become totally immune in this regard. Having to earn his keep in a foreign country by tutoring, he buried whatever he could of his country's old aristocratic prejudices and his aspirations to elegance and a life of pleasure, ostentation, and worldly successes from his youth in Paris and embraced his role with the same simplicity as if he had received it as an inheritance... in a word, with no regrets, no complaints, no grumbling. He drank from the Carioca

River with the same spirit of conformity with which he would have drunk from the Lethes. He forgot himself in order to don his new fate. But from the very beginning, he explored the most singular nooks and crannies of the country that was to become his second homeland, and which he loved as such! He was viewed as an underling even by those most capable of understanding – which is not the same as feeling – the intellectual creator's calling as essentially noble. Meanwhile, he proved himself indifferent to the social harlequinade, knowing quite well that *everyone dreams what he is*, as Calderón expressed it better than anyone else.

Yet what depth of feeling! While everyone was out of place – and he never aspired to hierarchical change, on the contrary, he believed that the social distribution was fair, that the positions and responsibilities were allotted to the best, even if they did not do their best, even if they failed to give all they could – when they did occupy their positions, he at least wanted his own. He was a conservative and Catholic, and when I met him he was shaken by the *Kulturkampf*, based on his German notion that the world's greatest politician – who for him was certainly Bismarck – could not be betrayed on that issue simultaneously by his national scent and conservative instinct. His dyed-in-the-wool conservatism was also part of his philosophy, so that according to his feeling about our institutions, we ourselves were incompetent: a feeling of idealistic veneration. From this simple public servant, who had nothing to call his own except his daily wages, and a foreigner to boot, came perhaps the only cry of *"Long Live the Imperial Constitution!"* that was heard – so feeble was his voice at his age – on November 15, when General Deodoro's troops paraded on Ouvidor Street. Whoever happened to hear that old man fearlessly voicing his protest might have concluded that he was some protégé of the Emperor, delusional with the catastrophe that would swallow him up with it. Yet he was not. He owed neither favors nor gratitude. Whatever he possessed, he had won by merit in public admissions contests, in which his competitors all threw in the towel while singing his praise. He was not spiteful, but a philosopher. He was the man who had best studied our country's psychology and had most conformed to it until that act, which he considered a national disaster, like the tearing of the temple veil for the Jews.

I once identified a key trait in his perspicacity for things Brazilian, recalling that it was he who made me realize that our interest for public things is smaller when the subject concerns us most closely. Thus, he told me, local affairs always interest *all of us* less than those of the province, and those of the province less than the national policy. To demonstrate how precarious our **self-government** was, what better than this indifference that increases in direct proportion to the interest we should feel? Another of his observations that reveals his quick spirit was our conversation on the English impermeability to foreign ideas and concepts. I interpreted the slowness of the English to grasp and understand a point of view, a foreign novelty, as perhaps a sign of less intellectual vivacity than the continental peoples. "On the contrary," he pointed out, and although the words are mine, the idea was his, "this repulsion of what comes from abroad, this suspicion of what does not conform to the instinct of the race, actually proves the English originality, the strength of the country's productivity, the pride in its national creations. It was this resistance that allowed England to give the world a Shakespeare." Perhaps it was this reflection that led me to think that cosmopolitanism in the sphere of intellectual conception is neither a creative element nor an enviable superiority. On the contrary, the difficulty in assimilating in feeling what has no affinity with our own production is rather a virtue than a fault. Permeability jeopardizes the solidity and conservation of one's own qualities, that is, one's own nature.

If I had to single out what I owe to Tautphoeus among his many efforts to educate me, I would highlight two acquisitions that in a certain sense could be called inner transformations. The first (and it was not even his suggestion, perhaps he was not even aware of my point of view, and if he had been, who knows if he would not have tried to dissuade me?) was that in his presence, thinking of him, I became accustomed to considering the historian's judgment as the definitive judgment, the one that finally matters, and thus the one to be rightly pursued *from the onset*. There can be no greater revolution for the spirit than this, to appear spontaneously before the solitary judge of the library of the future rather than the countless judges from today's public square. That judge may not cite our name, and the incomplete testimony may be unjustly favorable or unfavorable to us, but his opinion is what counts, what matters. The judgment by the crowd that praises or despises us today is nothing but dust on the highway. We need not be actors in order for this concept of the true level that decides on reputations to affect each of our actions, stimuli, and moral affinities:

the effect is the same for the spectator, onlooker, or indifferent passerby. On a smaller scale, of course, because this is the greatest of all possible differences in the reasons for inspiration and conduct – like the change from the pagan concept, in which worldly life is more important, to the Christian concept, wherein everlasting life is what truly matters. Having reduced the aspirations of one's own soul to those of the mind or the spirit, the metamorphosis is also profound between living (or bearing witness to life) with a view towards one's contemporaries, and living for posterity. When posterity is involved, of course it is always necessary to imagine the space of several generations, to leave the door open to oblivion. In the present, thousands or even millions judge us. Yet little by little the courtroom empties, until the great characters come to depend on the sentence from a single judge, a Mommsen, Ranke, Curtius, or Macaulay, cloistered in his library, seeking to awaken a retrospective interest in them, all pure enthusiasm, an actor's illusion, involving none of the sentiments, not a single one, nor the true passions they inspired.

I owe another transition to Tautphoeus. How can I explain it so that only the nuance is understood, and nothing more? Because I wish to believe that the seeds would have developed by themselves, but I feel that his beneficial irrigation seeped into the earth where perhaps they were germinating without my realizing it.

In the latter years of Tautphoeus' life, we had a little retreat in Paquetá, near the Castelo section, in a quiet spot in that beautiful landscape. It was an old one-story house to which one of the former owners, an Englishman, had added a veranda all around and in the center a small upper story with green shutters and a vine-covered balcony, which gave it the simple yet picturesque appearance of a foreign residence. It faced the sea, and the low-lying coast behind formed a soft background. The house was on a slight rise in the terrain, and the slope down to the beach was covered with a lawn, as carefully tended as any park. The island of Paquetá is a tropical jewel with no great interest to native Brazilians, but with an almost infinite variety for the foreign painter, photographer, or naturalist. It held a special appeal for me as a bit of landscape from the North of Brazil, nestled on the bay of Rio. Whereas everywhere in the entrance to Rio de Janeiro one sees the dark granite massifs covered with dense rainforest guarding the coast, on Paquetá the picture is different: beaches lined with coconut palms, cashew groves, and along the shore the willowy wild reeds alternating with ancient mango trees and solitary tamarinds. Yet next to these miniatures from the North, each little cove on the island is lined with rock covered with the same characteristic native vegetation of Rio.

Tautphoeus had always loved our nature. Ever since he arrived in the country he had explored Brazil's natural wonders. The night's darkness, the wee hours of the morning, and the distance were no obstacle to him when he tracked some subtle moonlight, a sunset, a trickle of water down the rock, a *jequitibá* tree hidden in the virgin forest. He lived his entire life in this intimate lover's conversation with the light and land of Brazil, a ray of sunlight on Corcovado or Sugarloaf as a mysterious greeting by the creative power to which he always replied. Watching him sitting, listening to the birds in the nearby forest, I subtly associated my teacher with my first English lessons and remembered the Sultan Mahmud's vizier. The outskirts of Rio de Janeiro held a special attraction for him. He was always ready for any excursion to the scenic spots where people invited him, and Rio has countless such places. To spend the afternoon under the centuries-old trees found on so many of the islands, watching the mountains' glorious hues at sunset, was a veritably voluptuous experience for him. Our house on Paquetá pleased him because the silence and isolation of the library allowed him to choose at will between the sea, the meadow, and the mountains: the long beaches, the nearby forest, or the grassy plain if he felt like taking a walk; the quiet water in the cove, like a Swiss lake, if he wished to take our boat and ask Mudo, our now-deceased oarsman, to sail to one of the tiny islands, with a full view of the Organ Mountain Range in Teresópolis from one side and the mountains in the city of Rio on the other. He always came on Saturdays and stayed for Sunday, and sometimes, on his short vacations, he stayed for days. We could see it was his farewell. His faculties were intact, and he gave the impression that his spirit would not wither away, but would be snuffed out suddenly in the middle of some more intense or prolonged contemplation or meditation. Still, his physical stamina was waning, and we could see how tired he was after thinking so long, and his involuntary tribute to doubt: whether he had taken full advantage of his time on earth, or had lived in vain. He had taken his taste for obscurity, modesty, and withdrawal all too seriously, had courted anonymity excessively. Perhaps he realized that oblivion was about to engulf him – except that in some rare spirits the memory of him would last longer, until they in turn were engulfed.

How gentle were those final days he gave us, how piercing, how profoundly melancholic, yet with a melancholy for the moments that we wish to make eternal, or so that others may enjoy them by our side, for them not to vanish entirely like falling stars! He often liked to sit on a bench by the sea, or should I say by the lake, from the impression it gave, and watch the dusk, without missing the slightest subtle change in the air, the sky, the water, the colors on the horizon, the murmurings and silence of the solitude. How often by day, as we walked through the woods near the house, as I opened the way for us to pass in the brushes, he would ask me not to disturb nature, to respect the intricate, unexpected wildness of it all, because that disorder was infinitely superior to anything art could attempt to depict. He found the most barren and arid landscape more beautiful than the gardens of Sallust or Louis XIV. Ah! If he had been the one to discover and lay claim to America, the axe would never have entered this land! And the torch? For him, slashing-and-burning was like torching someone at the stake. The fire licked up the precious resins, the sap, the life juices – the countless whimsical designs by unparalleled artists, all in their respective genres, all unique models of color and sensitivity. The fire appeared to consume him with a cruel, pulsating pain, all his subtle connections to nature and universal life, all the nerves of his outer intellect.

He truly loved Brazilian nature, and to no end. Many times I slipped into our conversations the idea of a trip to Europe to see if it would awaken some forgotten affinities or dormant memories. Yet his entire European side was dead, atrophied. What had replaced it, alive and errant, was a new, American, Brazilian sensitivity. Our land never ceased to enchant him. It told him secrets it did not tell us, that in order to feel, perhaps one had to have possessed and renounced a former incarnation, another world. If we Brazilians could only feel such love! Tautphoeus' perennial aging was one of the influences that developed in me the taste, the enchantment (although purely sentimental and naïve on my part) that contact with Brazil holds for me to this day. In Tautphoeus, that love was different: refined, spiritual, intellectual, aesthetic. In me, it became a simple affinity of the heart, a tenderness, a yearning for life, but this affinity owed a great deal to the spectacle of affectionate daydreaming by that wise old man – that ancient Greek, that philosopher born and raised in other climes – before the amenity and sweetness of the tropics, our rough-hewn picturesque scenery, the touches of mutation in natural stages, the modulation, the colors, our landscape's intimate solitude.

At the time of my literary vainglory, two things about him puzzled me. First, that despite all his erudition, he never published anything. Second, that he could be so submissively Catholic. Now, in his later years, during our walks in the forest and our *soirées* by my little cove, gilded by the moonlight, our conversations turned to religion. Oh, what fabulous monologues were his! The last time he crossed our *mare clausum* he returned home to die. The vestiges of his thinking remained with me for years, and I still sometimes feel the fleeting ripples. Through my talks with him, I came to understand that a great spirit can feel at will, free, in a revealed religion, and that writers as such do not represent the thinkers' elite, that next to them, or perhaps above them, is a kind of intellectual Trappist, with a vow of silence, taking refuge there and experiencing a disdain for the limelight, with its vulgar ostentation, its poorly disguised lust for money, it frivolous manners, its expropriation of creation by others, its lack of inner sincerity. To shun the stage or today's marketplace cannot be a sign of intellectual inferiority.

My lasting impression of Tautphoeus can be summed up in Goethe's conversation with Eckermann about Alexander Von Humboldt: "What a man he is! Long as I have known him, he never surprises me anew. One may say he has not his equal in knowledge and living wisdom. Then he has a many-sidedness such as I have found nowhere else. On whatever subject you approach him, he is at home, and lavishes upon us his intellectual treasures. He is like a fountain with many pipes, under which you need only hold a vessel, and from which refreshing and inexhaustible streams are ever flowing. He will stay here some days; and I already feel that it will be with me as if I had lived for years."[86] To hear him, to watch him, to live with him was literally to forget the present and join Socrates' followers. He was one of those copies, reproduced over and over and from era to era in different countries, but which nevertheless maintains the superiority and original primacy of the noblest of human models.

86 Quoted here from the English translation of *Conversations of Goethe with Eckermann and Soret*, London, 1883, pp. 177–178. T.N.

CHAPTER XXVI

THE LAST TEN YEARS (1889–1899)

The FALL OF THE EMPIRE had put an end to my career. The monarchist cause was to be my last contact with politics. I spent 1889 to 1890 entirely under the impact of November 15, following May 13, writing my soliloquies in a Thebes where I could walk hundreds of miles without a single soul with whom to speak. My strongest impression from 1891 was the death of the Emperor. From 1892 to 1893 there was a respite, and religion overshadowed everything else. It was the time of my mysterious, indefinable return to the faith, when a veritable dove called after the flood, bringing the olive leaf of life reborn. From 1893 to 1895 I suffered the shock of the Revolt and Saldanha's death, the subjects of my two books *Balmaceda* and *Intervenção*.[87] However, starting in 1893, the subject that was to become my life's literary devotion, my father's *Life*, had gripped me and would occupy me for six straight years, to the point of complete absorption. As I wrote a few pages back, my spirit now aspired in every way to definitive form and repose. On November 15 our monarchy had experienced what I called an assumption: it had lived and ended as a national incarnation. The wand left by the fairy godmother in the cradle of our nationhood had been broken and cast away, and who can say that she had not foreseen the outcome? Independence, National Unity, Abolition: no dynasty had ever inscribed such a perfect *cartouche* on its pyramid. When I thought of the role played by the Brazilian reigning house, Dom Pedro I, Dom Pedro II, Dona Isabel, and the necessary conditions of national unanimity, spontaneity, and purpose for it to play that role again

---

87 On Saldanha da Gama and Nabuco's book *A Intervenção estrangeira* (1896), see note 37 above. *Balmaceda* (1895) dealt with the war in Chile in 1891, at the end of which the defeated president José Manuel Balmaceda committed suicide. R.S.

in keeping with its legend, the problem exceeded my imagination, and I found it an assault on History to want to add a new panel to that triptych, except by the hand of a genius, a guarantee, a delicacy, a stroke of fortune against all odds.

On the other hand, during the years I worked on my father's *Life*, my attitude was subtly affected by the spirit of the old generations that created and founded the liberal regime that our generation had allowed to be destroyed. What I breathed in those vast archives was not an irreconcilable monarchist spirit, like a religion in itself or a state of bliss for those who stood out in the world for professing it. The monarchy during those times of incomparable political architects, stonemasons, and sculptors was a beautiful and pure form, but which could not exist on its own. Their patriotic interest, love, zeal, and fervor focused on the national substance, the country. Their vassalage to the monarchist principle was merely a tribute paid to the first of social conveniences. For such men, truly founding fathers, an earthquake could shake the institutions, but Brazil would exist forever, and it would be their duty to come to its aid in time of peril, whatever the storm raging around it, and the more wounded, maimed, and exhausted, the greater their duty not to abandon it. They never created a dilemma between the monarchy and the fatherland, because the fatherland could have no rival.

Those manly sentiments, that old loyalty, had a great impact on me, and as I breathed it, my desire increased to at least not leave my tomb walled off from the future. I understand Berryer's dying letter to Henry V, as I understand Chambord's letter concerning the white flag. The French monarchy had created a chivalry, an aristocratic point of honor, the spirit of a class apart, and even so it was like Berryer himself, like Chateaubriand, like the Duc de Aumale – *"La France était toujours là!"* – that ever since colonial times our statesmen and the Emperor reflected their absolute patriotic sentiment and had placed the fatherland above and beyond dispute with any other idea or sentiment. I, however, had no shred of legitimism, of divine right. My nature, the tonic accent, was different: liberal, not in the passing, political sense of the word, but in the eternal human sense, and as a liberal, my life's central aspiration could only be to never dissociate myself from my country's fate, whatever its form of government.

Thus, even as a monarchist, I distanced myself from politics little by little. My spirit had crystallized in facets that would always make me reject partisan politics as anti-political. What else could I have attempted alone, on my own? In 1879 I had enlisted in a campaign that I believed would last beyond my own lifetime. I thus made a sort of perpetual vow to serve a great national cause that was supposed to last more than thirty years, but in fact lasted only nine. Even so, I saved no energy, initiative, or imagination for other undertakings. Besides, abolition's universal thrust had isolated me from the parties, distanced me from their contentious sphere. By habit, I now aspired to live where there was more breathing room, where I could inhale moral unanimity, faith, human optimism, and the oxygen of great ideal winds.

I was also convinced that rival parties, men, and institutions in the same society tend to seek the same level, like liquids in communicating vessels, and that political people are one and the same, with each side's idealists and radicals representing imperceptible minorities. Finally, there was my inability to deal with the personal element, on which nearly all the results depend in politics. It was entirely impossible for me to retrieve the inner impulse, movement, or impetus of our old abolitionist volleys. I saw all the party struggles, grassroots *meetings*, agitated Chamber sessions, and oratorical tirades as belonging to the age of chivalry. The slightest political issue provoked an invincible timidity in me, and they all became national and international matters of conscience. A series of reflections, in the form of political maxims, signaled other danger warnings about any unknown surface on which I might dare to tread. Thus, from that point on, I gave up dealing with political parties and events. My sphere had become entirely subjective. "There are times in which to associate with others, even with those better than ourselves, means to betray our inner ideal, which we must refine and polish infinitely in our own way." This phrase that I wrote about André Rebouças' isolation, when I still could not have imagined his melancholic end, expresses much of my own feeling. One needs to steal part of life from the world, and it had better be the final part, to devote it to the thoughts and aspirations that we do not wish to die with us.

During the last ten years, my political interest has given way gradually to religious and literary interests, until almost nothing remains of it except what it has in common with them. When I say political interest, I mean the political spirit, since the emotion, the part I play in the country's fortune, increases with the vicissitudes, contingencies, and whirlwinds of each new drama. The playwright and actor disappear, but the spectator feels the urge grow and become pressing. I can thus finish the story of my political years here, and even that of all my formative years, because among the new influences that are bound to dominate the rest of my life, I had already found the religious influence in my childhood and in my youthful learning. For years, my literary interests waged a winning battle against politics, until abolition came and relegated them, along with everything else, to a remote background. After that great focus of attention expired, no other interest held the same power against my literary inclinations. Even so, perhaps there was merely a fusion between my literary interests and politics. In fact, history is the only field in which I would still cultivate politics, because I would not risk lacking indulgence, which is charity of the spirit, or tolerance, the form of justice I can achieve. My spirit crystallized under these two facets to which I just referred. When I speak of the letters, I mean simply what they signify for me: the beautiful, sensitive, human side of things within my reach, the resonance, the admiration, and the state of spirit in which they leave me. It was the inner need to cultivate kindness that perhaps led me to trade politics for literature once and for all and consider my public life at an end. I believed that for the rest of my days my intellectual calling – politics had never been anything else for me – would be to polish images, emotions, and memories that I might wish to take in my soul. I viewed life in different historical periods through diverse lenses: the first, through the heat of youth, pleasure, the intoxication of living, and curiosity for the world. Then came ambition, popularity, the emotion of the political stage, the effort and reward in the struggle to make men free (all seen through magnifying glasses). Later – by way of contrast – nostalgia for our past and the growing appeal of our nature, withdrawal from the world into the sweetness of the home, our friends' tombs and our children's cradles (all still seen through emotional prisms). As I bid farewell to the Creator, I hope to see life through the lenses of Epictetus, pure and undistorted: admiration and recognition...

BIOGRAPHICAL APPENDIX

ABDUL-HAMID II (1842–1918), 34th Ottoman Sultan and the last to rule with absolute power, from 1876 until deposed in 1909. His government was marked by a decline in both the power and extension of the Ottoman Empire.

ABRANTES, Marquis of (Miguel Calmon du Pin e Almeida, 1796–1865), Brazilian writer, politician and diplomat. Served as minister in several cabinets, including Finance and Foreign Affairs.

ALENCAR, José Martiniano de (1829–77), Brazilian lawyer, journalist and Romantic novelist who laid the foundations for Brazilian national literature. Famous for his "Indianist" novels *Iracema* and *O Guarani*, but also regionalist (*O Gaúcho*), historical (*A guerra dos mascates*), and urban novels (*Senhora*).

ALLEN, Charles Harris (1824–1904), Secretary of the British and Foreign Anti-Slavery Society, 1879–98.

AMPÈRE, André-Marie (1775–1836), French physicist, philosopher, scientist and mathematician.

ANDRADA E SILVA, José Bonifácio de (1783–1838), Brazilian statesman, the "Patriarch of Independence". Tutor of D. Pedro II

ANDRADE PINTO, José Caetano de (1826–85), Brazilian lawyer. Chamberlain to the Emperor and member of the Council of State.

ARNOLD, Matthew (1822–88), English poet, literary, cultural and social critic. Author of *Culture and Anarchy* (1869) and *Democracy* (1879).

AULD, Captain Thomas (1795–1880), American planter. Husband of Lucretia Auld, who inherited land and slaves from her father, Aaron Anthony, including Frederick Douglass.

BAGEHOT, Walter (1826–77), British journalist and economist, editor of *The Economist* (1860–77) and author of *The English Constitution* (1867). He had a huge influence on Nabuco's political thinking. Chapter II of this autobiography is devoted to him.

BAILEY, Frederick, *see* DOUGLASS, Frederick.

BANKS, Nathaniel Prentice (1816–94), American military and political leader. Governor of Massachusetts, Speaker of the House of Representatives, and general in the Union Army during the American Civil War.

BANVILLE, Théodore de (1823–91), French poet and writer. One of the last Romantic poets, disciple of Victor Hugo.

BARAIL, François Claude du (Comte du Barail, 1820–1902), French general and Minister of War during the presidency of Marshall MacMahon (1873–79).

BARBOSA, Rui (1849–1923), Brazilian jurist, politician, diplomat, writer and renowned orator. Outstanding figure in the abolitionist campaign. Brazilian representative at the 2nd Peace Conference at The Hague (1907) and presidential candidate in 1910 and 1919. Founding member of the Brazilian Academy of Letters and president 1908–19.

BARROS Cavalcanti de Albuquerque Lacerda, ADOLFO (1834–1905), Brazilian politician. President of the Provinces of Amazonas (1864–65), Santa Catarina (1865–67 and 1867–68) and Pernambuco (1878–79).

BARTHÉLEMY-SAINT-HILAIRE, Jules (1805–95), French philosopher, journalist and statesman.

BAZAINE, François Achille (1811–88), French soldier. Marshall of France who surrendered to the Prussians at Metz in 1870. He was condemned to death for treason in 1873, a sentence commuted to 20 years of prison in exile, from which he escaped.

BENTO de Souza e Castro, Antônio (1843–98), Brazilian lawyer, public prosecutor and judge. After the death of Luís Gama in August 1882, he took over the leadership of the abolitionist movement in São Paulo.

BERRYER, Antoine Pierre (1790–1868), French lawyer, politician and famed orator.

BILAC, Olavo Brás Martins dos Guimarães (1865–1918), Brazilian journalist and one of Brazil's most important poets.

BISMARCK, Otto Leopold von (1815–98), Prussian nobleman, diplomat, soldier and politician. Prime Minister of Prussia 1862–71, largely responsible for the unification of Germany, and Imperial Chancellor 1871–90.

BLANC, Baron (Alberto de Blanc, 1835–1904), Italian diplomat and politician.

BLANC, Louis Jean Joseph Charles (1811–82), French Utopian socialist who played an important role in the Revolution of 1848.

BOCAIUVA, Quintino Antônio Ferreira de Sousa (1836–1912), Brazilian journalist and politician. Minister of Foreign Affairs after the proclamation of the Republic (1889–91).

BORDALO PINHEIRO, Rafael Augusto Prostes (1846–1905), Portuguese professor, artist, caricaturist, journalist and playwright.

BOUTMY, Émile (1835–1906), French lawyer, scientist, politician and sociologist.

BRADLEY, Joseph Philo (1813–92), American lawyer and jurist. Justice of the Supreme Court and member of the Electoral Commission that ruled in favor of Hayes in the disputed 1876 presidential election.

BRESSANT, Jean Baptiste Prosper (1815–86), highly renowned French actor.

BRIGHT, John (1811–89), English politician. Member of the House of Commons from 1843 to 1889. On the radical wing of the Liberal party, he was one of the greatest orators of his generation and a sharp critic of British foreign policy.

BROGLIE, 4th Duc de (Jacques Victor Albert, 1821–1901), French historian and monarchist politician. Prime Minister twice, in 1873–74 and 1877.

BROWN, John (1800–59), American abolitionist. Hanged in Virginia after his conviction for attempting to seize an arsenal.

BURCKHARDT, Carl (1818–97), German art historian. Considered one of the fathers of cultural history, his most famous work *The Civilization of the Renaissance in Italy* (1860).

CAETANO dos Santos, João (1808–63), Brazilian actor, set designer and theatrical entrepreneur.

CAMPOS, MARTINHO Álvares da Silva (1816–87), Brazilian physician and politician. Deputy, senator and member of the Council of State, president of Rio province in 1881 and Prime Minster for six months in 1882.

CANTÙ, Cesa (1804–95), Italian historian, educator, writer, intellectual and politician. Author of *Universal History*, in 72 volumes, inspired by the ideals of liberal Catholicism.

CARLOS, Don (Carlos Maria de Borbón y Austria-Este, 1848–1909), Pretender to the Spanish throne 1868–1909 and to the French throne 1887–1909.

CARNEIRO LEÃO, Honório Hermeto, *see* PARANÁ.

CARO, MADAME (Pauline Cassin, 1835–1901), French writer. Wife of Elme-Marie Caro (1826–87), French philosopher, spiritualist and literary critic.

CARVALHO, Alberto Antonio de Morais (1801–78), Portuguese lawyer and liberal politician.

CARVALHO, Ana Rosa Falcão de (1810–57), owner of the Massangana sugar plantation in Pernambuco and godmother of Joaquim Nabuco.

CARVALHO BORGES, Antônio Pedro de (Baron Carvalho Borges, 1824–88), Brazilian soldier, mathematician, and diplomat. Headed various diplomatic missions in South America and Europe. Minster in Washington when Nabuco was attaché there in 1876–77.

CARVALHO MOREIRA, Arthur de (c.1844–1918), son of the Baron of Penedo, Brazilian lawyer and diplomat, friend of Joaquim Nabuco.

CASIMIR-PÉRIER, Jean (1847–1907), French politician. Prime Minister 1893-94 and fifth President of the Third French Republic, 1894-95.

CASTELAR Y RIPOLL, Emilio (1832–99), Spanish lawyer, professor, journalist, writer and politician. He was the penultimate President of the First Spanish Republic, from 1873 to 1874, when he resigned and went into exile in Paris.

CASTRO, LUÍS, Portuguese lawyer, journalist and editor, who settled in Brazil. Editor of the *Jornal do Commercio* in Rio de Janeiro for 20 years.

CASTRO ALVES, Antônio Frederico de (1847–71), Brazilian Romantic poet. Enthusiast of great causes of freedom and justice, many of his poems adopted abolitionist themes.

CAXIAS, Duque de (Luís Alves de Lima e Silva, 1803–80), Brazilian soldier and statesman. Fought in the War of Independence and the wars in the Rio de la Plata 1825–28 and 1851–52, Commander of the Armies of the Triple Alliance in the Paraguayan War (1864–70). Caxias was twice Minister of War and three times

Prime Minister, 1855–57, 1861–62 and 1875–78. He is the Patron of the Brazilian Army.

CHAMBORD, Comte de (Henri V of France [Henri Charles Ferdinand Marie Dieudonné d'Artois], 1820–83), grandson of Charles X (1824–30) and legitimate heir to the French throne from 1848 until his death.

CHAMFORT, Nicolas de (1740–94), French poet, journalist, humorist and moralist.

CHARLES EDMOND Henri de Coussemaker (1805–76), French jurist, musicologist and ethnologist.

CHATEAUBRIAND, François-René Auguste de (1768–1848), French writer, essayist, diplomat and politician.

CLAPP, João Fernandes, Brazilian merchant, journalist and politician. Together with José do Patrocínio, he created the *Confederação Abolicionista* in 1883 and became its president.

COBDEN, Richard (1804–65), English politician, advocate of free trade and peace, one of the greatest Liberal thinkers on international affairs.

COIMBRA, Estácio de Albuquerque (1872–1937), Brazilian lawyer and politician.

COLOMA, LUÍS Roldán (1851–1915), Spanish Jesuit writer and journalist. His novel *Pequeñeces* (1891) satirized the flaws of the Spanish aristocracy during the time of the Restoration.

CONSTÂNCIO ALVES, Antônio (1862–1933), Brazilian physician, journalist, orator and essayist.

CORDEIRO, João (1842–1931), Brazilian entrepreneur and politician. Active participant in the abolitionist movement in Ceará, as founder and President of the *Sociedade Cearense Libertadora*.

CORRÊA RABELLO (Francisco Corrêa Ferreira Rabello, 1844–92), Brazilian lawyer and politician.

COTEGIPE, Baron of (João Maurício Wanderley, 1815–89), Brazilian magistrate and Conservative politician. A senator and minister in several cabinets during the Second Reign, he was Prime Minister 1885–88, responsible for the law of 1885 that guaranteed freedom for slaves more than 60 years old after three years, with compensation for the owners. He opposed the total abolition of slavery to the bitter end.

COUSIN, Victor (1792–1867), French philosopher, politician, educational reformer and historian.

CURTIUS, Ernst (1814–96), German historian, archeologist and professor. Director of the Museum of Antiquities in Berlin and best known for his *History of Greece* (1857–67) in three volumes.

CZACKI, Cardinal Wlodzimierz (1834–88), Ukrainian Catholic Cardinal, papal nuncio in Paris 1879–82.

DANTAS, João dos Reis de Sousa (1828–97), Brazilian lawyer and politician.

DANTAS, Manuel Pinto de Sousa (1831–94), Brazilian lawyer and politician. senator, member of the Council of State, minister in several cabinets during the Second Reign, Prime Minister 1884–85, when he introduced a bill to free slaves at the age of 60 without compensation to their owners, which was twice rejected in the Chamber of Deputies.

DANTAS, Rodolfo Epifânio de Sousa (1855–1901), Brazilian lawyer, journalist and politician. Son of Senator Dantas. One of the founders of the *Jornal do Brasil* in 1891.

D'AUMALE, Duc (Henri Philippe Louis Eugène d'Orléans, 1822–97), French writer, politician and soldier. Leader of the Orleanists. In 1873, he presided over the court martial that sentenced Marshall Bazaine to death for treason, later commuted to 20 years of prison in exile.

DEODORO DA FONSECA, Manuel (1827–92), Brazilian soldier and politician. Hero of the Paraguayan War (1864–70), he proclaimed the Republic in 1889 and was the first President of Brazil 1889–91.

DICKENS, Charles (1812–70), English novelist. The most popular novelist of the Victorian age.

DISRAELI, Benjamin (1804–81), English politician. Leader of the Conservative Party, twice Prime Minister, 1868 and 1874–80.

DONOSO CORTÉS, Juan (Marquis of Valdegamas, 1809–53), Spanish philosopher, politician and diplomat.

DOUGLASS, Frederick (Frederick Augustus Washington Bailey, 1818–95), American abolitionist and social reformer, after escaping from slavery.

DUFAURE, Jules Armand Stanislas (1798–1881), French lawyer and statesman. Twice Prime Minister, in 1876 and 1877–79.

DUMAS *fils*, Alexandre (1824–95), French writer. Highly respected author of books and plays, son of Alexandre Dumas *père*.

DUPONT de l'Eure, Jacques-Charles (1767–1855), French politician. Prime Minister, February-September 1848.

ECKERMANN, Johann Peter (1792–1854), German poet. His best-known work was *Conversations with Goethe* (1836), the result of his association with Goethe during the last years of his life.

ELIOT, George (pseudonym of Mary Ann Evans, 1819–80), English novelist. *Middlemarch* (1872) is considered one of the greatest 19th-century novels.

ÉLISÉE RECLUS, Jean Jacques (1830–1905), French geographer and anarchist. His work includes the *New Universal Geography: the Earth and its Inhabitants* (1876–94), in 19 volumes.

EMERSON, Ralph Waldo (1803–1882), American clergyman, writer, "Transcendentalist" philosopher and poet. His works *Nature, Essays* and *Society and Solitude* had a great influence on 19th-century American intellectual life.

ESQUIROS, Henri- François-ALPHONESE (1812–76), French writer and politician. Author of *The Gospel of People* (1840), an essay on the life and character of Jesus as a social reformer.

EUSEBIO DE QUEIROS, *see* QUEIROS.

FABER, Frederick William (1814–63), English composer of hymns, theologian and writer. Although a convert to Catholicism, many of his hymns, including *Faith of Our Fathers*, are sung by Protestant congregations.

FALCÃO, Anníbal (1859–1900), Brazilian writer and politician. Abolitionist and republican. He is credited with writing the libretto, under a pen name, of *Colombo*, an opera composed by his friend Carlos Gomes (1836–96).

FARNESE, Flávio (1835–71), Brazilian politician, lawyer, poet and journalist. Founder of the newspapers *Atualidade* (1858) and *A República* (1871), and one of the founders of the Republican Party in 1870.

FEIJÓ, DIOGO Antônio (1784–1843), Brazilian Catholic priest and statesman. Regent of the Empire 1835–37.

FERREIRA DE MENESES, José (?–1881), Brazilian journalist and abolitionist. Son of slaves, he was the owner of the most powerful and popular abolitionist daily newspaper in Rio de Janeiro, *A Gazeta da Tarde*, which, after his sudden death in 1881, was purchased by José do Patrocínio.

FERREIRA VIANA, Antônio (1833–1903), Brazilian judge, journalist and politician. A philanthropist, he founded schools, hospitals, and charitable institutions, besides defending the abolition of slavery.

FISH, Hamilton (1808–93), American politician. Secretary of State to President Ulysses S. Grant (1869–77).

FRANCESCO II (1836–94), King of the Two Sicilies, 1859–61 before it was annexed to the Kingdom of Italy.

FRANCISCO OTAVIANO de Almeida Rosa (1825–89), Brazilian lawyer, journalist, diplomat, politician and poet. Senator 1867–89.

FREEMAN, Edward Augustus (1823–92), English historian. Author of *The Growth of the English Constitution from the Earliest Times* (1872).

GALLWEY, Peter (1820–1906), English Jesuit priest and writer. At the Jesuit church in Farm Street, London he had a profound influence on Joaquim Nabuco in 1892.

GAMA, LUÍS Gonzaga Pinto da (1830–82), Brazilian soldier, lawyer, journalist and poet. Son of a Portuguese father and African mother, he was a leader of the abolitionist movement in São Paulo.

GAMBETTA, Léon (1838–82), French political leader. Prime Minister 1881–82, who tragically died in office at the age of 44.

GARFIELD, James Abram (1831–81), American politician. After nine consecutive terms as Representative, he was elected the 20th President of the United States in 1881, but he was assassinated during his first year in office.

GARRISON, William Lloyd (1805–79), American journalist, abolitionist and social reformer. Editor of the radical abolitionist newspaper *The Liberator* and one of the founders of the American Anti-Slavery Society.

GLADSTONE, William Ewart (1809–98), British politician, leader of the Liberal Party, Prime Minister four times: 1868–74, 1880–85, 1886, and 1892–94.

GNEIST, Heinrich RUDOLF Hermann Friedrich VON (1816–95), German jurist, legislator, politician and scholar, whose teachings and publications, based on studies of the English system of government, had a great influence on the development of German administrative law.

GOIS E VASCONCELOS, Zacarias de (1815–77), Brazilian lawyer and Liberal politician, Prime Minister three times, 1862, 1864, 1866-68. Author of *Da Natureza e Limite do Poder Moderador* in favor of a stronger Parliamentary government.

GONTAUT-BIRON, Viscount of (Anne-Armand-Élie de Gontaut-Biron, 1817–90), French politician and diplomat.

GOSCHEN, George Joachim (1831–1907), English writer, politician, and businessman. He switched from the Liberal Party to the Conservative Party in 1886 over the question of Home Rule for Ireland.

GRAÇA ARANHA, José Pereira da (1868–1931), Brazilian writer and diplomat, author of *Canaã* (1902), a milestone of pre-Modernist literature.

GRANT, Ulysses Simpson (1822–85), American politician and soldier. Commander of the Union Army during the American War Civil, and 18th President of the United States (1869–77).

GREEN, Thomas Hill (1836–82), English philosopher heavily influenced by Hegel's metaphysical historicism and a politician associated with the Temperance movement.

GROTE, George (1794–1871), English historian and philosopher, noted for his works on Plato and Aristotle and his *History of Greece* (1846–56).

GUANGXU (1871–1908), Chinese Emperor of the Qing Dynasty, reigned under the regency of his aunt, the Empress Dowager Cixi, from 1875 until his death.

GUIMARÃES, APRÍGIO Justiniano da Silva (1832–80), Brazilian lawyer, journalist, writer and politician.

GUSMÃO LOBO, Francisco Leopoldino de (1838–1900), Brazilian journalist. An abolitionist and friend of Nabuco, he was editor of the *Jornal do Commercio* 1880-90.

HAMILTON, John Church (1792–1882), American historian and lawyer. Fifth child of Alexander Hamilton, one of the Founding Fathers of the United States, to whom he dedicated several books.

HAVET, Eugène (1813–89), French professor and scholar. Much of his work focused on religion, his main argument that the development of Christianity was more due to Greek philosophy than to the writing of the Hebrew prophets.

HAYES, Rutherford Birchard (1822–93), 19th President of the United States (1877–81). His election in 1876 was one of the most disputed in US history. *See* TILDEN below.

HENDRICKS, Thomas Andrews (1819–85), American politician. Governor of Indiana (1873–77) and 21st Vice-President of the United States under President Grover Cleveland (1885–89). He was the Democratic vice-presidential candidate defeated in the controversial election of 1876.

HENRI V of France, *see* CHAMBORD.

HEREDIA, José Maria de (1842–1905), Cuban-born poet who became a French citizen in 1893.

HUGO, Victor-Marie (1802–85), French novelist, poet, essayist and political activist.

HUMBOLDT, Alexander von (1769–1859), German geographer, naturalist and explorer.

ISABEL, Princess (Dona Isabel Cristina Leopoldina Augusta Micaela Gabriela Rafaela Gonzaga de Bragança e Bourbon, 1846–1921), daughter of Emperor D. Pedro II. She was Regent on three occasions and signed the law abolishing slavery in Brazil on 13 May 1888.

ITABORAÍ, Viscount of (Joaquim José Rodrigues Torres, 1802–72), Brazilian journalist and Conservative politician. Senator from 1844 and Prime Minister 1868-70.

JOÃO ALFREDO Corrêa de Oliveira (1835–1915), Brazilian lawyer and politician. Several times minister, president of the provinces of Pará and São Paulo, senator 1877–89 and Prime Minister 1888–89, introducing the legislation abolishing slavery.

JOHNSON, Andrew (1808–75), 17th President of the United States, after the assassination of Abraham Lincoln.

JUAN, Don (Juan Carlos María Isidro de Borbón y Braganza, 1802–87), Carlist claimant to the Spanish throne 1861–68 and to the French throne 1883–87. Father of Don Carlos of Spain.

LABOULAYE, Édouard René Lefèbvre de (1811–83), French jurist, poet, writer, republican and abolitionist. He conceived the idea of the Statue of Liberty in New York and the Luxemburg Gardens in Paris.

LAFAYETTE Rodrigues Pereira (1834–1917), Brazilian jurist, plantation owner, lawyer, journalist and politician. Prime Minister in 1883.

LAMAR, Lucius Quintus Cincinato (1825–93), American politician and jurist. Member of the House of Representatives, senator, and Secretary of the Interior in the first administration of President Grover Cleveland (1885–89).

LAMARTINE, Alphonse Marie Louis de Prat de (1790–1869), French writer, poet and politician. His poetry influenced Romanticism in France and throughout the world.

LAMENNAIS, Hughes Félicité Robert de (1782–1854), French philosopher and political writer.

LAVIGERIE, Cardinal Charles Martial Allemand (1825–92), French Catholic Cardinal.

LAVRADIO, 5th Marquis of (1794–1874), Portuguese nobleman and soldier.

LEDRU-ROLLIN, Alexandre-Auguste (1807–74), French lawyer and politician. Minister of the Interior February-May 1848, and Socialist candidate in the first ever presidential election in 1848 won by Louis-Napoleon Bonaparte.

LEMAÎTRE, Jules (Francois Jules Lemaître Elie, 1853–1914), French teacher, writer, critic and playwright.

LEO XIII, Pope (Vincenzo Gioacchino Raffaele Luigi Pecci Prosperi Buzzi, 1810–1903), Italian priest and social reformer. Pope from 1878 until his death.

LÉON SAY, Jean-Baptiste (1826–96), French politician and economist. Minister of Finance on four occasions from 1872 to 1882. Outstanding as editor and collaborator of *Dictionnaire des finances* and *Dictionnaire nouveau d'économie politique*.

LEWES, George Henry (1817–78), English philosopher, literary and theatre critic.

LILLY, William Samuel (1840–1919), English writer and politician. Converted to Catholicism in 1874, he served as secretary of the English Catholic Union.

LIMA, Manuel de OLIVEIRA (1867–1928), Brazilian diplomat and historian. Friend of Nabuco until they disagreed over relations with the United States and Panamericanism in 1906. Author of many books, including *Dom João VI no Brasil* (1909).

LINCOLN, Abraham (1809–65), 16th President of the United States (1861–65).

LITTRÉ, Émile Maximilien Paul (1801–81), French lexicographer and philosopher, famous for his *Dictionnaire de la langue française* (revised edition, 1877).

LUDWIG II (Ludwig Otto Friedrich Wilhelm von Wittelsbach, 1845–86), King of Bavaria from 1864 to 1886. Known as the "Mad King", he nevertheless left a huge legacy to the history of art and architecture, and was the patron of Richard Wagner.

MACAULAY, Thomas Babington (1800–59), English poet, historian and politician.

MACHADO DE ASSIS, Joaquim Maria (1839–1908), Brazilian writer, one of the most important figures in Portuguese-language literature. Best known for his short stories and his novels, including *The Posthumous Memoirs of Bras Cubas* (1881) and *Dom Casmurro* (1900). Founding member and first president of the Brazilian Academy of Letters, 1897–1908.

MACHADO PORTELA, Joaquim Pires (1827–1907), Brazilian writer and politician. Defeated Nabuco in the election of December 1884 in Recife.

MACIEL PINHEIRO, Luís Ferreira (1839–89), Brazilian lawyer and journalist.

MAC-MAHON, Marie Edme Patrice Maurice de (1808–1893), French military and political leader with the distinction of Marshall of France. President of the Third Republic (1873–79).

MAHAN, Alfred Thayer (1840–1914), US naval officer, geo-strategist and historian. His book *The Influence of Sea Power upon History* (1890) had enormous influence in shaping strategic thinking throughout the world.

MAISTRE, Joseph-Marie (1753–1821), French philosopher, lawyer and diplomat.

MANNING, Cardinal Henry Edward (1808–92), Anglican cleric who converted to Catholicism in 1851. Archbishop of Westminster, head of the Roman Catholic Church in Great Britain, from 1865 until his death.

MANUEL PEDRO Cardoso (1848–80), Brazilian lawyer, professor, journalist and politician.

MARBLE, Manton (1834–1917), American journalist. Owner and editor of the *New York World* 1862-76.

MARIANO Carneiro da Cunha, José (1850–1912), Brazilian lawyer and journalist. An abolitionist, he had been a classmate of Joaquim Nabuco at the Faculty of Law in Recife.

MARSHALL, James William (1822–1910), American politician. US Postmaster-General under President Ulysses S. Grant (1869–77).

MAUÁ, Baron and Viscount (Irineu Evangelista de Sousa, 1813–89), Brazilian merchant, shipbuilder, railway builder, industrialist and banker.

MAY, Thomas Erskine (1815–86), English Constitutional theoretician and historian. Author of the fundamental *Erskine May: Parliamentary Practice* (1844).

MEYER, Joseph (1796–1856), German industrialist and publisher.

MIGNET, François-Auguste-Marie (1796–1884), French journalist and historian.

MIGUEL I, Dom (1802–66), seventh child and third son of D. João VI and Carlota Joaquina. He was King of Portugal 1828–1834.

MILL, John Stuart (1806–73), English philosopher and economist, one of the most influential 19th-century liberal thinkers.

MOCENNI, Monsignor Mario (1823–1904), Italian Roman Catholic Cardinal and Vatican diplomat.

MOMMSEN, Christian Matthias Theodor (1817–1903), German historian, specialist on Ancient Roman history. Winner of the Nobel Prize for Literature in 1902 for his *History of Rome (Römische Geschichte)* published in 5 volumes 1854–56.

MONTEZUMA, Francisco Gê Acayaba de (Viscount of Jequitinhonha, 1794–1870), Brazilian lawyer, jurist and politician. Despite a long political career as member of the Council of State and senator, he only participated directly in government in 1837 as Minister of Foreign Affairs.

MOREIRA, Nicolau Joaquim (1824–94), Brazilian physician and writer. One of the first Brazilian authors to discuss anthropological ideas, then widely disseminated in Europe and the United States. He opposed the introduction of Chinese or Indian immigrants as an alternative to African slave labor.

MOREIRA DE BARROS, Antônio (1841–96), Brazilian politician. President of the province of Alagoas 1867–68 and Minister of Foreign Affairs 1879–80.

MORLEY, John (1838–1923), English writer, newspaper editor and Liberal politician. Biographer of Gladstone.

MURAT, Luís Morton Barreto (1861–1929), Brazilian journalist and poet. Participated in the campaigns for the abolition of slavery and proclamation of the Republic.

MUSSET, Alfred Louis Charles de (1810–57), French Romantic poet, novelist and playwright.

MUSURUS PASHA, Constantine (1807–91), Turkish diplomat. Ambassador in London from 1851.

NABUCO DE ARAÚJO FILHO, José Thomaz (1813–78), Brazilian magistrate and politician. President of the province of São Paulo, Justice Minister in several cabinets, member of the Council of State and senator 1858–78. Father of Joaquim Nabuco.

NEWMAN, Cardinal John Henry (1801–90), English clergyman who converted to Catholicism in 1845 and became a central figure in 19th-century English religious history.

OLINDA, Marquis of (Pedro de Araújo Lima, 1793–1870), Brazilian lawyer, journalist and politician. Regent (1837–40) and Conservative Prime Minister on four occasions: 1848–49, 1857–58, 1862–64 and 1865–66.

OLIVEIRA MARTINS, Joaquim Pedro de (1845–94), Portuguese politician and social scientist. One of the founders of the group "Os Vencidos da Vida" (Life's Vanquished), which included Eça de Queiros and Ramalho Urtigão.

OLLIVIER, Émile (1825–1913), French politician and writer. Prime Minister January-August 1870.

ORLÉANS E BRAGANÇA, D. Pedro de (1875–1940), firstborn son of the Imperial Princess, D. Isabel and the Conde d'Eu, and heir to the throne of the Brazilian Empire. In 1908 he abdicated in favor of his brother D. Luís Maria Filipe (1878–1920).

OTTONI, Cristiano Benedito (1811–96), Brazilian soldier, engineer, professor and politician.

OTTONI, TEÓFILO Benedito (1807–69), Brazilian journalist, merchant, politician and entrepreneur.

PARANÁ, Marquis of (Honório Hermeto Carneiro Leão, 1801–56), Brazilian lawyer, coffee planter, diplomat, magistrate and politician. Prime Minister from 1853 to 1856.

PARANHOS, see RIO BRANCO.

PARIS, Comte de (Louis Phillipe Alberto d'Orléans, 1838-1894), grandson of Louis-Philippe (1830–48) and pretender to the French throne from 1848 to his death. In 1871 he renounced his claim to the throne in favor of the Comte de Chambord.

PATROCÍNIO, JOSÉ Carlos do (1853–1905), Brazilian pharmacist, journalist, writer, orator and political activist. One of the important figures in the Brazilian abolitionist movement and one of Brazil's greatest journalists, owning two newspapers: *Gazeta da Tarde* and *A Cidade do Rio*.

PEDREIRA do Couto Ferraz, Luís (Viscount of Bom Retiro, 1818–86), Brazilian lawyer and politician. President of the province of Rio de Janeiro (1848–53), member of the Council of State and senator.

PEDRO II (Pedro de Alcântara João Carlos Leopoldo Salvador Bibiano Francisco Xavier de Paula Leocádio Miguel Gabriel Rafael Gonzaga, 1825–91), Emperor of Brazil 1840–89.

PEDRO LUÍS Pereira de Sousa (1839–84), Brazilian lawyer, journalist, politician, orator and poet. His works included *Os voluntários da morte*, an epic poem dedicated to Poland (1864).

PEIXOTO, Floriano Vieira (1839–95), Brazilian military and political leader. First Vice-President (1889–91) and second President of Brazil (1891–94).

PELLETAN, Pierre Clément EUGÈNE (1813–84). French writer, journalist and politician.

PENEDO, Baron of (Francisco Inácio de Carvalho Moreira, 1816–1906), Brazilian lawyer, politician and diplomat. Minister in London 1855–89, except during the period in which diplomatic relations were severed between the two countries, from 1863 to 1865.

PEREIRA, Lafayette Rodrigues, *see* LAFAYETTE, Counselor.

PIMENTA BUENO, José Antônio (Viscount and Marquis of São Vicente, 1803-78), Brazilian magistrate and politician. Prime Minister 1870–71.

PIMENTEL, Sancho de Barros (1849–1924), Brazilian lawyer and politician. President of the provinces of Piauí (1878), Paraná (1881–82), and Ceará (1882).

PRADO, ANTÔNIO da Silva (1840–1929), Brazilian lawyer, planter, politician and entrepreneur. As Minister of Foreign Trade and Agriculture in the João Alfredo cabinet in 1888, he encouraged European immigration to replace slave labor. Under the Republic, he was Mayor of São Paulo 1899–1911.

PRÉVOST-PARADOL, Lucien-Anatole (1829–70), French journalist and essayist. His book *La France nouvelle* (1865) was an important reference for Orleanists and also for French Liberals.

QUARAIM, Baron of (Pedro Rodrigues Fernandes Chaves, 1810–66), Brazilian magistrate, cattle rancher, journalist, diplomat and politician. Senator from 1853 to 1866.

QUEIRÓS Coutinho Matoso da Câmara, EUSÉBIO DE (1812–68), Brazilian magistrate and politician. Minister of Justice from 1848 to 1852 in the Marquis of Olinda cabinet and author of the law for the suppression of the slave trade in 1850.

QUINET, Edgar (1803–75), French historian and intellectual.

RAMALHO ORTIGÃO, José Duarte (1836–1915), Portuguese realist writer. One of the founders of the literary group "Life's Vanquished".

RAMPOLLA, Cardinal (Mariano Rampolla del Tindaro, 1843–1913), Italian Roman Catholic Cardinal and the Vatican's Secretary of State (1887–1910).

RANCÉS Y VILLANUEVA, Manuel (1824–97), Spanish journalist, politician and diplomat.

RANKE, Leopold von (1795–1886), German historian. Considered one of the greatest of 19th-century historians, the father of the scientific method in historical research, emphasizing primary sources.

REBOUÇAS, ANDRÉ Pinto (1838–98), Brazilian engineer. Of African descent (his father was the son of a freed slave), Rebouças was a close friend of Nabuco and a leading abolitionist.

REBOUÇAS, Antônio Pereira (1798–1880), Brazilian lawyer and politician. Father of André Rebouças and Antônio Pereira Rebouças Filho.

REBOUÇAS FILHO, Antônio Pereira (1839–74), Brazilian military engineer. Brother of André Rebouças.

RÉMUSAT, Comte de (Charles-François-Marie de Rémusat, 1797–1875), French politician and philosopher.

RENAN, Joseph Ernest (1823–92), French writer, philosopher and historian of Christianity. He had a huge influence on Joaquim Nabuco, who dedicates Chapter VII of this autobiography to him.

RIO BRANCO, Baron of (José Maria da Silva Paranhos Júnior, 1845–1912), lawyer, historian, diplomat and statesman. Son of the Viscount of Rio Branco, and close friend of Nabuco. He began his career as Consul in Liverpool 1876–93, and after several major victories in territorial disputes with Brazil's neighbours, he served as Minister of Foreign Affairs from 1902 to 1912.

RIO BRANCO, Viscount of (José Maria da Silva Paranhos, 1819–80), Brazilian politician, journalist, diplomat and statesman. He was Minister of Foreign Affairs 1855–57 and 1858–59, and Conservative Prime Minister 1871–75, during which time he enacted the Law of Free Birth (1871).

ROBESON, George Maxwell (1829–97), American lawyer and politician. Secretary of the Navy under President Ulysses S. Grant (1869–77).

ROBINSON, Lucius (1810–91), American lawyer and politician. Governor of New York (1877–79).

RODRIGUES ALVES, Francisco de Paula (1848–1919), Brazilian politician, 5th President of Brazil (1902–6), elected to a second term in 1918 but fell ill and died before taking office.

RODRIGUES TORRES, *see* ITABORAI.

ROTHSCHILD, Baron Lionel Nathan (1808–1879), British banker and politician.

RUSKIN, John (1819–1900), English writer, poet, artist, art critic and social critic. His essays on art and architecture were extremely influential in the Victorian Age.

SAINTE-BEUVE, Charles Augustin (1804–69), French literary critic and important figure in the history of French literature.

SALDANHA DA GAMA, Luís Filipe de (1846–95), Brazilian naval commander and one of the principal leaders of both the Naval Revolt and the Federalist Revolution against the government of Floriano Peixoto (1892–94).

SALDANHA MARINHO, Joaquim (1816–95), Brazilian lawyer, journalist, sociologist and politician.

SALES TORRES HOMEM, Francisco de (Viscount of Inhomirim, 1812–76), Brazilian lawyer, journalist and politician. He was the son of a priest and a mother who was the granddaughter of a slave. Deputy, senator, twice Minister of Finance, in 1858–59 and 1870–71, and an opponent of slavery.

SALISBURY, 3rd Marquis of (Robert Arthur Talbot Gascoyne-Cecil, 1830–1903), English politician, leader of the Conservative Party, three times Prime Minister, 1885–86, 1886–92 and 1895–1902.

SALVADOR DE MENDONÇA (Salvador de Menezes Drummond Furtado de Mendonça, 1841–1913), Brazilian lawyer, journalist and diplomat. One of the founders of the Republican Party in 1870, consul-general in New York 1876–89, Brazilian minister in Washington 1889–98.

SAND, George (pen name of Amandine, also Amantine, Aurore Lucile Dupin, Baroness of Dudevant, 1804–76), French novelist and feminist. She was married to the French writer Maurice Sand (pen name of Jean-François-Maurice-Arnauld, Baron Dudevant, 1823–89). Her lovers included writer Jules Sandeau and composer Frédéric Chopin.

SANDEAU, Leonard Sylvain Julien (JULES) (1811–83), French writer and novelist.

SARAIVA, Francisco Rodrigues dos SANTOS (1831–1900), Portuguese linguist, theologian, philosopher and poet. Author of the *Novíssimo dicionário latino-português: etimológico, prosódico, histórico, geográfico, mitológico, biográfico, etc,* many editions.

SARAIVA, José Antônio (1823–95), Brazilian lawyer, diplomat and politician. President of the provinces of Piauí, Alagoas, São Paulo and Pernambuco, Foreign Minister 1865–66, senator 1869–89, Liberal Prime Minster in 1880–82 and 1885. The Saraiva Law (1881) made voting for the Chamber of Deputies for the first time direct and restricted the suffrage to literate voters.

SCHERER, Edmond Henri Adolphe (1815–89), French journalist, literary critic, theologian and politician.

SCHURZ, Carl Christian (1829–1906), German-born American lawyer, journalist and politician. The first US senator born in Germany (elected in 1869), he fought for anti-racist causes.

SERRA, Joaquim (1838–88), Brazilian journalist, playwright and abolitionist.

SILVEIRA DA MOTA, José Inácio (1811–93), Brazilian lawyer and politician. Member of the Council of State and senator 1855–89, he was the author of the 1862 law prohibiting the sale of slaves in public auctions and the separation of children from parents and husbands from wives.

SINIMBU, Viscount of (João Lins Vieira Cansanção de, 1810–1906), Brazilian politician. President of various provinces, minister in several cabinets, Liberal Prime Minister 1878–80.

SOARES DE MEIRELLES, Pedro Rodrigues (1849–82), Brazilian lawyer. Republican and one of the five first editors of the newspaper *A República*, together with Quintino Bocaiúva, Aristides Lobo, Flávio Farnese and Luiz Vieira Ferreira.

SOARES DE SOUSA, Paulino José (Viscount of Uruguay, 1807–66), Brazilian jurist and politician. Minister of Justice 1840 and 1841–43, Foreign Minister 1843–44 and 1849–53, when he had to deal with British pressure for the abolition of the slave trade, senator from 1849 and member of the Council of State from 1853.

SODRÉ Pereira, JERÔNIMO de Azevedo (1840–1909), Brazilian physician and politician. The deputy who spoke in favor of the abolition of slavery in the Chamber of Deputies in 1879. President of the province of Sergipe in 1889.

SOUSA CARVALHO, Antônio Alves de, Brazilian lawyer, journalist and politician. President of the provinces of Espírito Santo, Alagoas and Maranhão. Founder and editor of the Rio de Janeiro newspaper *Diário do Brasil*.

SOUSA LEÃO, Domingos de, *see* VILA BELA.

SOUTO, TEODURETO Carlos de Faria (1841–93), Brazilian lawyer, journalist and politician. President of the provinces de Santa Catarina (1883) and Amazonas (1884).

SOUZA CORREA, João Arthur de (1856–1900), Brazilian diplomat. Minister in London from 1890 to 1900.

SOUZA PINTO, José Maria Frederico de (1806–54), Portuguese merchant, lawyer and writer. A naturalized Brazilian, he was the founder of the *Instituto dos Advogados do Brasil*.

SPENCER, Herbert (1820–1903), English philosopher and sociologist.

STRAUSS, David Friedrich (1808–74), German theologian. A disciple of Hegel, his *Life of Jesus* (1835) caused a scandal in German religious circles and influenced Ernest Renan in his own *Life of Jesus* (1863).

STUBBS, William (1825–1901), English clergyman and historian. Regius Professor of Modern History in the University of Oxford (1866–84), Bishop of Oxford (1889–1900).

SUMNER, Charles (1811–74), American lawyer and politician. Leader of the Massachusetts abolitionists and the radical Republicans in the Senate during the American Civil War.

TAINE, Hippolyte Adolphe (1828–93), French critic, historian and sociologist. His views on the contextual study of literature and art – the importance of "race, milieu et moment" – had a huge influence on literary and art criticism and intellectual culture generally in France and elsewhere.

TAUNAY, Viscount de (Alfredo d'Escragnolle Taunay, 1843–99), Brazilian writer, artist, military engineer, politician, historian and sociologist. Grandson of the French artist Nicolas-Antoine Taunay. During the War of Paraguay, he took part in the military operation immortalized in his book *A retirada da Laguna* (1871). President of the provinces of Santa Catarina and Paraná.

TAVARES BASTOS, Aureliano Cândido (1839–75), Brazilian politician, writer and journalist. Author of *Cartas do Solitário* (1862), *O vale do Amazonas* (1866), *Reflexões sobre a imigração* (1867), *A Província* (1870), *A situação e o Partido Liberal* (1872) and *Estudos sobre a reforma eleitoral* (1873).

TAVARES JUNIOR, Pedro Augusto (1858–?), Brazilian writer and politician. A Republican, he was briefly governor of Maranhão in 1889-90.

THACKERAY, William Makepeace (1811–63), English novelist with prestige comparable to that of Dickens.

THIERS, Louis Adolphe (1797–1877), French historian and statesman. He was three times Prime Minister during the reign of Louis Philippe (1830–48), played a crucial role in crushing the Paris Commune (1871) and became the first (provisional) President of the Third Republic (1871–73).

TILDEN, Samuel Jones (1814–86), American politician. Governor of New York and Democratic presidential candidate defeated by Rutherford B. Hayes in the controversial 1876 election. He was the first candidate to be defeated in the Electoral College (by one vote) after winning a majority of the popular vote.

TROLLOPE, Anthony (1815–82), English novelist, one of the most prolific and successful of the Victorian age.

UMBERTO II (Umberto Rainiero Carlos Emanuel João Maria Fernando Eugênio de Sabóia, 1844–1900), King of Italy 1878–1900.

URUGUAI, Viscount of, see SOARES DE SOUZA, PAULINO José.

VILA BELA, Baron of (Domingos de Sousa Leão, 1819–79), Brazilian politician. President of the province of Pernambuco three times, in 1864, 1867–68 and 1878–79.

VIOLLET-LE-DUC, Eugène Emannuel (1814–79), French architect associated with 19th-century revivalist architecture and one of the first theoreticians of the preservation of historical heritage.

WADDINGTON, William Henry (1826–94), French politician and diplomat of English ancestry. Prime Minister in 1879, ambassador to Britain 1883–93.

WALES, Prince of (Albert Edward, 1841–1910), first-born son of Queen Victoria (1837–1901), he ruled as Edward VII from 1901 until his death in 1910.

WANDERLEY, João Maurício, see COTEGIPE.

WHEELER, William Almon (1819–87), American lawyer and politician, the 19th Vice-President of the United States, with President Rutherford B. Hayes (1877–81).

ZACARIAS, see GOIS E VASCONCELOS.